T0373553

"The authors have done a tremendous job of not just offering a comprehensive and insightful overview of the recall itself, but more importantly of putting this event in the proper political, historical and societal context. This book is essential reading for anyone who wants to understand California—where we've been, how we got here and where we're headed."

Dan Schnur, *former Chair, California Fair Political Practices Commission*

"The true story of California's Recall Election is stranger than fiction. This book has lessons to teach, and we have much to learn."

Anjuli Verma, *University of California—Santa Cruz*

"Timely. Well-researched with excellent contributions. This book is a perfect example of how the politics of the Golden State affect us all. This latest California political earthquake—only the second ever recall of a Governor in that state—is just the latest example of the weaponization of democracy in our era of 'Protest Politics.' Gerston and colleagues provide a rich must-read about this growing dynamic in our politics."

David McCuan, *Sonoma State University*

California's Recall Election of Gavin Newsom

California went through a political earthquake of sorts when the state recalled Governor Gray Davis in 2003. In 2021, the state faced another political turning point with the threatened recall of Governor Gavin Newsom. Less than two years after Newsom's overwhelming election victory, more than two million Californians signed on to the recall effort, hoping to expel him from office in a special election. How could such a monumental turnabout be possible? Normally, the political headwinds would be much too strong for a movement to oust a governor who had decisively vanquished his opponent. But—with the COVID-19 pandemic dominating every aspect of society, including politics—these weren't normal times. Organizing a recall election is a demanding enterprise: it takes abundant political energy, tremendous amounts of anger with the status quo, and mounds of money. Yet, for the second time in less than two decades, such wheels were set in motion. What is it that makes California so dynamic yet so fragile? This book explains that paradox and, in the process, enlightens readers about the recall process, the challenges of federalism, and the pitfalls of direct democracy. It examines the underlying conditions that expose a state with poorly linked institutions, a bitterly divided society, and a governor who had to act under nearly impossible conditions, demonstrating his strengths and vulnerabilities along the way. It's a story that could happen only in California, a state with a history of "only" stories.

Designed to be useful in a variety of college courses, this book is the first to unveil the Newsom backstory and will appeal to pundits and politicos as well as interested general readers.

Larry N. Gerston is professor emeritus of political science at San Jose State University.

Mary Currin-Percival is associate professor of political science and director of the Institute for Public Affairs and Civic Engagement at San Jose State University.

Garrick L. Percival is professor and chair of the political science department at San Jose State University.

California's Recall Election of Gavin Newsom

COVID-19 and the Test of Leadership

Larry N. Gerston,
Mary Currin-Percival and
Garrick L. Percival

Routledge
Taylor & Francis Group

NEW YORK AND LONDON

Cover image: Genaro Molina/Getty Images

First published 2023
by Routledge
605 Third Avenue, New York, NY 10158

and by Routledge
4 Park Square, Milton Park, Abingdon, Oxon, OX14 4RN

Routledge is an imprint of the Taylor & Francis Group, an informa business

Library of Congress Cataloging-in-Publication Data
A catalog record for this book has been requested

ISBN: 978-1-032-10969-5 (hbk)
ISBN: 978-1-032-10968-8 (pbk)
ISBN: 978-1-003-21795-4 (ebk)

DOI: 10.4324/9781003217954

Typeset in Sabon
by Apex CoVantage, LLC

For Elisa, in-house editor with uncommon wisdom and for Andrew and Ethan

Contents

About the Authors

Larry N. Gerston engages the political process as an author and an analyst. He has written 12 academic books in addition to *California's Recall Election of Gavin Newsom*, including *California Politics and Government: A Practical Approach* (with Mary Currin-Percival and Garrick Percival); *Not So Golden After All: The Rise and Fall of California*; *Politics in the Golden State* (with Terry Christensen); *Recall! California's Political Earthquake* (with Terry Christensen); *Making Public Policy: From Conflict to Resolution*; *The Deregulated Society* (with Cynthia Fraleigh and Robert Schwab); *American Government: Politics, Process and Policies*; *Public Policy: Process and Principles*; *Public Policymaking in a Democratic Society: A Guide to Civic Engagement*; *American Federalism: A Concise Introduction*; *Confronting Reality: Ten Issues Threatening to Implode American Society and How We Can Fix It*; and *Reviving Citizen Engagement: Policies to Renew National Community*. He has penned more than 150 op-ed pieces for every major newspaper in California. Gerston is the on-air political analyst for NBC Bay Area television and KCBS radio. He speaks often on issues such as civic engagement and political empowerment. Gerston has also authored four children's books.

Mary Currin-Percival is associate professor of political science and director of the Institute for Public Affairs and Civic Engagement at San Jose State University. She earned her Ph.D. in political science from the University of California, Riverside. In addition to *California's Recall Election of Gavin Newsom*, she has co-authored *California Politics and Government: A Practical Approach*, 15th ed. Dr. Currin-Percival teaches courses in American institutions, research methods, and mass political behavior. She also coordinates the SJSU Votes! voter registration, mobilization, and education project. Her research focuses on teaching and learning in political science, public opinion, and elections. Dr. Currin-Percival's work has appeared in several journals including *PS: Political Science and Politics, Journal of Political Science Education,*

International Migration, Journal of Elections, Public Opinion and Parties, and *Digital Journalism.*

Garrick L. Percival is professor and chair of the political science department at San Jose State University. He earned his Ph.D. in political science at the University of California, Riverside. His work focuses on American politics, primarily the nexus between crime policy, racial politics, and inequality at the state and local levels of government. In addition to *California's Recall Election of Gavin Newsom*, Dr. Percival is the author or co-author of two previous books, including *Smart on Crime: The Struggle to Build a Better American Penal System*, and *California Politics and Government: A Practical Approach*, 15th ed. He is currently working on several research projects focused on local prosecutors and their relationship to California's de-incarceration efforts. His work has also appeared in *State and Local Government Review, State Politics and Policy Quarterly, Social Science Quarterly, Political Research Quarterly, Journal of Public Administration Research and Theory*, and the *Policy Studies Journal*, among other outlets.

Preface

The recall election of California Governor Newsom has been described in a variety of ways ranging from the classic exercise of citizen participation to an abomination of democracy. So, which is it? That depends on your definition of "democracy," a fundamental concept we often discuss with little agreement. For now, let's set aside that question and focus on the recall, a relatively rare event in American politics, yet more common in California. And perhaps after reading our account of the recall election, you'll be better equipped to answer to what extent, if any, the event exemplified the democratic process or why it did not.

The recall has become an essential instrument for voters to hold elected officials accountable through special elections. In California, recall supporters need no special reason to bring on voter action; all they need is a required number of voter signatures. Opponents of Governor Gavin Newsom turned to the recall as a means to remove him from office five times during his first year of office, never succeeding in acquiring enough signatures. When the sixth effort began in March 2020, we wondered whether this try, too, would fizzle for lack of signature support, or make it across the petition signing threshold. The effort qualified easily after unexpected twists and turns. That drew our interest.

At stake was the career of the highest elected official in the nation's most-populous state. But why? Initially, recall proponents framed the election about Newsom's management of various issues including taxes, water, immigration, guns, and homelessness gone amok. Although they shared libertarian/conservative political values in a very Democratic state, the only other bond among the malcontents was that *something* should be done about Newsom's management of _____ (fill in the issue). Still, why have a special election about the governor's future a bit more than a year before a regularly scheduled election, anyway? To that question the organizers simply would say, "We've had enough."

So, we began our writing adventure. We monitored several news accounts throughout the state daily; researched national, state, and in some cases local government reports; followed public opinion polls; and conducted interviews of people close to Newsom. We soon discovered that we were trying to analyze a moving target—the characters, events, and issues seemed to change over time, sometimes rapidly, forcing us to recalibrate our research and interpretation of events more times than we'd like to admit.

With the sudden onset of the COVID-19 pandemic, recall proponents now focused on the governor's management of the virus. Suddenly, what began as an outlier campaign blended with growing public frustration from a once-in-a-century public health curse and the search to blame someone for the chaos. As Californians increasingly found themselves unemployed, out of school, and, in too many cases, ravaged by the disease, the quality of Newsom's stewardship became the basis for determining his and the state's future. But would the voters agree?

And what about the governor? Never lacking confidence, he told Californians that they would be okay because he and the state's experienced public health authorities would shepherd the populous to safety. Follow the science, Newsom said.

Newsom underestimated the depth and relentlessness of the pandemic and overestimated his and the state's administrative apparatus ability to deal with it. His initial calculations and mandates to overcome them left people frustrated in some cases, angry in others. A few personal gaffes along the way led to public questioning about whether Newsom was just another hypocritical politician who told people to do one thing, while he did something else. Was the governor in over his head? Was he even the right person for the job? Then again, was there anyone who could have prepared for the pandemic's physical and emotional onslaught? Our own assessments of it all changed almost daily.

Still, the state's difficulties associated with the pandemic went beyond Newsom. After all, the governor wasn't responsible for the Trump administration that all but abandoned California and the other states in the midst of a national public health crisis. Nor was he responsible for local governments that ignored his executive orders, or residents unwilling to make sacrifices for the public good, or a state legislature that largely left the governor to deal with the mess. Still, when it came to elected officials in the state, Newsom, as we'll document, by far had the most authority and was expected to make things better. Yet, he struggled, and many residents became impatient, others downright angry.

Eighteen months after the beginning of the recall attempt and 21 months after the pandemic reached California's shores, the recall election occurred. Whatever misery accompanied Newsom for the largest part of the period seemed to lift as the critical election event neared. The recall campaign—labeled by public opinion surveys at one point as a nip-and-tuck effort—dissipated almost as quickly as an east wind chasing away California's famous coastal fog. Was it because of Newsom's ability to finally harness the pandemic, recognition of many Californians that the disease was too much for any mortal to manage, fear of what many viewed as unqualified (or even dangerous) candidates who might replace Newsom, Democratic partisans "coming back home" to support a Democratic governor, or something else?

In this book, we present the facts, issues, and personalities and leave that judgment to you, the reader. We only know this: that the pandemic represented an unprecedented challenge to a state burdened with besieged state institutions, poorly linked governments, and a frightened public. The pandemic also provided us with an opportunity to examine California politics and its governor under the worst conditions imaginable. This book represents the culmination of our findings.

Accounts like ours are not only the results of our research but also of the support of many around us. To that end, we are thankful for the work of Khaleed Rasheed, our research assistant who found material well beyond anything we asked of him. We also express our gratitude to Elisa Gerston, our in-house (literally for one of the authors!) editor, who helped us move this project along. We also extend our deep thanks to the reporters of the many publications you see cited in these pages. Reporters, it is often said, write the first draft of history; we relied heavily on their work and insight as we drafted this book in real time as the recall campaign unfolded. At Routledge/Taylor & Francis, we extend our thanks to Jennifer Knerr, Jacqueline Dorsey, and Emma Harder-Collins. We also want to thank Aruna Rajenden for help in putting together the final page proofs. Of course, while all of these people were helpful in producing our effort, we own responsibility for the final product.

Chapter 1

California

The Perpetually Restless Society

"Shake, Rattle and Roll"

Joe Turner

It's unlikely that rhythm-and-blues singer Joe Turner was thinking of California in 1954 when his hit soared to number one on the *Billboard R&B Chart*, but the title of the song embodies the essence of the state nonetheless. California is earthquake country. Along with a package of majestic mountains with redwood forests, fertile valleys that supply much of the nation's agriculture, and pristine beaches along the coast that double as movie backdrops, the state's topography resides on a series of temperamental faults and fissures that occasionally remind us of who's really the boss—nature. Some states suffer from hurricanes, others endure tornadoes, but those catastrophes typically present warning signs of looming disasters. California has no such leeway with earthquakes that erupt with little or no notification. They rumble several times per day throughout the day just about everywhere, usually with little consequence. But when a big one occurs, it can bring a large city or even a region of the state to its knees. Earthquakes are humbling experiences and prompt us to acknowledge that some things in life are totally out of our control.

In many respects, California's politics reflect its temperamental ecological composition. The political environment is simultaneously robust, fragile, and often on the cusp of disarray. As such, California politics are anything but neat and orderly. Instead, people operate with a kind of modulated chaos, constantly attempting to prevent the next political earthquake but clearly aware of an assortment of divisions that may tear into the state's population at any moment. It's an exciting venue, California, but a place where politics rarely find stable ground. The casual observer may view California as exciting, intriguing, and alluring; but for the politically inclined, however, it's a blended tease of anticipation, trepidation, and uncertainty.

DOI: 10.4324/9781003217954-1

It's over this domain that Gavin Newsom has presided as governor of what he calls the country's only "nation-state." Newsom's description of California may be a bit over the top, but not by much. Were California a nation unto itself, its $3.2 trillion gross state product would be equivalent to the fifth-wealthiest country in the world, behind only the rest of the United States, China, Japan, and Germany, yet ahead of the United Kingdom, India, France, and Italy. Elected in 2018 with a strong economy as a sturdy foundation, an acquiescent Democratic Party-controlled legislature, and a largely contented public, Democrat Newsom was poised to take his place on the political stage as the state's preeminent elected official of the nation's preeminent state. Even at that, some observers viewed his presence as the state's chief executive a brief stay before competing for the presidency.

He couldn't have asked for a better spot. In so many ways, California almost seems to foreshadow the nation's future. While the rest of the nation anticipates becoming a majority of minorities by mid-century, California is already there. While the rest of the nation sputters over moving from an industrialized economy to a service economy, California is already there. While the rest of the nation struggles to come to terms with immigration, California is already there.

Yet, California mirrors the nation in at least one crucial respect: political polarization. The state may be blue, but in many cases it's blue in name only. In fact, politically speaking, there are more shades of blue in California than in a painter's fan deck. Long-standing, papered- over divisions not only between political parties but within parties—particularly the Democrats—have left the state with uncertain political instability. In a state where registered Democrats outnumber Republicans by more than 20 points, a pathetically weak Republican Party has appeared to assure Democrats their continuation of power now and for who knows how long into the future.

Still, like one of California's unexpected earthquakes, Newsom's exalted political position was threatened by a recall election. It didn't matter that in 2018 Newsom destroyed Republican John Cox by 24 points for the state's top job. Nor did it matter that Newsom was the first Democrat to succeed another (Jerry Brown) in 130 years, ostensibly assuring an unbroken continuation of Democratic domination in state politics. All that mattered was that Newsom's reign was on the ropes.

Enter Gavin Newsom

Who is Gavin Newsom, anyway? If looks were the primary requirement to be governor, Newsom would probably win every four years, hands down. Tall and lean, he's often been described as a candidate straight out of central casting.[1] And with just enough gray in his hair to seem in contemplation over the state's most serious issues, Newsom surely had the physical stature for the job. Not since Ronald Reagan has a gubernatorial candidate appeared so, well, . . . gubernatorial! Jerry Brown? Too cerebral. Arnold Schwarzenegger? Too muscular. Gray Davis? Too calculating. But Newsom certainly looked the part.

Then again, being governor requires a lot more than being telegenic. You need to understand the state's complex institutional organization, endless interest groups, competing ethnic and racial factions, and overlapping political relationships. And you must possess that special informal "power to persuade"[2] that easily surpasses the official authority connected to the office. Being governor is not as difficult as herding cats, but it's not that far off either. Nevertheless, the question remains, did Newsom have that special quality to do the job? He certainly thought so. In fact, in his mind, no political job was too tough. As Newsom wrote in his book, *Citizenville*, "I truly believe that governing is easier than we like to think it is."[3] In 2018, the voters apparently agreed.

Looking back, Newsom's victory over John Cox was the easy part. Governing a one-of-a-kind state like California is another thing altogether, given the state's mammoth, yet fragile arrangement. Newsom's political foundation began to quiver just a bit on February 21, 2020, when opponents filed papers with the California Secretary of State to recall Newsom from office. This in itself was only a mild shock for two reasons. First, of the 19 states that provide for a recall of an executive branch officer, California has the lowest bar for qualifying such an election. Second, Newsom had been a target practically since the first day he assumed the governorship. During Newsom's short tenure, five other recall attempts emerged only to quickly fizzle out for lack of the necessary 1,495,000 signatures. But attempted recalls of a California governor were hardly new or successful. Since the initiation of the recall in 1913, 54 efforts have been attempted, with only one for governor actually qualifying for the ballot. That single effort culminated with the successful recall of Governor Gray Davis in 2003. Still, given such a thin record, there wasn't much to worry about, Newsom thought.

Outside California, recall elections of state governors are unusually rare events. Over the nation's history, only four such elections have been held. North Dakota Governor Lynn Frazier was recalled in 1921, while Wisconsin Governor Scott Walker escaped that fate in 2012. California's Gray Davis was recalled in 2003 in response to severe public criticism over his management of several major problems, not all of his doing, but for which he was blamed nonetheless.[4] Which takes us back to Newsom, the second California governor to be placed in the recall bull's eye. Even with a low bar, few in the Democratic establishment originally believed that what they viewed as a few Fox News cranks would have the wherewithal to gather enough valid signatures.

But the March 2020 effort was different; if not at first, certainly over time. The list of grievances originally was a potpourri of gripes, including Newsom's approach to immigration, California's high taxes, the state's homeless population, threats to gun rights, possible water rationing, an anti-vax undercurrent, and even concerns about the state restricting parental rights.[5] What about COVID-19? It wasn't an issue when signature gathering for the latest recall effort began. At the time recall papers were drawn, there were only 20 cases in the entire country. Needless to say, those numbers would accelerate dramatically over the following months, and by late Spring 2020, Newsom's management of COVID-19 was added to the recall complaint list. But still, a recall election?

In fairness to Newsom, the COVID-19 pandemic hit him differently than any other governor. The very first death in the nation occurred in California on February 6, 2020, but wasn't recognized as such until more than two months later. Medical science was of little help in those early days because there was no protocol for dealing with this particular virus. Beyond that, President Donald Trump had basically described the virus as much ado about nothing and offered little help. Of course, no state had resources equal to those of the federal government, so Newsom had no choice but to chart his own course. He was the first governor in the nation to order a statewide lockdown on March 19, 2020, a seemingly strict act, yet within weeks his directive was described by critics as "a deliberately light touch" compared to those in other states,[6] given that he did not initially close schools, restaurants, bars, or places with large gatherings.

Still, in responding to COVID-19, there were many more questions than answers, such as whether Newsom and the legislature could ever get on the same page at the same time when dealing with the myriad unpredictable developments associated with the pandemic. And could Newsom keep the state's 58 counties and nearly 500 cities all on the same COVID-19 management schedule as the state grappled with an extraordinary tragedy that seized so many more lives each and every day? These questions had never been asked nor answered on such a massive scale. Nevertheless, this was the governor's challenge: to somehow oversee an all-consuming, unprecedented health disaster.

With an ever-expanding list of particulars, the questions about Newsom's stewardship increased by the day. Was COVID-19 the primary reason for the recall effort, or was public concern over the pandemic the culmination of many anxieties masked by the state's complexities? Was Newsom the victim of misplaced public anger about COVID-19, or was he simply over his head in attempting to navigate the state through the historic pandemic? How much of the ability to contain the pandemic was simply beyond Newsom's control, given the national catastrophe? Was the recall a genuine citizens' effort to rescue the state from unsatisfactory gubernatorial leadership, or was the reform tool simply a cynical way for Republicans to wrestle control of the state that they couldn't win through a regularly scheduled election? And, was Newsom's eventual victory over the recall proponents more the result of an ill-planned revolt with no basis, Newsom's masterful exaction of governance in the midst of crisis, good campaign strategy, some combination of these, or something entirely else? Those are among the questions we endeavor to answer in this book.

The Many Californias

Picture a jigsaw puzzle with pieces that don't quite fit and you've framed California. Collectively, the state is massive. At just over 100,000,000 acres, California is the third-largest state in the nation, behind only Alaska and Texas. Demographically, it's anything but tidy. Yes, it's a single state, but its largesse provides virtual gated havens for populations with very different—at times, almost incompatible—values. Most casual observers view California politically in terms of north and south, with an imaginary line from Tehachapi mountains just below Bakersfield zigzagging its way toward Santa Barbara separating the two regions, but that's overly simplistic. Self-described "true" northern Californians with small-town rural values see the fictional separation extending from San Francisco southeast toward Yosemite and down to the remainder of the state, leaving out just about every city above 100,000 residents, including Sacramento. Then there are the "Jeffersonians," residents of twelve extreme northern California counties who, for nearly a century with inhabitants of seven southern Oregon counties, have sought to secede from both states and form the state of Jefferson.

Such dreams of division are hardly new to California. In fact, secessionists have advanced variations of the theme more than two hundred times since California joined the Union. And it's not just a historical footnote, either. California voters rejected a version of division as recently as 2014, when venture capitalist Tim Draper spent $5 million attempting to qualify a statewide ballot initiative to divide California into six states: Jefferson, North California, Silicon Valley, Central California, West California, and South California. The proposed measure failed to gather enough signatures, but for many the aspiration of breaking up California remains real. Secessionists are serious; they see other parts of the state as out of sync with their values.

Never mind that no such separation could occur without approval of the U.S. Congress, something that last happened in 1863 when West Virginia was permitted to separate from Virginia in the midst of the Civil War.[7]

California's dedicated secessionists may have a point, at least to a degree. There's plenty of data showing that core values of the Golden State residents can differ markedly by where they live. They diverge on traditional wedge issues like water, gun control, housing, homelessness, same-sex marriage, immigration, and taxes. Smaller pockets bicker over the state's vaccination policy, recent relocations of inmates from state prisons to county jails, an inadequate water supply, and the state's "death with dignity" policy for those who are terminally ill. On a liberal-to-conservative scale, coastal Californians are considered the most liberal, and most decidedly so near the Bay Area. Greater Los Angeles leans to the left fairly often, with liberalism becoming more moderate as the focus shifts south through Orange County and San Diego County. Then things become a bit fuzzy. For example, conservative Democrats dominate the Central Valley, but they share little common philosophical ground with their liberal Democratic counterparts in the Bay Area. In fact, politically, most Central Valley Democrats are closer in values with Republicans, irrespective of their party labels. The far north also offers its own brand of politics, with a hefty dose of libertarianism that condemns "Big Government" in just about every respect as well as any institution that tells folks there how to live.[8]

California's disparate political values were clearly demonstrated by the residential origins of voter recall signatures in the state's 58 counties. Bear in mind that for a recall election of a statewide elected official to take place in this state, there must be valid recall petition signatures equal to 12% of the votes cast in the previous gubernatorial election. Given the vote total in 2018, the 12% recall signature number for the Newsom recall was 1,495,000. So, what did we learn?

The participation rates varied greatly. In the rural, extreme north part of the state and Central Valley counties, between 10% and 16% of the voters signed Newsom recall petitions. In the Bay Area, most county recall signatures came in at between 1% and 3%. Farther south, 3.1% of Los Angeles County voters signed recall petitions, while the rates in Orange and San Diego Counties were 7.3% and 5.9% respectively. Just to the east in semi-rural, fast-growing Riverside County, the rate jumped to 10%. Of significance is that those counties with high signature rates also voted heavily for Republican presidential nominee Donald Trump in 2016 and Republican gubernatorial candidate John Cox in 2018, relative to the rest of the state.[9] Demographically, we see that in the early going, at least, support for the Newsom recall came disproportionately from northern, rural regions of the state. Clearly, these areas were the hot spots of the Newsom recall effort, but they alone would not be enough to send Newsom packing. Proponents counted on discontent spreading to political independents and the more Democratic parts of the state—a tall order, given a huge Democratic majority. But then again, there are so many shades of blue in California.

Home of the Politics of Reform

The attempted recall of Governor Gavin Newsom was just the latest chapter of California's love affair with political reform. In fact, much of today's politics in California stem largely from the long-standing dedication by many to make democracy work in this state differently—almost more intimately—than in most states. Political reform came to California first in the opening years of the twentieth century. The Progressive Party, a fledgling political party offering itself as an alternative to the Democratic and Republican parties, proposed political and economic reform by placing more power directly into the hands of the people instead of the traditional elected officials. A caveat: today's "Progressives," a segment of the Democratic Party, also is dedicated to political and economic redistribution of power, but beyond that bears little resemblance to its namesake from more than one hundred years ago.

Led by future Governor Hiram Johnson, the Progressives of the early twentieth century believed that big business, the media, and a corrupt legislature viewed California as their personal turf and legislated accordingly for their self-interests. These reformers argued that "Direct Democracy" was the only way to counter the sinister relationship and protect the public good. They introduced the initiative, referendum, and recall as tools to provide the public with the means to have the final say over the policymaking process in the event that its needs were overlooked or abused by elected officials.[10] Those tools are with us today. By gathering an appropriate number of signatures, voters are able to make policy directly (initiative), reject the will of the legislature (referendum), or remove an elected official from office (recall). About half of the states have adopted various forms of the initiative and referendum, while 19 states have embraced the recall.

The Progressive Party in California pretty much died out by the mid-1920s, but Progressive-inspired reforms have continued to guide California politics, and most commonly through the initiative. In 1974, voters via the initiative created the Fair Political Practices Commission (FPPC), a state agency dedicated to regulating campaign finance, conflicts of interests, lobbying, and governmental ethics. In 1990, Californians voted to place term limits on legislators (now 12 years) and members of the executive branch (two 4-year terms). And in 2010, the voters changed the direct primary process so that the "top two" winners would face off in the general election regardless of their political party affiliation or lack thereof. All of these efforts have been designed to control power while installing a level of confidence in the political system.

Oddly enough, none of the reforms have worked as intended. The FPPC has been criticized for not sufficiently promoting transparency; foes have disparaged the term limits law for creating a "turnstile" governmental system that creates instability and a lack of continuity, while almost cavalierly disposing of valuable legislative expertise; and "top two" primary opponents have pointed to primary elections that often have often resulted in placing two members of the same party on the ballot, with the other major party left out and minor parties all but obliterated. The point is that reform in California sometimes produces unanticipated consequences.

This takes us to the Newsom recall effort. Most states have guardrails on the recall process that allow efforts to move forward only for good reason such as malfeasance, misconduct, incompetence, or failure to carry out duties as described by dictates of the office. Not so in California, where absolutely no reason or justification is required for pursuing the removal of an elected official. In addition, unlike most states that use the recall, the California version is actually a two-pronged event. The first question asks voters whether an elected official should be removed from office; a simple majority sends the official packing. On the possibility that the governor is removed, the second question asks the voters to choose a successor from a list of candidates who have qualified for the election.

The second question is the tricky part. Of importance is that contrary to most states with the two-pronged approach, California law does not allow the recalled governor's name to appear among the list of replacement candidates. That leaves the governor's political party allies in a dilemma: specifically, does a member of his party become a recall candidate just in case the governor is recalled? If so, will that take away votes from the governor that he otherwise would have received? In the recall of California Governor Gray Davis in 2003, Democratic Lieutenant Governor Cruz Bustamante ran as a replacement candidate with the banner, "No on recall, Yes on Bustamante." Bustamante came in second after winner Arnold Schwarzenegger. With a prominent Democrat on the ballot, we'll never know how many would-be Davis voters decided to abandon Davis and cast their lot with Bustamante.

Finally, there's one more twist: the recalled governor's successor can win the post by winning fewer votes than the number of votes required to oust the governor. That's because while it takes a majority to remove the governor in a recall election, it only takes a plurality among the many candidates on the ballot to win the replacement election. And it's easy to become a candidate—for $4,200 in fees or 7,000 signatures, you, too, can run as a replacement candidate. Perhaps that's why there were 135 such candidates on the ballot to replace Davis in 2003 and 46 candidates appeared on the 2021 Newsom recall attempt.

Put all of these elements together with one of the lowest recall signature requirements in the nation, and the election has the potential of becoming quite the political spectacle.

A State of Extremes

By January 1, 2022, COVID-19 had taken the lives of 76,000 Californians and infected more than 5,200,000 others. Hard as it was to accept these numbers, they actually reflected well on the state. The death statistic amounted to 10.6% of the nation's total. Inasmuch as Californians represent about 12.5% of the national population, state residents managed the pandemic better than most states. Needless to say, "better pandemic management" in California meant little to those who contracted the virus, and worse yet, those who died, but it does say something about the state compared to others.

Whereas California fared better on controlling COVID-19, the state suffered more financially than most others. In February 2020, the national unemployment was 3.5%, compared with 3.9% in California. Two months later with the onslaught of the pandemic, national unemployment soared to 14.7%, compared with 16% in California. Still, a small portion of Californians actually thrived financially in spite of the disease. How do we explain this seeming contradiction?

Economists have provided an answer. Most recessions eventually return the economy to a form similar to what existed prior to the downturn. A resumption that occurs quickly is known as a "V" recovery for the swift return to "normal." A resumption that takes place after an extended period of recession is described as a "U" recovery for the period in which commercial and consumer activity stalls until there is enough momentum to generate recovery. Either way, a post-recession economy returns with recovery looking pretty much like the economy appeared before the recession. But many economists viewed the national recuperation from the COVID-19 pandemic as a "K" recovery. With this model, the long line of the letter angling down and to the right underscore the lack of recovery for most people. The shorter line of the letter angling up and to the right points to a much smaller group that actually profits from the bad economy.[11]

For Californians, there is nothing encouraging or helpful about a "K" recovery from COVID-19. That's because the state has a long history of a very uneven economy that has provided vast wealth for a few with vast poverty or near-poverty for a large portion of the state. The COVID-19 pandemic only exacerbated these long-standing tendencies. To better appreciate California's extremes, we focus on income and taxation patterns, education differences, and housing and homelessness. Combined, they underscore the condition of the state even before the arrival of COVID-19, which only exacerbated the state's major problems.

Income and Taxation Patterns

On the surface, California appears to be a high-income state. According to U.S. Census Bureau statistics for 2018, the median income in California was $75,277, third behind Maryland ($83,242) and Connecticut ($76,348), and well above the national median income of $61,937. But it's not simply a matter of "top line" numbers. Inflation-adjusted household income data gathered by the California Budget and Policy Center not only shows a historic income disparity between those at the top and the bottom in California, but an acceleration of that disparity in recent years. In 2006, the top 5% of the state earned an average of $426,851, while the bottom 20% of California households earned $16,441. Simply put, those at the very top earned 27 times those at the bottom. Fast forward to 2018, when the top 5% of California households had average incomes of $506,421 versus the lowest 20% of households that earned $15,562. By 2018, the top income rung earned 32 times those at the bottom. Even more startling, when controlled for inflation, the poorest 20% of the state actually experienced a *drop* of income.[12]

Income isn't the only factor to explain survivability, especially when considering poverty. The nation's official poverty rate established by the Census Bureau has ranged in the 12–13% range for several years. The national poverty rate in 2019 was 12.3%, equal to $25,750 for a family of four. The poverty dollar figure is determined by using a three-times multiplier for food costs plus the number of people in a family and a few other factors. With that determinant alone, California's poverty rate in 2019 was 12.5%, slightly above the national average. But when the Census Bureau includes the geographic cost of living, medical costs, taxes, and anti-poverty measures like food stamps and unemployment insurance, the state's true poverty rate is 18.1%, the highest in the nation.[13]

Examine the difficulties caused by the COVID-19 experience and we see a bad situation that has only worsened. By December 2020, job losses were the highest among low-income workers, particularly those in leisure/hospitality, personal services such as auto repair, beauty/barber shops, and dry cleaning, and farm workers. Financial disruption also had a racial component. Whereas 56% of Whites and 61% of Asian Americans declared themselves in "good financial shape" in the midst of the pandemic, only 29% of Latinos and 32% of African Americans enjoyed similar circumstances.[14] In a state already saddled with an increasing division between the "haves" and "have nots," COVID-19 has only deepened the chasm.

While many Californians suffered from low incomes, those at the top encountered another problem—high taxation. Like most states, California has a progressive income tax. However, at 13.3% for the wealthiest earners, California's income taxes are the highest in the nation. The highest earners are particularly valuable to the state's treasury. As a matter of fact, the top 1% of income earners in California represent .4% of all households, yet pay 50% of the state's income taxes. Nevertheless, with Governor Newsom claiming a $54 billion budget shortfall in May 2020 because of the pandemic, legislators proposed a massive tax increase on the rich, raising the top rate to 16.3% of those earning $5 million or more annually.[15] If passed, the new tax rate would bring in an additional $6 billion annually to the California treasury. As time went on, aid from the federal government more than offset anticipated income losses. The call for higher taxes went away, but the memories of a proposed increase stayed with an already anxious public.

Education Levels

Civil rights activist Malcolm X once said, "Education is the passport to the future, for tomorrow belongs to those who prepare for it today." To the extent that he is right, a large contingent of Californians won't be traveling very far with their credentials. Compared to the other 49 states, California is a near-bottom dweller. In a 2020 research project of the 50 states released by Wallethub, a financial assessment company, California ranked 37th in its quality of public education, wedged between Missouri and Idaho. Among the three other most populated states that compete with California, New York ranked 12th, Florida 22nd, and Texas 28th, respectively.[16] "Wait a minute," you say, "that's one crummy study." Fair enough. Well, here's another: a recent analysis released by *USA Today* ranked California's public education 35th, between Arkansas (34th) and Texas (36th).[17] Of course, each study has slightly different methods for determining its conclusions—for instance, note that Texas ranks 28th in one analysis and 36th in the other. But let's face it, on the whole, California isn't about to set any public education overachievement records!

As bad as the general data are, they are even more troubling when the education achievements of California students are measured by race. Consider recent data provided by the California Department of Education. During the 2018–2019 academic year, 40% of students in grades 3–8 were proficient on the state math test. However, scores varied noticeably by race: from 75% of Asian Americans, to 55% of Whites, to 27% of Latinos, to 20% of African Americans. In reading, while the average proficiency score proficiency was 52%, 77% percent of Asian Americans were proficient, compared to 65% of Whites, 41% of Latinos, and 33% of African Americans.[18] Remember, these data existed before the COVID-19 pandemic struck the state.

Public education difficulties in California only worsened with COVID-19. Eight months into the pandemic with virtually all public schools shut down, more than a half million households with students—mostly in low-income and rural areas—lacked internet access.[19] With the best internet access were Asian American (87%) and White (75%) families, with Latino (71%) and African American (62%) families trailing.[20] One other distressing fact: as of March 31, 2021, only 22.6% of California's public school students had returned to school on a part-time or full-time basis, ranking the state 50th—dead last.[21] By the same date, nearly half of the nation's students had gone back to school. Of course, California's students returned to school over time, albeit at a much slower pace than their peers in other states, and not necessarily on the same schedule. In fact, evidence indicated that wealthy, White districts were returning faster than poor, minority districts, further accentuating the disparities in California's public education.[22] Nevertheless, for more than a year, COVID-19 presented special challenges to California students and their parents—challenges that didn't rise to the same extent elsewhere. What this means downstream, particularly with respect to long-term effects, remains to be seen.

For his part, Governor Newsom began advocating the return of students to public schools as early as December 2020 and offered $2 billion worth of state-provided incentives as an inducement. However, the state legislature didn't authorize any funds until March 2021. Even then, few school districts were willing to take him up on the offer, inasmuch as many teachers awaited vaccinations and schools still lacked safety protocols. Thus, between an uncertain legislature and an adamant teachers' union, Newsom was unable to move the ball. Meanwhile, frustration grew over the lack of direction, especially among those students and families with the fewest resources.

Housing and Homelessness

Housing and homelessness represent a double-edged sword for Californians. With respect to housing, the state is short more than 3.5 million housing units, and shows no sign of closing the gap. In January 2020, Governor Gavin Newsom spent virtually all of his State of the State address urging the legislature to pass legislation making it easier to build more housing. Despite a flurry of bills on topics ranging from restructured zoning to high-density housing near transit corridors, nothing escaped the legislature. Of the 500,000 new units proposed by Newsom, just over 100,000 units were created—a decrease of 9% from 2019.

The differential between housing need and availability grows every year. With an inadequate supply, the prices of housing have soared and continue to do so. In 2021, the median price of a home in California exceeded $700,000, more than double the national average. Ironically, during 2020 when COVID-19 reduced the state workforce by 1.5 million, the median single-family home price in California grew by more than 11%. One more piece of housing data: according to the California Association of Realtors, as of 2019, only 31% of California households could afford to purchase a median-priced California home, contrasted with 56% of national households.[23] And that was *before* COVID-19!

Then there's the homelessness component. When considered on a per capita basis, California has 38 homeless persons per 10,000 residents. The more than 160,000 identified homeless ranks California as having the third-highest homelessness rate among the fifty states, behind only New York and Hawaii.[24] That's almost as many as the entire population of Hayward (171,000) and more than Pasadena (141,000). During the pandemic, the state's homeless population increased by 7%; during the same period, the national homeless population grew by 2%. About one fourth of the nation's homeless population lives in California, with most of the dispossessed living in the state's largest cities where temporary assistance is most available.[25] Data accumulated shortly before the pandemic showed that about a quarter of homeless adults with children worked full- or part-time; the percentage was lower for adults without children.[26] Given the massive surge in unemployment with the pandemic, it's reasonable to assume that the percentage of the homeless who were working decreased, only adding to the burdens placed on people and governments alike.

The state legislature occasionally provides block grants for local governments to address homelessness through shelters and temporary housing, but there is no ongoing program to replenish funds as they are expended. Then, like so many other aspects of California state government, people often have difficulty seeing any connection between state and local relationships. Aid to the homeless is a classic example, because most voters don't realize that the aid is made available by the legislature and governor. What they do see, however, are large numbers of people living in tents and temporary shelters. The voters' anguish about the issue was seen through their disapproval of Governor Newsom's management of homelessness. Consider the data accumulated in a poll taken in late September 2020. While voters approved the effort Newsom had undertaken as governor, 55% said he had done a poor/very poor job handling homelessness, compared with 11% who agreed he had done a good/excellent job.[27]

Three Examples of the Same Theme

Whether income and taxation anxieties, uneven education levels, or housing and homelessness worries, all of these elements point to the extremes that define California. Finding ways to manage these extremes is difficult enough under normal conditions—not that "normal" anything is found with great abundance in California. Under the incredible stress of a pandemic, however, governing is all the more difficult. That challenge fell to Governor Gavin Newsom.

Plan of the Book

The recall election of California Governor Gavin Newsom was not just another election; in fact, it took on national dimensions. Originally, much of the recall energy originated with people considered by most observers to be well outside the political mainstream, but over time the recall movement attracted respectable sums of money and endorsements from outside the state. Nationally known Republicans, independents and even some Democrats joined ranks with the early proponents, albeit for different reasons. For many proponents, the recall was seen as the precursor to the 2022 national midterm elections and perhaps even an early indication of the issues framing the 2024 presidential campaign. Some Republican leaders hoped that if not victory, a solid showing would make Republicans competitive in California and elsewhere in areas previously thought as unwinnable. Thus, while the recall election was not a national referendum, many thought that it at least took the political temperature of a vast swath of voters.

The remaining chapters of this book direct attention to the many elements leading up to the election, the campaign itself, and the consequences of the election's outcome. Chapter 2 delves into the emergence and development of Gavin Newsom from his college days through his business career and entry into politics. Chapter 3 continues the Newsom saga with respect to his election to the governor's post and the years of office leading up to the arrival of COVID-19 pandemic in California. In Chapter 4, we discuss the assault of COVID-19 on the state's residents, medical community's capacity, and political response by the governor. Chapter 5 focuses on how dealing with COVID-19 upended California governance. Chapter 6 shifts to the origins and evolution of the recall movement as a growing political storm in California. Chapter 7 examines the recall campaign from the moment of its authorization to its end. Chapter 8 concludes our study with some observations on the difficulties of managing California in the midst of a pandemic.

A Final Word

As students of politics and government, we fully appreciate the complexities found in all political environments. Each is unique, defined by competing values, unique divisions and bonds, and, not surprisingly, approaches to governance. To this extent, California is no different than most political and governmental arrangements. However, given the state's largesse and impact on the rest of the nation and world, what happens in California often ripples elsewhere disproportionally. And although we don't expect our analysis to fully explain the many intricacies and nuances of leadership, elections, and political behavior in California, we hope that the story of the recall election of Governor Gavin Newsom contributes a bit to the discussion.

Notes

1. "Governor Newsom, the Next Governor of the Republican Resistance," *The New Yorker*, October 29, 2018, www.newyorker.com/magazine/2018/11/05/gavin-newsom-the-next-head-of-the-california-resistance.
2. In his seminal work, *Presidential Power*, Richard Neustadt argues that beyond the president's official power, the most important power of the chief executive is the power to persuade. Much the same could be said about the governor of California. New York, New York: John Wiley & Sons, 1980, pp. 27–29.
3. Gavin Newsom and Lisa Dickey, *Citizenville* (New York, NY: Penguin Publishing Company, 2013), p. 101.
4. See Larry N. Gerston and Terry Christensen, *Recall! California's Political Earthquake* (Armonk, New York: M.E. Sharpe Publisher, 2004).
5. "The origin of the Newsom recall had nothing to do with COVID-19: Here's why it began," *The Sacramento Bee*, March 21, 2021, www.sacbee.com/news/politics-government/capitol-alert/article250130094.html.
6. "In confronting coronavirus, Gov. takes California on its own path," *Los Angeles Times*, March 20, 2020, times.com/california/story/2020-03-18/california-governor-gavin-newsom-coronavirus-crisis-response.
7. Article IV, Section 3, Clause 2 of the U.S. Constitution states that "The Congress shall have Power to dispose of and make all needful Rules and Regulations respecting the territory or other Property belonging to the United States; and nothing in this Constitution shall be so construed as to Prejudice any Claims of the United States, or of any particular State."
8. Eric McGhee offers a detailed discussion of California's regional political values and trends in "California's Political Geography 2020," Public Policy Institute of California, San Francisco, CA, February 2020.
9. For a county-by-county breakdown, see "The California counties fueling the Newsom recall," *SF Gate*, March 22, 2021, www.sfgate.com/politics/article/Gavin-Newsom-recall-progress-update-California-21-16042186.php.
10. For an excellent account of the Progressive movement in California, see George E. Mowry, *The California Progressives* (Berkeley, CA: The University of California Press, 1951).
11. For a description on the "K" economic recovery from COVID-19, see "How a 'K-shaped' recovery is widening U.S. inequality," *The Washington Post*, December 20, 2020, https://www.bloomberg.com/news/articles/2020-12-10/how-a-k-shaped-recovery-is-widening-u-s-inequality-quicktake.
12. "Income Inequality Significantly Increased for Californians in 2018: Millions of People Can't Afford Their Basic Needs," *California Budget and Policy Center*, Sacramento, CA, September 2019, https://calbudgetcenter.org/resources/income-inequality-significantly-increased-for-californians-in-2018/.
13. See "In states such as California and Maryland, poverty may be worse than you think," *USA Today*, November 12, 2019, www.usatoday.com/story/money/2019/11/12/15-states-where-poverty-is-worse-than-you-might-think/40569843/.

14. "Income Inequality and Economic Opportunity in California," *Public Policy Institute of California*, December 2020, www.ppic.org/publication/income-inequality-and-economic-opportunity-in-california/.

15. "Is it time to raise taxes on the rich? California Democrats call for new millionaire's tax," *Sacramento Bee*, August 3, 2020, www.sacbee.com/news/politics-government/capitol-alert/article244604892.html.

16. "States with the Best & Worst School Systems," *Wallethub*, July 27, 2020, https://wallethub.com/edu/e/states-with-the-best-schools/5335.

17. "Best and worst schools: Which schools get the best grade based on the education rankings?" *USA Today*, February 16, 2020, www.usatoday.com/story/money/2020/02/16/states-with-the-best-and-worst-schools/41019857/.

18. "Only half of California students meet English standards and fewer meet math, test scores show," *Los Angeles Times*, October 9, 2019, www.latimes.com/california/story/2019-10-09/california-school-test-scores-2019.

19. "Up to 1 million California students may still lack connectivity during distance learning," *EdSource*, October 15, 2020, https://edsource.org/2020/california-still-lacks-connectivity-for-more-than-300000-students-during-distance-learning/641537.

20. "Who is Losing Ground with Distance Learning in California?" *Public Policy Institute of California*, October 2020, www.ppic.org/wp-content/uploads/who-is-losing-ground-with-distance-learning-in-california-october-2020.pdf.

21. "Burbio's K-12 School Opening Tracker," March 31, 2021, https://cai.burbio.com/school-opening-tracker/.

22. See "California students in richer areas far more likely to be back in classrooms," *CalMatters*, February 24, 2021, calmatters.org/education/k-12-education/2021/02/california-school-reopening-wealth-gap/ and "Schools in more affluent areas move faster to reopen than those in low-income areas," *Los Angeles Times*, February 11, 2021, www.latimes.com/california/story/2021-02-11/divide-emerges-covid-school-reopening-rich-poor-areas.

23. "California's Future: Housing," *Public Policy Institute of California*, January 2020, www.ppic.org/wp-content/uploads/californias-future-housing-january-2020.pdf.

24. "State of Homelessness: 2021 Edition," *National Alliance to End Homelessness*, Washington, DC, 2020, https://endhomelessness.org/homelessness-in-america/homelessness-statistics/state-of-homelessness-2021/.

25. See "California's Homelessness: Challenges in Context," *Legislative Analyst's Office, California State Legislature*, January 21, 2021, https://lao.ca.gov/handouts/localgov/2021/Homelessness-Challenges-in-Context-012121.pdf.

26. "Working While Homeless: A Tough Job for Thousands of Californians," *NPR*, September 30, 2018, www.npr.org/2018/09/30/652572292/working-while-homeless-a-tough-job-for-thousands-of-californians.

27. "Poll shows Californians give Newsom high marks on COVID-19, low marks on addressing homelessness," *Los Angeles Times*, September 29, 2020, www.latimes.com/california/story/2020-09-29/california-voters-berkeley-poll-newsom-high-marks-coronavirus-low-marks-homelessness.

Chapter 2

Gavin Newsom

Innovator or Illusionist?

You could go through a whole litany of things that sparked me wanting to do something important

—Barack Obama

What drives political ambition? What causes someone to see in themselves a person who can instigate political and social change? In his rise to the presidency, Barack Obama spoke often about factors that fueled his ambitions and is longing to leave a mark. The absence of his father and the fact that he grew up in places with few other black children around are two of his cited examples.

Of course, each politician will have different factors at play. For Gavin Newsom early political success seemed to beget more success and more ambition. Prior to the September 14, 2021 recall election, he had a perfect record in winning races for San Francisco supervisor, San Francisco mayor, lieutenant governor, and most recently, governor of the most populated state in the nation. Newsom has never publicly expressed a desire to be President, but given his trajectory, it would be hard to think otherwise. And with each electoral victory up the political ladder, that quest had seemed a bit more achievable. Until the recall moment.

The recall posed a serious challenge to Newsom's political future. A solid rejection of the threat by the voters would leave Newsom well situated for re-election as governor in 2022 and in position for a presidential run in 2024, 2028, or who knows when. After all, he's only 54 years old which, in national politics, is just the beginning of one's prime. But a loss in the recall election or even a narrow victory would quite possibly leave his ultimate achievement in jeopardy, if not out of reach.

But of course, it's not that simple. In politics, every election is both its own story and in all likelihood part of a larger narrative. On the one hand, it has a beginning with the declaration of candidacy, a middle with a campaign, and an end with victory or defeat. On the other hand,

DOI: 10.4324/9781003217954-2

whether it's a candidate's first race or the next step in a series of races, there's always a beginning *before* the beginning, chiefly the path that he or she took en route to the latest challenge. The events that occur on that path tell us much about the candidate's values, character, growth, and circumstances that accompany and enabled his or her pursuit of destiny. This takes us to Gavin Newsom.

In this chapter, we examine Newsom's personal background beginning with his childhood in San Francisco. We also examine some of the political and financial connections that his grandfather, William Newsom, II and father, William Newsom, III established. We pay close attention to the Newsom family connection to the wealthy Getty family, especially the influence the Gettys had upon the success of the PlumpJack Group, Newsom's real estate, restaurant, and winery businesses.

Next, we explore Newsom's political growth and election advancements, beginning with his appointment to the San Francisco Parking and Traffic Commission in 1996 by Mayor Willie Brown. A six-month stint led to an appointment to the San Francisco Board of Supervisors, where Newsom was seen as an outsider by other members. Despite having little political experience and having not been part of the San Francisco Democratic Party leadership, Newsom was elected Mayor of San Francisco in 2004. We then examine some of his more controversial and groundbreaking decisions that created controversy on both sides of the political spectrum.

Following Newsom's San Francisco career, we turn to Newsom's venture into state politics, which briefly included a gubernatorial candidacy in 2010, before turning his attention to the lieutenant governor's position. Our study of Newsom's tenure as lieutenant governor includes a discussion of his performance, his tense relationship with Governor Jerry Brown, and his general dissatisfaction with the office and its duties.

Of interest is the way Newsom's values changed over time, from being a political moderate as a supervisor and mayor to much more liberal as lieutenant governor. Some observers viewed his metamorphosis as a sign of growth, others as shrewd calculation. Either way, particularly in the early years, Newsom had issues with his colleagues, often leaving them with the sense that Newsom viewed himself and his ideas as superior to theirs.

Deep Family Roots

Reno, Nevada has long defined itself as "the Biggest Little City in the World." But Reno couldn't hold a candle next to San Francisco. Consider the difference. Reno has 225,000 people living within 111 square miles, with a density of 2,450 residents per square mile. San Francisco has 880,000 residents within a 47-square-mile boundary and a population density of 18,440 residents per square mile—second among U.S. cities only to New York.

But this detour is about more than numbers. A city with a large population and small footprint can find a lot of the same people in the same locations again and again. That interaction is particularly present with San Francisco's social and cultural elites, whose values often spill over into the political realm. Gavin Newsom is a beneficiary of this group.[1] However, before we get to the present, we must explore the past, where Gavin Newsom's political roots go back two generations.

Gavin Newsom's background begins with his grandfather, William Alfred Newsom II, a general contractor and bank investor in San Francisco, who relied on Edmund G. "Pat" Brown, an attorney, for legal matters. Upon striking up a friendship, Newsom II helped finance Pat Brown's second run for San Francisco District Attorney in 1943 (he lost his first D.A. campaign in 1939). This time Brown won. Their relationship continued, with Newsom II ultimately managing Brown's gubernatorial campaign in 1958. In 1959, Brown awarded Newsom II the lucrative Squaw Valley concession contract prior to the 1960 Olympics, which was criticized by the state legislative analyst as unfair to the state.[2] Brown and Newsom II remained close friends even after Brown was defeated for a third term by Ronald Reagan in 1966.

This takes us to the next generation. Jerry Brown, son of Pat Brown and a governor himself beginning in 1975, and William "Bill" Newsom III knew each other courtesy of their fathers' close relationship. In fact, Jerry Brown and Bill Newsom attended St. Ignatius High School along with Gordon Getty, the son of oil magnate J. Paul Getty. So close were Bill Newsom and Gordon Getty that during their high school years, Getty often slept at the Newsom home, where William Newsom II functioned almost as a father figure.[3] Years later, after Bill Newsom and his wife, Tessa, divorced, the Getty family "informally adopted" Bill's son Gavin in a similar fashion.[4]

In yet another sign of the intertwined families, Governor Jerry Brown appointed William "Bill" Newsom III Superior Court judge in 1975 and to the California Court of Appeal in 1978, where he served until his retirement in 1995. Bill Newsom was a strong supporter of criminal justice reform and rehabilitation for felons and environmental causes.[5] He was also an environmentalist, serving on the board of several organizations including Earthjustice, the Environmental Defense Fund, and Sierra Watch. A staunch defender of California mountain lions, he was a founding board member of the Mountain Lion Foundation and founder of the Wildlife Conservancy. He was a fan of Gavin Maxwell, Scottish naturalist and environmental writer, and the inspiration for his son's name. Bill also loved river otters, and Gavin Newsom recalled his first pet Potter the Otter sleeping curled up in his bed when he was a child.[6]

Bill Newsom later served as a Getty family attorney, and as an example of the trust the Getty family placed in him, he assisted the family after the 1973 kidnapping of J. Paul Getty's grandson, John Paul Getty III. He and others traveled to Southern Italy to deliver the nearly $3 million in ransom for his release.[7] In the 1980s, Bill Newsom helped with a change in state trust law that allowed Gordon Getty to claim his share of the Getty Family Trust divided between the Getty siblings. He then managed the Gordon P. Getty Family Trust, which later provided seed money for early business ventures undertaken by Gavin Newsom and Gordon Getty's son, William "Billy" Getty.[8]

Bill Newsom made other strong connections through St. Ignatius High School, such as his old high school chum, congressman and state legislator John Burton. A powerful Democrat, Burton later served as state chair of the Democratic Party between 2009 and 2017 and was also an important influence on Gavin's early political career.

Everyone has roots. In Gavin Newsom's case, his roots included a combination of wealthy and politically powerful Bay Area stewards. None of this is to take away anything from Newsom's future successes in politics and business. Still, his background provides a rich foundation for Newsom's present life.

A Humble Beginning

Gavin Newsom's beginning revealed little of what he would become. Born in 1967 to Tessa Newsom (née Menzies) and William Alfred Newsom III, he showed intelligence and a strong work ethic. But his self-confidence was challenged by the difficulties he faced in school due to a learning disability. Gavin's parents were married for only a couple of years, separating when he was two years old, and divorcing three years later. Bill Newsom's new job as Superior Court judge took him to Placer County, while Tessa Newsom, Gavin, and his younger sister Hilary remained in San Francisco. Tessa paid most of the expenses, sometimes working three jobs as a waitress, a paralegal, and a secretary, as Bill struggled to recover financially party due to his failed State Senate run in 1968.[9] In 2003, Hilary Newsom Callan recalled, "Our father was very important in our lives, but we were raised by my mother. . . . She was there 24/7. . . . There were Christmases when my mom told us not to be disappointed because there wouldn't be any gifts. Both parents did the best they could for us but there was no silver spoon."[10]

Newsom's severe dyslexia made education a challenge. He attended multiple schools, including kindergarten and first grade at the French-American bilingual school where his dyslexia created such difficulties that he had to transfer out. Reading aloud was the most difficult obstacle; he was placed in remedial reading classes at Notre Dame de Victoire in the third, fourth, and fifth grades.[11] He was diagnosed with dyslexia at age five, but Tessa, fearing he would use his dyslexia as a "crutch," didn't tell him. She also feared that it might stigmatize him. Newsom discovered his diagnosis when he was in fifth grade after going through some of his mother's papers.[12]

Newsom dealt with his family's financial struggles and his challenges in school in various ways. In middle school, he drank raw eggs à la Rocky Balboa "to toughen himself up." Then, inspired by *Remington Steele*, a television series, he began wearing blazers and suits to school and started using hair gel to achieve that Gavin Newsom look. "The suit was literally a mask," he once said. "I am still that anxious kid with the bowl-cut hair, the dyslexic kid—the rest is a façade. The only thing that saved me was sports."[13] He was a double threat—a star basketball and baseball player and was able to attend Santa Clara University funded by a partial baseball scholarship and student loans. Although he blew out his arm in his second year, he still finished school and graduated with a degree in political science.

After graduating, Newsom's first job was delivering podiatric orthotics. He then worked for real estate firm Shorenstein & Co. and "did everything from clean bathrooms to remove asbestos."[14] He also earned his real estate license during this time period. In 1991, while he was still working at Shorenstein, Newsom created PlumpJack Group, named after an opera written by Gordon Getty. Newsom, with PlumpJack partner Billy Getty, opened his first wine store on Fillmore Street in San Francisco in 1992. Newsom has referenced his hospitality experience as good training for politics, especially in crisis management.[15] He has also noted specific instances in which his experiences made him more understanding of why people get frustrated with government. For instance, when he was on the San Francisco Board of Supervisors, he recalled how the permit for the Fillmore wine shop was delayed by the San Francisco Health Department over the required installation of a sink (since wine was deemed a "food"). Newsom's sink cost $27,000 and ended up being used to water plants.[16]

Getty Invests in Gavin

Gordon Getty was an early financial supporter of Newsom, with the Getty Trust providing "seed money" for the PlumpJack restaurant and Fillmore wine shop.[17] PlumpJack expanded into restaurants and other investments, including the purchase and expansion of Squaw Valley Inn and a winery in Oakville in the heart of Napa Valley. The Getty Trust was a lead investor in 10 of 11 Newsom's businesses. Newsom also invested in Getty businesses, buying $10,000 worth of stock in the initial public offering when the family-owned Getty Images went public in 1996.[18] During 1997–2000, the Getty Trust paid him $169,000 for investment advice.[19]

The Gettys also covered some personal expenses for Newsom, including his wedding reception when he married prosecutor Kimberly Guilfoyle and a $1 million loan to assist with the purchase of their Pacific Heights home. Newsom's relationship with Getty has only fed his critics' depictions of him as elitist. Newsom argued that he built these businesses, though. "[I] conceived of [the businesses], wrote the business plans, found the investors, and by no means are the investors exclusive to the Getty family. Quite the contrary."[20] The Gettys may not have been the only investors, but it's hard to deny their centrality in Newsom's business career.

Connecting With Willie Brown

Newsom's political and family connections and his financial success led to a long and fruitful relationship with former Assembly Speaker and later San Francisco Mayor Willie Brown. Brown recalls that he met Newsom through Gavin's father Bill Newsom when Bill ran for the state legislature. Brown became closer to Gavin when Brown ran for mayor. As Brown described it, Gavin Newson and Billy Getty were "rich kids who owned a house together, owned bars and liquor stores, and were great volunteers. Newsom . . . made an offer to me at the end of every day: 'If you want to go bar-hopping, I know all the bars.' And that's the role he played. . . . He knew all the bartenders, the door people . . . all over the city in the pursuit of voters. And he was in a position financially to pick up the tab. But I came to know Newsom in a social setting involving pursuit of votes for me. . . ."[21]

After his successful election, Brown appointed volunteers to various commissions. Some had significant responsibilities such as the Police Commission and the Planning Commission. Others offered more title than clout. Brown appointed Newsom to Parking and Traffic and Getty to Park and Recreation commissions because "[I] knew neither one of them wanted to be burdened with extensive time on committee meetings. I could tell very clearly this was not their deal. I wouldn't stick them on the Port Commission or Airport Commission or Fire Commission, any of those. . . ."[22] Whatever Newsom's work ethic, it didn't fit with commissions of significance, which is why Brown appointed Newsom to the lesser-known body.

Lonely on the Board [of Supervisors]

The next step in Newsom's early political career came more from luck and timing than electoral success. San Francisco Supervisor Kevin Shelley won election to the State Assembly, leaving a vacancy for the mayor to fill. Brown appointed 29-year-old Newsom to replace Shelley six months after beginning his term on the Parking and Traffic Commission, his only formal political experience. Newsom wasn't involved with the Democratic Party at the time, but he had "other traits that Brown [valued]: energy optimism and an easy familiarity with San Francisco's upper crust."[23] Another fact: Newsom was a straight White male and Kevin Shelley's departure left the board without one. "If you're going to run a city like San Francisco, you'd better balance the city, reflecting the diversity of the city in every category—diversity, ethnicity, religiously, wealth. You want sex and gender. You gotta do it right,"[24] Brown explained. With his new post, Newsom was the youngest member on the Board of Supervisors. Parking and Traffic may not have been very exciting, but it did create the opportunity for Newsom to move up San Francisco's political ladder—fast.

Newsom was elected to the board in 1998 and re-elected in 2000 and 2003. In those days, he was a centrist, business-friendly Democrat, and as such, alienated the most Progressive members of the board. He often had difficulty even gaining a "second" on his motions. Some of this wasn't too surprising, given his allegiance to the moderate Brown. In fact, Newsom voted with Mayor Brown almost all of the time, earning a reputation for being tied to Brown. He also had the "rich boy" reputation. Even Brown acknowledged that Newsom was the most unpopular member of the board: "They saw him as an elitist. And he didn't make any friends with them either. . . . His access to wealth, his access to the social circle of San Francisco; his association with the powers that be—Nancy [Pelosi], Dianne Feinstein, Barbara Boxer. None of those were street people. So, Newsom was clearly evidence of a chosen group."[25]

Rather than discourage the perception of being a snob, wittingly or not Newsom provided fodder for the discussion. For example, in September 2004 shortly after his election to mayor, *Harper's Bazaar* published an article about Newsom and his then-wife Kimberly Guilfoyle, titled "New Kennedys." The piece contained several flashy photos, including one of the couple whimsically lounging on a rug in the Getty mansion.

All the while, Newson's business-friendly votes offended the Progressive majority of the board. For his part, Newsom claimed he was only acting as a "fiscal watchdog." For example, he offered a controversial "Care Not Cash" welfare reduction proposal in 2002. The plan targeted over 3,000 single homeless adults receiving welfare in an effort to stop recipients spending welfare money on heroin and alcohol while reducing deaths. Care Not Cash would have reduced local welfare payments by about 80% and replace this money with services such as shelter and food. The board rejected the proposal as an attack on the poor. Newsom then led the fight to place the issue before the voters in late 2002, and it passed handily. Newsom followed with what Progressives viewed as an anti-homeless ballot measure in November 2003, which banned "aggressive" panhandling throughout San Francisco and all forms of begging in specific areas such as on public transportation, near ATMs, and in parking lots. That measure also passed. Again and again, the majority Progressive faction of the Board of Supervisors tussled with Newsom. In the words of former fellow board member Tom Ammiano, "There were members of the board who woke up every morning wanting to f*** Gavin Newsom over."[26] Then-moderate Gavin Newson was a far cry from the liberal elected governor in 2018.

Mayor of San Francisco

In 2003, Willie Brown was termed out, so the mayoral race was wide open. Supervisor Gavin Newsom entered the race as did Board of Supervisors President Matt Gonzalez, Supervisor Tom Ammiano, and former Supervisor Angela Alioto. San Francisco City Treasurer Susan Leal and former San Francisco Police Chief Tony Ribera were also candidates in the November 4, 2003 election. The top two finishers were Newsom with 41.9% of the vote and Gonzalez with 19.8% of the vote. With no candidate receiving at least 50% of the vote, a runoff election was scheduled for December 9, 2003. Though local elections are officially nonpartisan in California, the powerful Democratic Party with 55% of the city's registered voters clearly supported Newsom; Gonzalez received support from the Green Party, which contained 3% of the city's registered voters.

The runoff was much closer than political party affiliations would have suggested. Newsom out-raised and outspent Gonzalez by raising nearly $4 million in contributions, almost a 10-to-1 advantage.[27] In addition to unofficial support by the Democratic Party, Newsom was backed by dozens of unions, real estate groups, and other corporate interests. He also received numerous endorsements from prominent Democrats, including former President Bill Clinton and his Vice President Al Gore.[28] Gonzalez had the support of Progressive groups like homeless activists and environmentalists. He was also endorsed by a majority of the Board of Supervisors, who were much more liberal than Newsom. Newsom won the runoff by the narrow margin of 53% to 47%.

Care Not Cash

Immediately Newsom went to work with an activist program. Homelessness in San Francisco had only increased over the past decade, despite efforts to control it. The condition had caught flak from the business community as an affront to tourism, which has always been a critical element of San Francisco's economy. He returned to the Care Not Cash concept. Now with the power to act, Newsom put together a 10-year program to reduce homeless cash grants of between $320 and $395 down to about $60. The saved funds would be used for food and the procurement of shelter. Once again, Progressive members opposed the idea, as did homeless advocacy groups. Others argued the program would reduce the amount of funds homeless San Franciscans were currently spending on food, shelter, and other services. But now-Mayor Newsom was able to get the plan through, although at a cost. He was yelled at on the street, victimized by graffiti spray painted on his garage, with his likeness burned in effigy.[29] In the short term, Newsom was vindicated. A study by the *San Francisco Chronicle* found that by the end of the year, the city's homeless rate had plummeted 40% from 2,497 to 1,515.[30] Three years remained on the 10-year plan when Newsom left the mayor's office in 2011 to be lieutenant governor. At that time, the Budget and Legislative Analyst of San Francisco found that the homeless population in San Francisco had nearly quadrupled to 6,415 from 1,515 at the end of 2004.[31] Care Not Cash was a stunning failure.

Same-Sex Marriage

Although Mayor Gavin Newsom had repeatedly frustrated Progressives with moderate policies, he was not that easy to label. Defying state law in February 2004, Newsom directed the city clerk to issue marriage licenses to same-sex couples. Newsom said he was inspired to act after President George W. Bush proposed a constitutional amendment to ban same-sex marriage.[32] He ordered performance of same-sex marriages knowing full well that in March 2000, California voters had passed Proposition 22, a statutory initiative defining marriage as only between a man and a woman. However, Newsom believed that denying marriage licenses to gays and lesbians violated their equal protection under the California Constitution.[33] Thus, the city clerk was authorized to conduct same-sex marriages. About 4,000 licenses were issued between February 12 and March 11, 2004 before the California Supreme Court ordered San Francisco officials to cease issuing marriage licenses until the legal issue was resolved. On August 12, the state's high court ruled that the mayor had overstepped his authority.[34]

But there was another angle. In May 2008, the state supreme court agreed with Newsom that Proposition 22 violated the state's constitution and declared that same-sex couples had a right to marry. Same-sex marriage opponents didn't give up though. They obtained over 1.2 million signatures for a proposed state constitutional amendment. Proposition 8, which eliminated the rights of same-sex couples to marry, passed by a margin of 52.3% to 47.7% on November 4, 2008, making same-sex marriage unconstitutional in California. It was then upheld by the California State Supreme Court.

Ultimately, the case went all the way to the U.S. Supreme Court, where the justices left in place a lower federal court ruling that Proposition 8 was unconstitutional. Shortly thereafter, on June 26, 2015, same-sex marriage was legalized across the nation when the U.S. Supreme Court, in *Obergefell v. Hodges*, ruled 5–4 that the 14th Amendment required all states to recognize same-sex marriages.

Gavin Newsom was an innovator—some might even say a trailblazer—on same-sex marriage and took a lot of heat from both the Left and the Right for his actions as Mayor of San Francisco. But there is little doubt that his actions were of monumental importance in the battle for marriage equality.

Sanctuary City

San Francisco was first declared a "sanctuary city" in 1989 by the Board of Supervisors and then-Mayor Dianne Feinstein. When he became mayor, Newsom reaffirmed San Francisco as a sanctuary city. "I will not allow any of my department heads or anyone associated with this city to cooperate in any way shape or form with these [federal immigration] raids," Newsom declared. "We are a sanctuary city, make no mistake about it."[35]

The sanctuary city policy was controversial and cited by opponents as a contributing factor in several brutal crimes. Cases occurred in which the city shielded undocumented immigrants accused of serious crimes from federal authorities. A particularly gruesome case occurred in 2008, when an undocumented immigrant from Honduras with a juvenile record was accused of stabbing a 14-year-old boy to death, yet never referred to federal officials. After enduring serious criticism from the right, Newsom "declared that he had ordered juvenile justice officials to report illegal immigrant offenders to federal authorities" and "pledged a 'top-to-bottom' review of the city's sanctuary policies and practices."[36] In fact, in early July that year, Newsom had announced a policy change whereby the city would turn over to federal authorities undocumented juvenile immigrants who were convicted of felonies.[37] Simply put, Newsom did a one-eighty on the sanctuary city concept.

Then in 2009, Newsom vetoed legislation which prohibited city officials from reporting undocumented youth arrested on felony charges to federal authorities for possible deportation. The legislation, introduced by Supervisor David Campos, and adopted by an 8–3 vote, required that undocumented arrested juveniles could only be reported if there was a conviction. Newsom vetoed the legislation because it conflicted with federal law; the Board of Supervisors responded by overriding his veto by the same 8–3 vote.[38]

The sanctuary city policy was later cited as a contributing factor in the 2015 murder of Kate Steinle, 31, who was shot while walking with her father down San Francisco's Embarcadero. Police arrested Juan Francisco Lopez-Sanchez, who had been deported five times and had a more than twenty-year history of run-ins with authorities. Federal officials asked city officials to notify Immigration and Customs Enforcement (ICE) authorities before releasing Lopez-Sanchez from jail. But in compliance with the sanctuary city policy, the San Francisco Sheriff's Department did not notify federal authorities before releasing Lopez-Sanchez since there was no federal warrant for his arrest.

Over time, Newsom bobbed and weaved on the sanctuary city issue, sometimes fighting with his own Board of Supervisors, other times fighting with federal authorities. As such, he became a target for both liberal and conservative groups, leaving people confused over the city's direction.

Re-election

Newsom was re-elected mayor in 2007. It was the first mayoral election in San Francisco history to use ranked-choice voting, where no run-off is needed because voters' second and third choices are considered. Progressives, including former Supervisor Matt Gonzales and Supervisors Ross Mirkarimi and Chris Daly declined to run. Nonetheless, Newsom faced a colorful group of opponents. A professional "showman," a nudist, and the owner of a sex club were among the other 12 candidates on the ballot. Newsom, facing no serious challenger, won with 72% of the vote. In his victory speech, he listed his priorities for his second term—the environment, homelessness, health care, and education.[39]

Newsom pursued an aggressive agenda during his second term. Among Newsom's successes were the Community Justice Center and his environmental programs. Opened in March 2009, the Community Justice Center in the Tenderloin District allowed individuals who are caught committing nonviolent felonies to avoid jail time and instead get help with their problems such as drug addiction or alcoholism or mental illness.

Newsom also developed a strong environmental record during his second term in June 2009, he signed the country's first mandatory composting law. Residents and businesses were required to separate recycling from trash and also compost food waste and plant trimmings, using a three-bin system. The goal was "zero waste" and, as of 2018, San Francisco sent less trash to the landfill than any other major U.S. city.[40] In addition, city buses began to "run on B20, a blend of diesel and biodiesel, which is made from recycled oil and fat."[41] San Francisco also became a leader in converting city vehicles and taxis to hybrid or electric and passed strict green building regulations.

Big Ideas

As mayor, Newsom had a fondness for memorizing facts and statistics and keeping notes at the ready, partly as a strategy to manage his dyslexia. But he was also known to be a "big ideas" person, even before his political career. In the 35-page PlumpJack handbook, he encouraged employees to take risks and rewarded them for proposing new ideas, even those that failed. As mayor though, Newsom was accused of getting so wrapped up in the big ideas that he lost track of the everyday details of running the city or getting to know his colleagues.[42]

Some of those "big ideas" weren't necessarily Newsom's, at least in the eyes of others. For example, Care Not Cash was Amos Brown's plan, according to Willie Brown, and universal healthcare was Tom Ammiano's.[43] Newsom also liked to share his big ideas and sometimes even the details of proposed policies, perhaps not realizing that the average person was not the policy wonk he was. In 2008, Newsom gave a seven-and-a-half-hour State of the City address on YouTube because he had so many ideas to share with San Franciscans. And he was known to carry with him an "accountability matrix," a binder of documents which tracked his various ideas and their progress.[44] However, former San Francisco supervisor Chris Daly who regularly clashed with Newsom on the board, complained the former mayor's penchant for "regurgitating irrelevant statistics" and business-school jargon was simply a means to muddy issues when politically useful: "I sat next to Gavin for two years on the Board and have too much personal experience to be a believer in him as some sort of 'progressive hero.'"[45] Whatever the truth, such perceptions likely contributed the often-expressed view of Newsom as inauthentic, an attribute not particularly desirable in the world of politics.

Lieutenant Governor

With the end of his second mayoral term on the horizon (he was scheduled to be termed out of office in 2011), Newsom, like most politicians facing term limits, started looking for his next political gig. For the politically ambitious, the gaze is almost always upwards. In April 2009, Newsom would try to make the biggest leap available to him in California politics: a run for governor. He certainly wasn't the first San Francisco mayor to eye the top prize, although the last person to win was James Rolph, Jr., who served as mayor for nearly twenty years before election to the governorship in 1930.

Newsom's run for governor that year effectively ended before it even got started. With the state reeling from the Great Recession, massive budget deficits, and the public's disenchantment with the leadership of the soon-to-be-termed-out Arnold Schwarzenegger, Attorney General (and two-time former governor) Jerry Brown entered the race promising to bring his lifetime's worth of governing experience to clean up the mess.

Newsom initially framed the potential matchup between "a stroll down memory lane" with Brown or a "spring to the future" with him.[46] But the message didn't resonate; voters were looking for an experienced hand.

Recalling the governor's race, Willie Brown warned Newsom against bucking Jerry Brown, perhaps the most politically experienced elected official in California history: "He [Newsom] didn't take my advice. . . . I explained to Newsom you can announce, but you better say 'only if Jerry doesn't run' because that's your constituency."[47] Struggling to raise the kind of money needed to run a competitive statewide campaign and seeing Brown was going to secure the nomination with relative ease, Newsom bowed out.

Five months later, Newsom announced a run for lieutenant governor. He talked glowingly about the job. "Being in a position where you can fight for cities and counties, where you can organize counties around homeless policy and health policy and education reform, and you can have the bully pulpit, to me that's not just symbolic," Newsom said at the time of his announcement. "You can actually make a real impact."[48] Facing Republican Abel Maldonado and a variety of third-party challengers, Newsom won with 50.1% of the vote.

Sizing Up the Office

Despite Newsom's ostensible enthusiasm for the job, the lieutenant governor of California is an odd political office in a number of ways. On one hand, it's the state's number-two executive office. On the other hand, the office has little power. If for any reason the governor becomes disabled and can't fulfill the duties of job, the lieutenant governor takes the reins, but that possibility is more theoretical than real. The lieutenant governor also serves in an "acting" capacity when the governor travels out of state, another responsibility with little real sizzle. The lieutenant governor heads several state commissions, is a member of the governing bodies of the University of California and California State University systems, and serves as President of the State Senate, but those positions are largely ceremonial and typically lack any regular substantive responsibilities.

If the job as California lieutenant governor is seen as anything in the modern era, it's as an "executive-in-waiting" position. History suggests that maybe it shouldn't be seen this way. Gray Davis was one of only two lieutenant governors who had ever moved up to the governorship in 1998. Moreover, the office is independently elected, meaning California's number two doesn't run on the same ticket as the governor. Although lieutenant governors might develop close partnerships with the governor (and wield political influence that comes with such a relationship), or be the beneficiary of "political grooming" in the rarified political circles of Sacramento politics, this is far from guaranteed.

Newsom had no such benefits with Brown in a relationship that might be best described as "distant." Despite ties between the Brown and Newsom families that dated back years, tension between the two men grew after Newsom's short flirtation with governorship in 2010.[49] Reliving their history, Newsom believed the distance stemmed from Brown's paternalistic view of Newsom as "just a kid," although Brown never said as much.[50]

Regardless, once in office Brown rarely asked his lieutenant governor for advice or counsel. As if to remind Newsom that he was *lieutenant* governor, Brown rejected appointing Newsom to a board governing the state's new health insurance exchange (created after the adoption of the Affordable Care Act in 2010) and denied Newsom's request to create a state council on homelessness.[51] Brown said that the role of the lieutenant governor was limited by design, suggesting there was nothing personal.

In his first years as lieutenant governor Newsom failed to carve out a clear role for himself. Newsom once said, "I feel like I've succeeded in finding a million ways not to do something." He once was asked by a friend (during a commercial break taping a current events television show) how often he worked in Sacramento; he replied, "Like one day a week, tops. There's no reason . . . it's just so dull."[52] Newsom actually avoided Sacramento and worked instead in San Francisco, at a desk in a workspace for tech start-ups. Newsom was once even stopped by a woman who asked him to take a picture with her son. The boy asked, "What does a lieutenant governor do?" While gazing straight at the camera Newsom reportedly replied, "I ask myself that every day."[53]

With no real substantive responsibilities, Newsom had few policymaking opportunities, except for times when Governor Jerry Brown was out of state. Even then, one must be careful not to upset the boss. Thus, in those rare moments, Newsom did manage to declare an official state vegetable (artichoke, if you're wondering) and fruit (avocado) while Governor Jerry Brown was away on travel to China. Otherwise, Newsom focused on keeping his name and face in the news. He was a regular on cable television and inside politics shows like "Meet the Press."

When longtime U.S. Senator Barbara Boxer announced she would not seek re-election in 2015, the open Senate seat was undoubtedly enticing to Newsom. His name, along with Attorney General Kamala Harris, immediately surfaced as leading contenders to replace her. But saying that "my head and my heart" remained firmly in California and not Washington D.C., Newsom turned his attention back to the governorship, thus leaving the progressive lane of the Democratic Party wide open for what would be a successful Senate run for Harris.[54] In February 2015, 15 months after re-election as lieutenant governor, he announced his candidacy for governor. "I have zero interest in becoming the next governor to become governor," Newsom said with a seemingly altruistic tone. "I want to try to do something meaningful and purposeful and help people do extraordinary things in their lives."[55] Truth to be told, Newsom's announcement was timed to dissuade other candidates from running and most importantly, to allow him to begin fundraising.

Building a Resume

Once Newsom announced, he needed a platform to build enthusiasm for his candidacy. What better way than to enmesh oneself back into debates over hot-button issues that animate America's culture wars? And that's exactly what Newsom did, only this time instead of same-sex marriage, he focused on legalizing recreational marijuana and stricter regulations on guns and ammunition.

In 2012, Newsom became the first statewide elected official to publicly endorse the legalization of marijuana. He became deeply engaged on the issue and helped to galvanize public support for Proposition 64—the California Marijuana Legalization Initiative—which passed with 57% of the vote in 2016. The law made it legal for adults 21 and over to use marijuana for recreational purposes. That same year Newsom formed a campaign committee that raised more than $4.5 million to pass Proposition 63, an initiative that outlawed large ammunition magazines, mandated background checks for people who buy bullets, and imposed fines for not reporting guns that were lost or stolen.

His work on gun control, not surprisingly, placed him in direct conflict with the powerful National Rifle Association. And Newsom, quite predictably, became a punching bag for activists and provocateurs on the political right. Seemingly lost at sea for most of his tenure at lieutenant governor, Newsom appeared reenergized by his jump back into the ideological wars over policies he deemed important.

Newsom once described his love for "Big Hairy Audacious Goals."[56] It was perhaps fitting for a man with the reputation for having some of the best locks in politics. Now, as his campaign dawned for the one office he had long coveted, the stakes for Newsom couldn't have been higher.

Notes

1. See "Must Reads: How eight elite families funded Gavin Newsom's political ascent," *Los Angeles Times*, September 7, 2018, www.latimes.com/politics/la-pol-ca-gavin-newsom-san-francisco-families-20180907-story.html.
2. "Column: Maybe not a bond, but there's a connection between Jerry Brown and Gavin Newsom as governors of California," *Los Angeles Times*, January 6, 2019, www.latimes.com/politics/la-pol-ca-road-map-jerry-brown-gavin-newsom-connection-20190106-story.html.
3. "Newsom's portfolio: Mayoral hopeful has parlayed Getty money, family ties and political connections into local prominence," *San Francisco Chronicle*, February 23, 2003, www.sfgate.com/politics/article/NEWSOM-S-PORTFOLIO-Mayoral-hopeful-has-parlayed-2632672.php.

4. "Gavin Newsom's keeping it all in the family," *CalMatters*, January 6, 2019. Updated July 8, 2019, https://calmatters.org/commentary/2019/01/gavin-newsoms-keeping-it-all-in-the-family/.

5. "William Alfred Newsom III, retired judge and father of Gov.-Elect Gavin Newsom, dies at 84," *Los Angeles Times*, December 12, 2018, www.latimes.com/politics/la-pol-ca-obit-william-newsom-20181212-story.html.

6. "Thank Newsom's childhood pet—an otter—for helping protect California land and waters," *The Los Angeles Times*, October 12, 2020, https://www.latimes.com/california/story/2020-10-12/skelton-gavin-newsom-pet-otter-conservation-lands-california.

7. "Newsom's portfolio: Mayoral hopeful has parlayed Getty money, family ties and political connections into local prominence," *San Francisco Chronicle*, February 23, 2003, www.sfgate.com/politics/article/NEWSOM-S-PORTFOLIO-Mayoral-hopeful-has-parlayed-2632672.php.

8. Dan Walters, "Gavin Newsom's keeping it all in the family," *CalMatters*, January 6, 2019. Updated July 8, 2019, https://calmatters.org/commentary/2019/01/gavin-newsoms-keeping-it-all-in-the-family/.

9. "Newsom's portfolio: Mayoral hopeful has parlayed Getty money, family ties and political connections into local prominence," *San Francisco Chronicle*, February 23, 2003, www.sfgate.com/politics/article/NEWSOM-S-PORTFOLIO-Mayoral-hopeful-has-parlayed-2632672.php and "Gonzalez, Newsom: What makes them run: From modest beginnings, Newsom finds connections for business, political success," *San Francisco Chronicle*, December 7, 2003. Updated January 13, 2012, www.sfgate.com/politics/article/Gonzalez-Newsom-What-makes-them-run-From-2510021.php.

10. "Gonzalez, Newsom: What makes them run: From modest beginnings, Newsom finds connections for business, political success," *San Francisco Chronicle*, December 7, 2003. Updated January 13, 2012, www.sfgate.com/politics/article/Gonzalez-Newsom-What-makes-them-run-From-2510021.php.

11. Ibid.

12. "Belmont/Newsom comes out: He's dyslexic / S.F. Mayor speaks of school woes," *San Francisco Chronicle*, April 21, 2004, www.sfgate.com/education/article/BELMONT-Newsom-comes-out-He-s-dyslexic-S-F-2790200.php.

13. Tad Friend, "Gavin Newsom: The next head of the California resistance," *The New Yorker*, October 29, 2018, www.newyorker.com/magazine/2018/11/05/gavin-newsom-the-next-head-of-the-california-resistance.

14. "Gonzalez, Newsom: What makes them run: From modest beginnings, Newsom finds connections for business, political success," *San Francisco Chronicle*, December 7, 2003. Updated January 13, 2012, www.sfgate.com/politics/article/Gonzalez-Newsom-What-makes-them-run-From-2510021.php.

15. Jada Yuan, "86 minutes with Gavin Newsom," April 29, 2011, https://nymag.com/news/intelligencer/encounter/gavin-newsom-2011-5/.

16. "Newsom's way," *SFGate*, March 11, 1997, www.sfgate.com/business/article/NEWSOM-S-WAY-3129914.php.

17. Dan Walters, "Gavin Newsom's keeping it all in the family," *CalMatters*, January 6, 2019. Updated July 8, 2019, https://calmatters.org/commentary/2019/01/gavin-newsoms-keeping-it-all-in-the-family/.

18. "Newsom's portfolio: Mayoral hopeful has parlayed Getty money, family ties and political connections into local prominence," *San Francisco Chronicle*, February 23, 2003, www.sfgate.com/politics/article/NEWSOM-S-PORTFOLIO-Mayoral-hopeful-has-parlayed-2632672.php.

19. "Gonzalez, Newsom: What makes them run: From modest beginnings, Newsom finds connections for business, political success," *San Francisco Chronicle*, December 7, 2003. Updated January 13, 2012, www.sfgate.com/politics/article/Gonzalez-Newsom-What-makes-them-run-From-2510021.php, and "Newsom's portfolio: Mayoral hopeful has parlayed Getty money, family ties and political connections into local prominence," *San Francisco Chronicle*, February 23, 2003, www.sfgate.com/politics/article/NEWSOM-S-PORTFOLIO-Mayoral-hopeful-has-parlayed-2632672.php.
20. "Newsom's portfolio: Mayoral hopeful has parlayed Getty money, family ties and political connections into local prominence," *San Francisco Chronicle*, February 23, 2003, www.sfgate.com/politics/article/NEWSOM-S-PORTFOLIO-Mayoral-hopeful-has-parlayed-2632672.php.
21. Interview with Willie Brown. May 20, 2021.
22. Ibid.
23. "S.F.'s new supervisor: Bold, young entrepreneur," *SFGate*, February 4, 1997. Updated January 30, 2012, www.sfgate.com/news/article/S-F-s-New-Supervisor-Bold-Young-Entrepreneur-2855573.php.
24. Interview with Willie Brown. May 20, 2021.
25. Ibid.
26. Tad Friend, "Gavin Newsom: The next head of the California resistance," *The New Yorker*, October 29, 2018, www.newyorker.com/magazine/2018/11/05/gavin-newsom-the-next-head-of-the-california-resistance.
27. "Donated dollars nourish contest/Newsom outraises Gonzalez by a factor of nearly 10 in Mayor's race," *SFGate*, December 2, 2003, www.sfgate.com/politics/article/Donated-dollars-nourish-contest-Newsom-2510373.php.
28. "S.F. campaign notebook," *SFGate*, December 3, 2003. Updated January 12, 2012, www.sfgate.com/politics/article/S-F-CAMPAIGN-NOTEBOOK-2510156.php.
29. "Gavin Newsom's approach to fixing homeless in San Francisco outraged activists: And he's proud of it," *Los Angeles Times*, October 23, 2018, www.latimes.com/politics/la-pol-ca-gavin-newsom-homelessness-san-francisco-20181023-story.html.
30. "Signs of hope replace despair, Mayor's homeless plan a start/Mayor's homeless plan to move people from streets to supportive housing brings cleaner blocks—but the toughest cases need more help," *SFGate*, December 5, 2004, www.sfgate.com/news/article/Signs-of-hope-replace-despair-Mayor-s-homeless-2666742.php.
31. "Policy Analysis Report," *Budget and Legislative Analyst*, Board of Supervisors, City and County of San Francisco, July 26, 2013, https://sfbos.org/sites/default/files/FileCenter/Documents/48249-BLA.Homeless%20Services.072613.pdf.
32. "The battle over same-sex marriage/Uncharted territory/Bush's stance led Newsom to take action," *SFGate*, February 15, 2004. Updated January 29, 2012, www.sfgate.com/news/article/THE-BATTLE-OVER-SAME-SEX-MARRIAGE-Uncharted-2823315.php.
33. Ibid.
34. *Lockyer v. City and County of San Francisco*, August 12, 2004, https://caselaw.findlaw.com/ca-supreme-court/1240046.html.
35. "Newsom pledges to make SF a sanctuary for illegal immigrants," *SFGate*, April 22, 2007, www.sfgate.com/bayarea/article/Newsom-pledges-to-make-SF-a-sanctuary-for-illegal-2600279.php.

36. "Suspect in boy's slaying avoided deportation: Juvenile Justice: Sanctuary city arrested for assault last year, he's now accused in slaying," November 14, 2008, www.sfgate.com/crime/article/Suspect-in-boy-s-slaying-avoided-deportation-3185379.php.
37. "S.F. mayor shifts policy on illegal offenders: Update: Sanctuary City Newsom concedes the city was wrong to shield young immigrants convicted of felonies from possible deportation," *SFGate*, July 3, 2008, www.sfgate.com/news/article/S-F-mayor-shifts-policy-on-illegal-offenders-3278495.php.
38. "San Francisco board overrides mayor's veto of sanctuary expansion," *Los Angeles Times*, November 11, 2009, www.latimes.com/archives/la-xpm-2009-nov-11-me-sf-sanctuary11-story.html.
39. "Newsom's 2nd act: His priorities: Environment, homelessness, education, housing, rebuilding S.F. General," *SFGate*, November 7, 2007. Updated February 10, 2012, www.sfgate.com/news/article/NEWSOM-S-2ND-ACT-3236820.php.
40. "How San Francisco sends less trash to the landfill than any other major U.S. city," July 14, 2018, *CNBC.com*, www.cnbc.com/2018/07/13/how-san-francisco-became-a-global-leader-in-waste-management.html.
41. Muni hybrid buses, www.sfmta.com/getting-around/muni/muni-hybrid-buses.
42. Tad Friend, "Gavin Newsom: The Next Head of the California Resistance," *The New Yorker*, October 29, 2018, www.newyorker.com/magazine/2018/11/05/gavin-newsom-the-next-head-of-the-california-resistance.
43. Interview with Willie Brown. May 20, 2021, and Friend, ibid.
44. "Gavin Newsom's lively term as SF mayor offers clues to how he'd lead state," *San Francisco Chronicle*, May 25, 2018. Updated May 26, 2018, www.sfchronicle.com/news/article/Gavin-Newsom-s-lively-term-as-SF-mayor-offers-12944142.php.
45. Ben Christopher, "Behind the smile: Why Gavin Newsom is striving for his 'Big Hairy Audacious Goal,'" *CalMatters*, October 23, 2018. Updated 23, 2020, https://calmatters.org/politics/2018/10/gavin-newsom-profile-california-governor-election/.
46. "Gavin Newsom was a rising star: Now he's Lieutenant Governor," *Los Angeles Times*, July 15, 2013, www.latimes.com/local/la-me-gavin-newsom-20130715-dto-htmlstory.html.
47. Interview with Willie Brown. May 20, 2021.
48. "It's official: Newsom running for Lt. Governor," *San Francisco Examiner*, March 12, 2010, www.sfexaminer.com/news/its-official-newsom-running-for-lt-governor/.
49. "From Brown to Newsom, California to see new style, substance," January 6, 2019, https://apnews.com/article/politics-ap-top-news-us-news-california-sacramento-373035f611c44d43b1c849aed8448285.
50. Ibid.
51. Ibid.
52. "Gavin Newsom on Sacramento: 'It's Just So Dull,'" *Huffpost*, May 29, 2012, www.huffpost.com/entry/gavin-newsom-on-sacramento_n_1554208.
53. "As lieutenant governor, Gavin Newsom has had few duties: And he skipped many of them," *Los Angeles Times*, April 20, 2018, www.latimes.com/politics/la-pol-ca-gavin-newsom-lieutenant-governor-attendance-20180420-story.html.
54. "Newsom won't run for Calif. senate seat: All eyes on Harris," *Politico*, January 12, 2015, www.politico.com/story/2015/01/gavin-newsom-not-running-barabara-boxer-seat-114178.

55. "Gavin Newsom is the first to enter 2018 race for Governor," *Los Angeles Times*, February 11, 2015, www.latimes.com/local/politics/la-me-pol-gavin-newsom-20150212-story.html.
56. Ben Christopher, "Behind the smile: Why Gavin Newsom is striving for his 'Big Hairy Audacious Goal,'" *CalMatters*, October 23, 2018. Updated 23, 2020, https://calmatters.org/politics/2018/10/gavin-newsom-profile-california-governor-election/.

Chapter 3

Becoming Governor

Newsom's Ambitious Agenda

If you limit your choices only to what seems possible or reasonable, you disconnect yourself from what you truly want, and all that is left is compromise.

—Robert Fritz

Robert Fritz, author, composer, and filmmaker, encourages admirers of his work to think big. He teaches the value of having a broad imaginative vision, the idea that creativity and leadership require thinking beyond what seems possible in the moment. For Fritz, compromise and half-baked solutions do a disservice to meaningful problem solving.

Gavin Newsom would likely agree with much of Fritz's views. In fact, Newsom's campaign for governor was filled with rhetorical and visual symbolism. The 50-year-old native Californian offered himself as the picture of a new generation of energetic leadership, suggesting a stark contrast to 80-year-old departing Governor Jerry Brown. In 2018, Newsom beat back several Democratic challengers before turning his attention and massive campaign war chest to his general election opponent, Republican businessman John Cox. As Newsom is wont to do, he made big promises on the campaign trail—on housing, education, child care, homelessness, clean energy, climate change, jobs, immigration, and criminal justice reform. His campaign tagline, "Courage for a Change," seemed to underscore the idea that he was planning big, audacious changes in California's governance.

But while Fritz views compromise as the result of poor focus, in politics compromise is a fundamental feature of the political process, not a hindrance. If Gavin Newsom didn't realize this before he became governor, he did shortly after he reached the state's highest office. He had to coordinate with the other branches of state government, harmonize with various local governments and agencies, work with the feds, please public opinion, and fend off various competing interests often at odds with his assessment of the state's needs. Governing a huge state like California,

DOI: 10.4324/9781003217954-3

Newsom would soon learn, is a lot more interdependent than simply setting a series of goals and getting results.

In this chapter, we chronicle the next direction for Gavin Newsom.
No longer the political moderate chief executive of a city defined by a
fractious board of supervisors, Newsom began anew with a blank slate.
Regarding his politics, Newsom turned left. With an overwhelming liberal Democratic legislature, he presented a similar posture, leaving behind
the more tempered stance he displayed as San Francisco mayor. Should he
win the state's highest office, Newsom would be in a dramatically different political environment, so he began to adapt accordingly.

One other significant point emerges here: Newsom's ability to define
and beat his opponents. In politics, strategy is just as important as governance; without executing the former correctly, the latter doesn't occur.
Accordingly, we see early in the gubernatorial campaign how Newsom
was able to exorcise fellow Democrat Antonio Villaraigosa, his biggest
threat, in favor of Republican John Cox, only to reinvent Cox's fairly
peripheral connection with Donald Trump. That strategy would be
tweaked 18 months later in Newsom's fight to defeat the recall.

We next turn to Newsom's first year as governor. His many lofty policy
proposals notwithstanding, the new governor struggled to gain traction
with a highly Democratic state legislature perhaps because of what some
viewed as an aloof posture—the same behavioral trait observed by others during his time as San Francisco mayor. Yes, Newsom used executive
powers for largely peripheral issues, but the major policies he proposed
en route to his election remained unsolved at the end of his first year.

The June Primary Election

California's election system operates with a "Top Two Primary." Adopted
by the voters in 2012, this nomination method awards general election
slots to the two candidates with the most votes in the primary irrespective of their political party affiliation. Unlike states that provide voters
nominees from each political party, under the top-two system it's possible
that two candidates with the same political party label could face off in
the November general election. As such, candidates need to campaign
with a different calculus. Out of more than twenty candidates running in
the 2018 election cycle, it appeared that Democrats had a much stronger
field than Republicans, suggesting the possibility of an intraparty contest
in November. The Newsom campaign clearly understood this possibility
and its potential consequences, which we will discuss later in this chapter.
For now, we turn to the list of candidates.

Gavin Newsom launched his gubernatorial campaign in February
2015, shortly after his re-election to the lieutenant governor's position.
By announcing early, Newsom hoped to minimize the possibility of any

serious opposition. He focused on big goals such as a statewide initiative to toughen gun laws in California. And he showed early signs of success. Proposition 63, which required background checks for ammunition purchases and banned possession of large-capacity ammunition magazines, passed in 2016; however, the proposition was ruled unconstitutional in 2019 by the federal courts.[1] Nevertheless, Newsom's commitment to reducing gun access endeared gun control proponents to the candidate. On another front, Newsom actively promoted legalization of recreational marijuana, which passed as Proposition 64 in 2016. Here, too, he was in sync with public opinion. On a separate public policy front, Newsom proposed adoption of a universal healthcare program for Californians early in his campaign.[2] Of all the gubernatorial candidates, Newsom stood apart for his "big" ideas. How many were politically possible remained to be seen.

Running against Newsom in the 2018 primary was a mix of Democratic and Republican candidates with varying degrees of political experience and support. Democrat Antonio Villaraigosa, who early in the race appeared to be Newsom's most formidable opponent, was the recent two-term Mayor of Los Angeles (2005–2013) and the former Speaker of the California State Assembly (1998–2000). His campaign focused on reforming publication education (he was a strong supper of charter schools), making modest changes to the state's health care policies, and tackling poverty and the state's uneven economy.[3] Once a liberal member of the state legislature, Villaraigosa approached the campaign as a bit more of a centrist than Newsom, whom Villaraigosa attacked as a "snake oil salesman" for promising the voters whatever they wanted to hear.[4]

Democrat John Chiang was State Treasurer and former State Controller (2006–2014). Before that, he served two terms on the State Board of Equalization. In 2011, he withheld state lawmakers' pay when they failed to produce a balanced budget by the June 15 deadline. Seen as a hero to state workers, Chiang also refused an order by then-Governor Arnold Schwarzenegger to furlough state workers three days a month during the state budget crisis two years earlier, though his actions were overruled by California Supreme Court.[5]

In another time, Villaraigosa or Chiang may well have been "the candidate to beat" for the election victory. Newsom clearly realized this and organized his campaign with more concern for these two individuals than any Republican.

The other candidates on the Democratic side developed little traction, never reaching potential voter support above single digits. Diane Eastin served as California Superintendent of Public Instruction from 1995 to 2003 and in the State Assembly from 1986 to 1994. In the Assembly, she served as chair of the Education Committee. Democrat Amanda Renteria was the former California Department of Justice Chief of Operations and the former political director for Hillary Clinton's presidential campaign. She also previously worked as an economic policy advisor for U.S. Senator Dianne Feinstein (D-CA). Eight other lesser-known Democrats were just that—lesser known.

On the Republican side, two viable candidates emerged: John Cox and Travis Allen. Venture capitalist John Cox was not a newcomer to the campaign trail. When he lived in Illinois, Cox ran for office three times between 2000 and 2004—once for the U.S. House of Representatives, once for the U.S. Senate, and once for a job as Recorder of Deeds in Cook County—a position he curiously said should be terminated. He lost all three times. In 2008, he ran for president but his campaign went nowhere. With respect to his California candidacy, Cox proposed a "neighborhood legislature" which would consist of 12,000 "citizen legislators" elected from neighborhoods, added to the 80-member State Assembly and 40-member State Senate.[6] Despite Cox's poor election record, he had one quality that others lacked—money, and lots of it. With an estimated worth north of $100 million, Cox contributed $5.8 million to his campaign.

Orange County Republican State Assemblymember Travis Allen, first elected in 2012, was an outspoken conservative and Trump supporter. A central theme of his campaign was a call to repeal the newly adopted gas taxes and vehicle fees. These fees and taxes were projected to raise $5.2 billion annually for road repairs and mass transit.[7] Anti-tax themes always resonated well with most California Republicans and the Allen campaign drew its energy from that sector. The other four Republican candidates as well as a long list of candidates from minor political parties and no affiliation received little attention other than their names on the ballot.

Primary elections are times when candidates are busy trying to rack up as many endorsements as possible, particularly from their political party organizations. But in this case, no Democratic or Republican candidate secured the endorsement of the Democratic or Republican state party. At the Democratic statewide convention, the delegation was locked into a tight race between Chiang (30%) and Newsom (39%), with neither overcoming the party's 60% threshold.[8] At the Republican state convention in San Diego, John Cox won 55.3% of delegates' votes, but that still wasn't enough to earn the endorsement.[9]

Newsom may not have achieved endorsement status among Democrats, but he did secure key endorsements from Sen. Kamala Harris (D-CA) and major labor unions—a key Newsom constituency—such as the Service Employees International Union (SEIU), California Professional Firefighters, California Federation of Teachers, and the California Nurses Association. Chiang's endorsements included Rep. Ted Lieu (D-CA), California National Organization for Women, Silicon Valley Asian Pacific American Democratic Club, AAPI (Asian-American/Pacific Islander) Democratic

Club of San Diego, Association for Los Angeles Deputy Sheriffs, and California Association of Professional Employees. Villaraigosa's endorsements included Rep. Karen Bass (D-CA), the California Hispanic Chamber of Commerce, California Charter Schools Association Advocates, and the Peace Officers Research Association of California.[10]

With respect to the Republican candidates, President Donald Trump, House Minority Leader Kevin McCarthy (R-CA), Howard Jarvis Taxpayers Association, and the California Pro-Life Council endorsed Cox; California Board of Equalization President Diane Harkey, several Republican members of the State Assembly, and the Republican Party of Santa Barbara County endorsed Allen.[11]

Major California newspapers were split between the top two Democrats pretty much along geographical lines. Former San Francisco Mayor Newsom was endorsed by the *San Francisco Chronicle* and the *San José Mercury News*, while former Los Angeles Mayor Villaraigosa was endorsed by the *Los Angeles Times* and the *San Diego Union Tribune*. The *Sacramento Bee* favored both Gavin Newsom and John Chiang. On the Republican side of the primary campaign, the *Orange County Register* backed John Cox.

The top seven candidates raised and spent more than $90 million. Outside spending by unaffiliated groups, which cannot officially coordinate with the campaigns while raising unlimited amounts of funds, spent almost $32 million on the gubernatorial primary, with much of it in the last couple of weeks before the election, a record amount of money. Families and Teachers for Villaraigosa was the top-spending outside group. Associated with the California Charter School Association Advocates, this committee spent over $22.7 million promoting Villaraigosa and opposing Newsom and Cox. Citizens Supporting Newsom spent $5.6 million and was funded primarily by the Service Employees International Union and Blue Shield.[12]

Polls showed a tight contest between Newsom and Villaraigosa until March, when several surveys indicated a Cox surge. Still, among those with opinions, Newsom held the edge in nearly every survey until the election. Importantly, a high percentage of respondents said they were "undecided" or said "other candidate" when asked.[13] In a Public Policy Institute of California poll conducted May 11–20, 2018 showed 15% of likely voters were still undecided, suggesting the race was still in flux.[14]

Newsom's campaign made a strategic decision to elevate Cox late in the primary, hoping Cox would secure enough votes to earn a top-two position. That's because Newsom's campaign felt far more enthusiastic challenging a Republican than a more formidable Democratic challenger. The campaign spent money lavishly on television advertisements attacking Cox, hoping the approach would activate the Republican base. It seemed to help.

One strategy from the beginning was to tie Cox to Trump. Newsom's goal was to portray them as best friends even if they were worlds apart in their demeanor. Cox was a self-described "Jack Kemp" Republican who sought consensus based on policy solutions centered on limited government and lower taxes. Trump, by contrast, threw rhetorical bombs at every chance; he came to power by directly challenging the establishment of the modern Republican Party. President Trump, in other words, was not a Jack Kemp Republican.

Despite their differences in values and style, it wasn't far-fetched for Newsom to connect Cox to Trump. In 2016, Cox had actually voted for the Libertarian candidate Gary Johnson, arguing then that he wasn't a Trump supporter. But three weeks before the primary election, and sensing he needed to tap into Trump's broad support among California conservatives, Cox called his vote for Johnson "a mistake." In exchange, Trump wrote on Twitter, "California finally deserves a great Governor, one who understands borders, crime, and lowering taxes. John Cox is the man—he'll be the best Governor you've ever had."[15] Cox said he was "honored and deeply grateful for the endorsement," and looked forward to working with Trump to "make California great again."[16] Trump's late endorsement of Cox late in the gubernatorial primary race and "appeared to elevate Cox's status."[17] More significantly, while the budding alliance between Cox and Trump may have galvanized Republican voters, it was a gift to the Newsom campaign, considering California's widespread antipathy for President Trump. But the Newsom campaign also gained a bonus from their new strategy: The emphasis on the Cox/Trump axis foreshadowed Newsom's approach to Larry Elder in the 2021 recall election.

While many expected the race to come down to Villaraigosa and Newsom, the two Democrats did not receive the most votes. Instead, Republican Cox came in second, setting up a Democratic/Republican choice for November. Knowing the electorate was heavily Democratic, the Newsom campaign smelled a November victory. "The primary reminded us just how partisan our elections tend to be," said Mark Baldassare, the chief executive of the Public Policy Institute of California, "and how deeply divided our parties are in the types of candidates they choose."[18]

The primary election was held on June 5, 2018. Barely more than a third of the registered voters exercised the franchise, a bit higher than the previous two gubernatorial primaries but well within historical norms. Newsom emerged in first place by winning 33.7% of the vote and clearly confirming the strength of his candidacy. Cox ran almost eight points behind but did well enough to secure a strong second with 25.4%. Villaraigosa's campaign lost whatever momentum it had and came in a distant third with 13.3% of the vote. The other candidates in order of vote percentage were Allen (9.5%), Chiang (9.4%), Eastin (3.4%), and Renteria (1.3%). The rest of the field received less than 1% of the vote.[19] Not surprisingly, Newsom ran strong in the Bay Area, securing over 50% of the vote in Alameda, Marin, San Francisco, San Mateo, Santa Cruz, and Sonoma counties and with nearly 50% in Santa Clara County (48.5%) and Contra Costa County (49.9%). Villaraigosa's strongest numbers were in Fresno (20.2%), Imperial (31.1%), and Los Angeles (21.8%) counties.[20]

Reflecting the partisan and ideological split in different parts of California, Cox performed well in small rural, more conservative counties such as Amador (41.7%), Colusa (43.3%), Glenn (47.3%), Shasta (44.3%), and Modoc (49.9%). But those counties did little substantially to his vote total. For instance, he only received 1,422 votes from his near-majority win of Modoc County.[21]

The General Election

Newsom and Cox had passed the critical first real test in the 2018 gubernatorial campaign. But there were now five months of bruising battles ahead. Newsom's Democratic opponents quickly got behind his campaign. "I'm asking you to get behind Gavin Newsom," Villaraigosa said in his concession speech on election night.[22] Newsom, obviously basking in his primary victory, immediately began to frame some of the issues that would come to dominate the general election campaign. Building on the themes he discussed during the primary campaign, Newsom promised to pursue single-payer health care and deal with the housing affordability crisis and homelessness, pledging a "Marshall Plan for affordable housing."[23] He seemed to chastise the Democratic Party for thinking too small and for being too timid. "My whole life, we've faced down skeptics. Defeatist Democrats who say we need to 'pick our battles.' To me, this is more than a political campaign. It's about Democrats acting like Democrats—in a battle for America's soul against a president without one."[24] Ironically, battling "for the soul of America" became fellow Democrat Joe Biden's campaign theme in 2020 in his quest for the U.S. presidency.

As the campaign moved into fall, Newsom continued to tie Cox to President Trump. Now, instead of using President Trump as a way of energizing Republicans, he hoped to make the President a focus for Democrats. Indeed, for as much as Newsom framed his progressive-oriented campaign around important, seemingly intractable problems, it was also in his mind fundamentally a statement about the values of California, and by extension, what America stood for. To make that rhetorical and conceptual leap, President Trump served as the ideal foil. "California's vision and America's values are one and the same," Newsom said. "But our values, as you know, are under assault. We're engaged in an epic battle, and it looks like voters will have a real choice between a governor who will stand up to Donald Trump and foot soldier [John Cox] for his war on California."[25]

For his part, Cox immediately attacked Newsom for being a political insider. He was someone all too comfortable in Sacramento: "Mr. Newsom you've had eight years, and your party has made a colossal mess of this once golden state." Cox declared that what the state really needed was a governor with some business sense: "Business people have been elected to office as governor all across the nation to clean up the messes that the politicians have made," he added.[26] One of those "messes" was SB1, a new law supported by Newsom in 2017 that increased the gas tax and vehicle licensing fees to help invest in infrastructure. To that end, Cox had spent $250,000 of his own money to help qualify a referendum (Proposition 6) for the November 2018 election that, if passed, would repeal the new gas tax. For Cox, the new gas tax exemplified how "out of touch" the Democratic Party was to the concerns of average middle-class Californians. He hoped repealing the law would attract voters of all political stripes who were disenchanted with rising gas prices.[27] Apparently, Cox was "out of touch," not the Democratic Party, considering that the voters rejected the referendum 57% to 43%.

Though Cox made a big deal out of the Trump endorsement just before the primary election, as the general campaign wore on, he talked less about President Trump and core Republican issues like gun rights and abortion. Instead, he focused on narrow pocketbook issues like repealing the new gas tax which hurt "forgotten Californians," such as "that teacher, that cop, that blue-collar union worker who is paying the gas tax increase."[28] In a related theme, Cox attacked the Department of Motor Vehicles (DMV), which was facing several scandals due to agency ineptitude and poor software. One problem centered on the DMV's bungling implementation of the 2015 California Motor Voter Act through incorrect registration of thousands of voters. These problems, Cox emphasized, stemmed from an incompetent state government bureaucracy. "The biggest issue of this campaign is affordability," Cox said about two months before the election. "Paying $700 a year more for gas, or waiting in line for hours at the DMV instead of being at work or with your family, those are all products of the affordability crisis faced by millions of Californians forgotten by the Sacramento political class."[29]

Whereas Cox focused on "forgotten Californians," Newsom promised to "renew the California dream," which included plans for affordable housing, access to health care, child care, and after-school programs, and the expansion of jobs. These are "the manifestation of pocketbook issues" Newsom said. He attacked his opponent for talking about issues without offering detailed plans to address them, even noting some of "Cox's plans have the form and substance of fog."[30] Over and over again, the Democratic candidate implied that his Republican opponent wasn't up to the job of running the nation's largest state.

But Newsom had his own problems focusing on authenticity—a concern that would follow him through the recall election. While he pushed for expansive, progressive initiatives, Newsom was criticized at different points of the campaign for flip-flopping on the issues, depending on whom he was speaking with and where he was speaking. In a speech to the powerful California Nurses Association he offered a full-throttled support for a single-payer health care system and universal coverage. Yet, a short time later Newsom told journalists he was not entirely endorsing the idea because of concerns about the program's cost.[31] Even on sanctuary cities, which Newsom wholeheartedly endorsed during the gubernatorial campaign, progressives complained that his record didn't quite seem to match his rhetoric. They remembered that as mayor, Newsom referred undocumented juveniles charged with serious felony crimes to federal immigration officials for deportation. The practice persisted after high-profile killings in 2008 at the hands of a 21-year-old undocumented immigrant. Former San Francisco County Supervisor Dave Campos was critical at the time. The policy "led to the deportation of many youth, including many youth who were wrongly convicted" Campos said. "[Newsom has] been trying to position himself as a champion of sanctuary cities. Don't rewrite history."[32] Such concerns led some voters to question his genuineness.

As the election neared, Newsom pulled away from Cox. A September Public Policy Institute of California poll showed Newsom with a 12-point lead (51% to 39%) among likely voters.[33] Newsom's growing advantage allowed him to pivot away from Cox. Increasingly confident, Newsom agreed to debate his opponent only once during the general election campaign.[34] After all, why risk things when you're leading? Instead, he squared his attention on President Trump. This allowed Newsom to talk about big national issues that energized the Democratic base. Immigration, women's reproductive rights, and health care and more "are under attack by an administration determined to move our country backwards," Newsom said. "Let's show Donald Trump what our bold progressive future really looks like."[35]

In addition to leading in the polls, Newsom was also, and not surprisingly, way ahead in the money race. Combining his tally from the primary and general elections Newsom raised a total of $58.2 million. Among his biggest campaign contributors were the California Teachers Association, Service Employees International Union, and California Nurses Association.[36] Cox, by contrast, was far behind, raising $16.8 million. Cox's largest donor was himself; he contributed another $700,000 to his campaign during the general and $5.8 million overall. Even for a man worth an estimated $100 million, this was a substantial investment in his own campaign. Beyond that, his self-funded effort signaled the challenges Republicans have raising competitive sums of money for a statewide race in which the odds are long.[37]

The general election held on November 6, 2018 saw 64.54% turnout among registered Californians, with just over 65% of the voters casting their decisions by mail.[38] It was the highest turnout in a midterm election in California in 36 years, indicating a high level of voter engagement in the first major election following Trump's 2016 presidential victory.[39] The overall results showed a landslide victory for Newsom with 61.9% of the vote. Predictably, given his San Francisco roots, Newsom ran strong in Bay Area counties, securing between 75% and 86% of the vote. Newsom also fared well in large urban areas throughout the state, including voter-rich southern California.

Cox's support came from more rural, conservative counties, particularly in the far northern parts of the state. Down south, he did win a majority of voters in Riverside and Kern Counties—two traditionally Republican counties—but just barely. Newsom still won a significant number of voters in these counties and even won a majority in previous GOP strongholds Orange County (50.1%) and San Diego County (56.9%).[40] When viewed from the full arc of the campaign, Newsom's focus on President Trump seemed to be a smart strategy: a general election exit poll showed two thirds of voters said President Trump was a factor in how they voted and 67% of those surveyed disapproved of the president's performance.[41] Newsom was the clear favorite among these voters who disapproved of President Trump.

Becoming Governor: Bold Vision Meets Compromise

Newly minted Governor Gavin Newsom entered office on January 7, 2019 promising big things. In his inaugural address he implied everything was on the line: "People's lives, freedom, security, the water we drink, the air we breathe—they all hang in the balance," Newsom said. He added, "The country is watching us. The world is waiting on us. The future depends on us. And we will seize this moment."[42] Such over-the-top objectives would be foundational in the Newsom administration. Less certain was how many would become reality.

But there was another side to Newsom's style, namely his knack for appearing out of touch from the lives everyday Californians. Just before the inauguration, the state's first family announced they would be moving into the renovated Victorian-style governor's mansion in Sacramento. But a few months after assuming office, Newsom announced the move was actually only temporary, and that the family had quietly purchased a $3.7-million, 12,000-square-foot home on 6-plus-acre lot in Fair Oaks—about a 15-minute drive from the capitol. The home was described as more "kid friendly,"[43] although with that size and cost, one would assume it had many more attributes than being good for the kids.

As to governance, Newsom assumed office with sweeping objectives. Yet, despite having overwhelming Democratic majorities in the state legislature, it was unclear how exactly the new governor planned to turn his sweeping ideas into legislative successes. At least on the outside, he appeared not to worry: "I'm not consumed by process, I'm consumed by outcomes. Judge us on what we do," Newsom said.[44] But without legislative support, what *could* he do?

To begin with, Newsom did have some independent powers associated with his office. While he waited for the legislature to act on his proposals, the new governor turned to executive action. Indeed, many state constitutions permit governors to utilize executive action, whereby they can dramatically reshape policy. This is exactly what Newsom did. He put an end to hydraulic fracking and yanked California's National Guard Troops on the U.S./Mexico Border, a decision that directly pitted him against President Trump.

With more than 700 people on California's death row and with the state close to resuming executions (given protracted legal battles over the state's lethal injection protocol, California hadn't executed a condemned person since 2006), Newsom signed an executive order in March 2019 imposing a moratorium on all executions. It was a bold, if not controversial move. Newsom also was a longtime opponent of the death penalty but Californians had twice recently (in 2012 and 2016) voted to uphold it. "I cannot sign off on executing hundreds and hundreds of human beings," Newsom said, while also noting the deep racial inequities in both death sentences and executions.[45] Supporters of the death penalty accused the governor of usurping the will of the voters.

With respect to other major public policy areas, Newsom sought to change policy through the budget. His first proposed state budget was a doozy. State coffers were flush with cash (a parting gift from Jerry Brown) and Newsom signaled he was intent on spending it. He proposed big new spending for early childhood education programs, a second year of free community-college tuition, housing and homelessness programs, and a boost to paid family leave.

But what about the legislature, the state's primary policymaking institution? That's where Gavin Newsom found unexpected problems. When he was governor, Jerry Brown had learned to court legislators across the political spectrum, mixing patience with a quiet urgency. It was an effective strategy that came with his years of experience in Sacramento politics. By contrast, Newsom didn't have a deep network of friends in the legislature. He spent relatively little time in Sacramento cultivating relationships. To make himself more available, he distributed his cell number to dozens of lawmakers. But this created its own problems when legislators regularly called and texted about their pet issues and projects with little or no response. Newsom had a penchant for making promises that weren't first filtered through his staff; this further compounded communication and coordination problems. So, what developed was a communications conundrum. On the one hand, Newsom took bold executive actions that left the legislature in the dust; on the other hand, he didn't go out of his way to court legislative support from fellow Democrats. These mixed messages did not win friends.

In one such example, Newsom held a May 2019 press conference announcing California would finally end charging sales taxes on diapers and menstrual products, a policy that would disproportionately benefit low-income families. "We can afford to do it because it's the right thing to do," Newsom declared.[46] But days later he revealed the tax break would only last two years, angering Democratic lawmakers who had secured agreement from him for this symbolically important policy change.

He also found himself in direct conflict with the legislature on major issues which, despite strong Democratic majorities, had its own institutional prerogatives shaped by more parochial district-level interests. In his first days on the job, Newsom threatened to withhold transportation funding to cities that weren't building enough housing. He pledged to build 3.5 million homes over seven years—a rate that would more than quadruple construction levels when he took office. "This is a new day and we have to have new expectations, new requirements," Newsom stated. "If you're not hitting your goals, I don't know why you get the money," he went to say.[47] But Democratic lawmakers balked at the idea, saying it would violate voters' trust, given their recent support for an increase in the gas taxes to pay for badly needed transportation projects.[48] Newsom was forced to delay the plan until 2023. Newsom's desire to move quickly and without legislative consultation was not a good way to begin his tenure.

Another unnecessary conflict for Newsom centered on California's proposed high-speed rail system. Newsom was also forced to walk back his plan to scale down the state's controversial high-speed rail project after strong pushback from labor unions and other groups. The original design extended from Los Angeles to San Francisco, at a projected cost of $40 billion, but over time, the anticipated costs soared to $100 billion. Seeing increasing public displeasure with the project, the governor pledged to build a much shorter (less-expensive) segment between Fresno and Merced. Longtime critics of the rail project took his words to mean the whole thing was dead, while construction unions wailed at the possibility of thousands of lost jobs. Under siege, Newsom backed off, later blaming the media for misconstruing his words. Under pressure he was forced to express his "full commitment" to high-speed rail while also emphasizing he was "refocusing" the project to get at least one point-to-point segment completed.[49]

With respect to the state budget, the single most important policy endeavor by the state legislature, Newsom made headway on a number of important issues. The $214.8 billion budget, the largest in the state's history, brought new investments to tackle the state's housing and homelessness problems. School spending rose above $12,000 per student as the state's education system continued to slowly climb back from painful cuts instituted during the depths of the Great Recession. More money was also budgeted to expand child care and all-day kindergarten classes across the state. Higher education saw a boost, with added spending creating a second free year of community college for full time students and adding some 15,000 extra spots in the UC and CSU systems. Health insurance subsidies were also expanded so more Californians could buy coverage. And perhaps most importantly, for the long-term financial health of the state, $19 billion was placed into the state's rainy-day fund, while another $3 billion was used to pay off old debt. There were also some setbacks. While funding was increased to fight homelessness and support more affordable housing, the money allocated remained far short of what many experts say was needed. Newsom also wanted to raise $140 million by adding a new tax on water users to clean up toxic water supplies in poor communities. But with state now sitting on a healthy budget surplus, many members of the legislature balked at creating a new tax.[50] The tax proposal failed, but some additional money for clean water was drawn from a fund designed to curb greenhouse gas emissions.

The governor also used the budget to reshape his own office, including money for more staff. Newsom proposed staffing his team with 132 employees (40 more than the number compared to Brown's last year in office) with a budget that would grow to more than $24 million. The governor's office under Jerry Brown, and under a $27-billion state budget deficit, was staffed with as few as 81 employees and operated on a $12.7 million budget. A larger staff with a bigger budget meant the new governor could reopen five regional field offices where staff could directly address constituents' concerns.[51]

Throughout 2019, the new governor's style involved bounding from one big issue to the next, while immersing himself into the minutia of policy debates right up to the last minute. "He has this questing, ceaselessly curious and hard-driving personality," said one former staff member. "It's Gavin Newsom's policy making style. He's always tinkering with policy until the last minute to always get it right."[52] But that also left policy activists not knowing exactly which way to turn. "I expected a sort of a steadier, more methodical governor. I found the decisions he made, the statements he made, more erratic than expected," said Kathryn Phillips, the director of the Sierra Club of California.[53] Newsom, though, maintained support with top legislative leaders who preached patience and implied a bit of controlled chaos was to be expected with any new governor.

But Newsom had supporters, some of whom were in key positions of power. Toni Atkins, the Senate President Pro-Tempore, said she liked the speed by which Newsom worked. It reflected his ambitious nature. "I guess I see him as really energetic, couldn't wait to take his job, ready to go," Atkins said. Likewise, Assembly Speaker Anthony Rendon suggested Newsom's scatterbrained reputation was really just a sign he was interested in far more issues than his predecessor.[54] Yet, the legislature was slow to address most of Newsom's policy agenda.

Beyond policymaking via executive order and normal legislative channels, governors are also tested by unplanned events or crises—natural disasters or economic recessions to name just two—that are thrust upon them. How elected officials govern through crises can affect their standing with the public and perceptions about their leadership and competency.[55] Sure enough, Newsom's first year was fraught with unforeseen challenges. Less than a month into his term, the energy giant Pacific Gas & Electric, which serves over 16 million people over 70,000 square miles, filed for bankruptcy because of legal liabilities tied to its role in sparking massive, deadly wildfires. Most tragic of these was the Camp Fire in November 2019 which killed 85 people and destroyed the town of Paradise.[56] The image of out-of-control wildfires and blacked-out communities led some commentators to describe California as a near "failed state."[57] At one point, PG&E Chief Executive Bill Johnson said blackouts might be needed for another decade before equipment could be upgraded to the level needed. Newsom blasted PG&E, saying, "It doesn't take a decade to fix this damn thing."[58] In a letter demanding rebates for PG&E customers Newsom accused the company of "neglect," "mismanagement," and placing "profit over public safety."[59] Over the course of 2019, the governor spent months wrangling over the terms of PG&E's exit from bankruptcy.

As Newsom's first year in office came to a close, it was thus a mix of progress and setback with plenty of messiness you could expect of an ambitious, easily distracted governor unfamiliar with the nuances of Sacramento legislative politics. His overall performance though received mostly positive marks with the public. A November 2019 Public Policy Institute of California poll of likely voters showed 48% approved of his job performance while 33% disapproved, a number that was modestly higher than Jerry Brown's first year in office.[60] At the time it appeared many of the problems that bedeviled recent California governors—skyrocketing housing costs, homelessness, fires, energy, climate change, and criminal justice reform—would continue to consume his administration as the new year dawned. What truly beckoned, however, nobody would have predicted. COVID-19 would make the governor's first-year battles seem quaint in comparison.

Notes

1. "California ban on large-capacity gun magazines back in play: Court to reconsider," *The San Francisco Chronicle*, Updated February 25, 2021, www.sfchronicle.com/news/article/California-ban-on-large-capacity-gun-magazines-15980134.php.
2. "Meet the candidates running to be California's next governor in Tuesday's primary," *The Los Angeles Times*, January 24, 2018, www.latimes.com/politics/la-pol-ca-california-governor-list-2018-story.html.
3. "Five things you need to know about Antonio Villaraigosa," *Sacramento Bee*, May 18, 2018, www.sacbee.com/article193603054.html.
4. Villaraigosa was referring to Newsom promising a single-payer healthcare system to nurses when he knew it was wishful thinking. See George Skelton, "Villaraigosa is right, single-payer healthcare in California is a political pipe dream," *Los Angeles Times*, March 12, 2018, www.latimes.com/politics/la-pol-ca-skelton-single-payer-healthcare-antonio-villaraigosa-gavin-newsom-20180312-story.html.
5. "Meet the candidates running to be California's next governor in Tuesday's primary," *The Los Angeles Times*, January 24, 2018, www.latimes.com/politics/la-pol-ca-california-governor-list-2018-story.html.
6. Ibid.
7. Ibid.
8. "After close race for endorsement between Newsom and Chiang, Democratic Party fails to back a candidate," February 25, 2018, https://ktla.com/news/politics/newsom-chiang-locked-in-close-race-for-democratic-partys-endorsement-for-ca-governor/.
9. "California Republican Party won't endorse in race for governor," *CalMatters*, Updated June 23, 2020, https://calmatters.org/politics/election-2018/2018/05/california-republican-party-wont-endorse-in-race-for-governor/.
10. "California gubernatorial election, 2018 (June 5 top-two primary)," *Ballotpedia*, https://ballotpedia.org/California_gubernatorial_election,_2018_(June_5_top-two_primary).
11. Ibid.
12. "Track the money that fueled the California primary for governor," *Los Angeles Times*, June 4, 2018, www.latimes.com/projects/la-pol-ca-california-governor-2018-money-primary/.
13. "California Governor – Open Primary," *Real Clear Politics*, November 5, 2018, www.realclearpolitics.com/epolls/2018/governor/ca/california_governor_open_primary-6299.html#polls.
14. Mark Baldassare, Dean Bonner and Alyssa Dykman, "PPIC Statewide Survey: Californians and Their Government," May 2018, www.ppic.org/wp-content/uploads/s-518mbs.pdf.
15. "Trump endorses Republican John Cox for Californian governor," *Los Angeles Times*, May 18, 2018, www.latimes.com/politics/la-pol-ca-john-cox-trump-endorsement-20180518-story.html.
16. Ibid.

17. "Meet the candidates running to be California's next governor in Tuesday's primary," *Los Angeles Times*, January 24, 2018, www.latimes.com/politics/la-pol-ca-california-governor-list-2018-story.html.
18. "5 takeaways from California's primary, for Californians," *New York Times*, June 6, 2018, www.nytimes.com/2018/06/06/us/5-takeaways-from-californias-primary-for-californians.html.
19. Secretary of State Alex Padilla, "Statement of the Vote," *Statewide Direct Primary Election*, 2016. June 5, 2018, p. 17, https://elections.cdn.sos.ca.gov/sov/2018-primary/sov/2018-complete-sov.pdf.
20. Ibid.
21. Ibid.
22. "It's Newsom vs. Cox in November as Villaraigosa tumbles in governor's race," *Los Angeles Times*, June 5, 2018, www.latimes.com/politics/la-pol-ca-governor-california-20180605-story.html.
23. "Gavin Newsom and John Cox to compete in California election for governor," *The New York Times*, June 6, 2018, www.nytimes.com/2018/06/06/us/politics/california-primary.html.
24. Ibid.
25. "It's Newsom vs. Cox in November as Villaraigosa tumbles in governor's race," *Los Angeles Times*, June 5, 2018, https://www.latimes.com/politics/la-pol-ca-governor-california-20180605-story.html.
26. Ibid.
27. "Newsom, Cox spending much of their time campaigning for other candidates and causes in California's race for governor," *Los Angeles Times*, August 9, 2018, www.latimes.com/politics/la-pol-ca-newsom-cox-governors-race-20180809-story.html.
28. "Do Gavin Newsom and John Cox even want the same job? Their visions of California's governorship radically differ," *Los Angeles Times*, September 21, 2018, www.latimes.com/politics/la-pol-ca-campaign-issues-california-governor-race-20180921-story.html.
29. Ibid.
30. Ibid.
31. Indeed, costs for a single-payer health care system were estimated to be $400 billion a year.
32. "Gavin Newsom criticized for flip-flopping on California's most pressing issues," *Los Angeles Times*, August 20, 2018, www.latimes.com/politics/la-pol-ca-governor-race-gavin-newsom-issues-shift-20180820-story.html.
33. Public Policy Institute of California, "Californians and Their Government," *Survey*, September 2018, www.ppic.org/publication/ppic-statewide-survey-californians-and-their-government-september-2018/.
34. "Gavin Newsom and John Cox clash in their only head-to-head governor's race debate," *Los Angeles Times*, October 8, 2018, www.latimes.com/politics/la-pol-ca-california-governor-debate-20181008-story.html.
35. "Do Gavin Newsom and John Cox even want the same job? Their visions of California's governorship radically differ," *Los Angeles Times*, September 21, 2018, www.latimes.com/politics/la-pol-ca-campaign-issues-california-governor-race-20180921-story.html.
36. "Gavin Newsom raised $50 million running for governor: He still has $15 million left over," *The Sacramento Bee*, February 1, 2019, www.sacbee.com/news/politics-government/capitol-alert/article225389760.html.
37. "Track the millions flowing into California's race for governor," *Los Angeles Times*, November 5, 2018, www.latimes.com/projects/la-pol-ca-california-governor-2018-money/.

38. Secretary of State Alex Padilla, "Statement of the Vote," *General Election*, November 6, 2018, p. 3, https://elections.cdn.sos.ca.gov/sov/2018-general/sov/2018-complete-sov.pdf.
39. "California's November election turnout was highest in a midterm in 36 years," *CapRadio.org*, www.capradio.org/articles/2018/12/14/californias-november-election-turnout-was-highest-in-a-midterm-in-36-years/.
40. Ibid., pp. 21–23.
41. "5 takeaways from the California's governor's race," *Los Angeles Times*, November 7, 2018, www.latimes.com/politics/la-pol-ca-takeaways-john-cox-gavin-newsom-20181107-story.html.
42. "Gavin Newsom's ambitious and uneventful first year as California governor," *Los Angeles Times*, January 5, 2020, www.latimes.com/california/story/2020-01-05/first-year-california-governor-gavin-newsom.
43. "Gov. Gavin Newsom and family to pass on the governor's mansion, head to Sacramento suburbs," *Los Angeles Times*, January 19, 2019, www.latimes.com/politics/la-pol-ca-governor-gavin-newsom-sacramento-house-governors-mansion-20190119-story.html.
44. "Gavin Newsom's ambitious and uneventful first year as California governor," *Los Angeles Times*, January 5, 2020, www.latimes.com/california/story/2020-01-05/first-year-california-governor-gavin-newsom.
45. "Saying the death penalty no longer an 'abstract question,' Gov. Newsom halts executions in California," *CalMatters*, March 12, 2019, https://calmatters.org/justice/2019/03/gavin-newsom-halts-executions-california/.
46. "Newsom faces criticism for not delivering on grand promises," *Los Angeles Times*, May 13, 2019, www.latimes.com/politics/la-pol-ca-gavin-newsom-budget-diapers-tampons-taxes-california-20190513-story.html.
47. "Gov. Gavin Newsom threatens to cut state funding from cities that don't approve enough housing," *Los Angeles Times*, January 10, 2019, https://www.latimes.com/politics/la-pol-ca-gavin-newsom-housing-money-budget-20190110-story.html.
48. "Newsom delays threat to block transportation funds to cities that flunk housing goals," *Los Angeles Times*, March 11, 2019, www.latimes.com/politics/la-pol-ca-gavin-newsom-housing-plan-201903011-story.html.
49. "Newsom blames the media, not his own words, for confusion over high-speed rail's future," *Los Angeles Times*, February 15, 2019, www.latimes.com/politics/la-pol-ca-gavin-newsom-bullet-train-explanation-20190215-story.html.
50. "California Gov. Gavin Newsom has signed his first budget. Here's where the $215 billion will go," *Los Angeles Times*, June 27, 2019, www.latimes.com/politics/la-pol-ca-california-government-spending-budget-20190627-htmlstory.html.
51. "Gov. Gavin Newsom is expanding the size and role of the California governor's office," *Los Angeles Times*, February 11, 2019, www.latimes.com/politics/la-pol-ca-gavin-newsom-staff-hires-20190211-story.html.
52. "Gavin Newsom's ambitious and uneven first year as California governor," *Los Angeles Times*, January 5, 2020, https://www.latimes.com/california/story/2020-01-05/first-year-california-governor-gavin-newsom.
53. Ibid.
54. Ibid.
55. John T. Gasper and Andrew Reeves, "Make it Rain?: Retrospection and the Attentive Electorate in the Context of Natural Disasters," *American Journal of Political Science*, 55, 2 (2011): 340–355.

56. "PG&E says its equipment likely caused Camp Fire, as investigation continues," *NPR KQED*, February 28, 2019, www.npr.org/2019/02/28/699026147/pg-e-says-its-equipment-likely-caused-camp-fire-as-investigation-continues, and "Officials: Camp Fire, deadliest in California history, was caused by PG&E electrical transmission lines," *CNBC.com*, Updated May 16, 2019, www.cnbc.com/2019/05/15/officials-camp-fire-deadliest-in-california-history-was-caused-by-pge-electrical-transmission-lines.html.

57. See Noah Smith, October 29, 2019, https://twitter.com/noahpinion/status/1188806445208240129; "This columnist thinks California is in big trouble: The fix? Kill Prop 13!," www.ocregister.com/2019/10/22/california-is-in-big-trouble-again-3/.

58. "Gavin Newsom rejects PG&E bankruptcy plan, demands 'radically restructured' California utility," *Sacramento Bee*, December 16, 2019.

59. "Comforting California, Newsom bashes a familiar villain: PG&E," *CalMatters.org*, October 31, 2019, https://calmatters.org/environment/california-wildfires/2019/10/pge-newsom-california-wildfire-blackouts-criticism/.

60. Public Policy Institute of California, "Californians and Their Government," *Survey*, 2019, www.ppic.org/data-set/ppic-statewide-survey-data-2019/.

Chapter 4

The Plague of COVID-19

Life is like an onion; you peel it one layer
at a time, and sometimes you weep.

—Carl Sandburg

It's unlikely that Gavin Newsom was thinking about an onion when he began his second year as California governor. Yet, along the lines of Carl Sandburg's description of life, Newsom would do more than his share of metaphorical weeping as he and the rest of California suffered through the various layers of COVID-19. Like just about everyone other than a few epidemiologists, Newsom was caught off guard by the pandemic. The governor didn't see it coming. Indeed, February 4, 2020, was a pretty typical day for a California governor who was still settling into his job. Newsom spent part of the day making non-newsworthy appointments to several state boards and commissions, just a small slice of the more than 3,000 executive appointments the governor typically makes during a four-year term.[1] Unbeknownst to Newsom, COVID-19, a virus that would go on to kill more than one million Americans, was about take its first (known) victim in the United States, Patricia Dowd, 57, of Santa Clara County.

Just several days earlier, Dowd was scheduled to travel to Stockton with her brother to attend a funeral for a high school friend. She abruptly canceled after falling ill. She would die just days later. Dowd's cause of death was originally labeled a heart attack. This made her passing all the more shocking. To her friends and family she had appeared to be in excellent health, regularly participating in spin classes and aerobics.[2]

It wasn't for another ten weeks, on April 21, when Santa Clara County health officials announced results from an autopsy, that the public learned Dowd had been infected with COVID-19. For epidemiologists the news about the cause of Dowd's death had chilling implications: it meant the coronavirus was spreading on the West Coast in early January, weeks before public health officials originally thought.[3]

DOI: 10.4324/9781003217954-4

When the coronavirus began making international headlines in late 2019, focus was placed on China where the virus originated. But for weeks the Chinese Communist Party covered up news about the virus and its earlier knowledge that it could spread from human to human.[4] Only on January 3, 2020 did the Chinese government officially announced that officials in Wuhan, Hubei Province were tracking a mysterious "pneumonia-like" illness of unknown origins which had sickened dozens of people in the city.[5] State television reported about a coronavirus that was "different from previous human coronaviruses."[6] China's first death from the coronavirus came on January 11 but the government didn't acknowledge human spread of the virus until January 20.[7] The government put Wuhan on complete lockdown on January 23, preventing flights and trains from leaving the city and suspending buses, subways, and ferry service. But this wasn't nearly enough. The virus was already quickly spreading across parts of Asia, the United States, and major swaths of Europe. By the end of January, the World Health Organization (W.H.O.) declared the coronavirus a global health emergency. And on February 11, the W.H.O. gave the virus an official name: COVID-19.[8]

By early February COVID-19 was unleashing a global health crisis that left officials scrambling to contain something they didn't fully understand. Back in Washington D.C., President Trump suspended entry into the United States from any foreign national who had traveled to China within the past 14 days.[9] Months into the pandemic President Trump would routinely tout his "early" travel ban from China as a sign of quick-thinking leadership. On closer inspection, however, President Trump's travel ban was not very "early" nor did it completely stop travel from China. And it came a full month after China first officially announced the outbreak. Even after restrictions were imposed, hundreds of thousands of travelers continued arriving in the U.S. directly from China.

In the San Francisco Bay Area, public health officials called a news conference on March 16 to announce the first shelter-in-place order in the nation. Over the previous week, data (as limited as it was) showed signs the virus was growing exponentially in Santa Clara County. With her voice breaking with emotion and knowing the order would upend the everyday lives for millions in the Bay Area, Santa Clara County's Director of Public Health, Dr. Sara Cody, announced a shelter-in-place order. "At the time we had very little testing, so we had enough information to know that we were likely in very bad shape, but not enough to measure how bad," Cody said, reflecting on the order a year later. "We had no treatment, no vaccine, we didn't have enough personal protective equipment. We just didn't have the tools. And shelter-in-place, that's a pretty big tool to use, but very effective."[10] Six other Bay Area counties quickly joined the shelter-in-place order.

Newsom Issues a Statewide Shutdown

Watching all this unfold was Governor Gavin Newsom who on March 19 issued a first-in-the-nation *statewide* stay-at-home order. The unprecedented shutdown announcement was streamed online and carried live on television and radio stations across the state.

"This is a moment when we need to make tough decisions. This is a moment when we need some straight talk and we need to tell people the truth" Newsom said at a press conference in Sacramento. The order called on all Californians to stay home and only leave for "essential trips" including trips the grocery store, to seek medical attention, or to exercise outside.[11]

Californians' lives were turned upside down. Schools closed across the state. Children were thrown into remote learning environments leaving parents scrambling to juggle work responsibilities while also tending to their kids' educational needs. Concerts were cancelled. Bars were closed. Professional sports, including the start of the 2020 baseball season, were called off. Major entertainment venues and tourist destinations like the Hollywood Bowl and Disneyland were shuttered until further notice. State business, including operations of the Department of Motor Vehicles, ceased operations.

The shelter-in-place order was by far the most intrusive step taken by Newsom, or any governor for that matter, up to that point. The order was built on top of an official "state of emergency" declaration issued by the governor on March 5 after a man died from the virus after falling ill on the *Grand Princess* cruise ship. Several days after the ship made port, a mad scramble ensued to find others who might have also have been infected. On the next return trip from Hawaii, the *Grand Princess* was held off the coast of San Francisco while public health officials screened passengers for possible infection.[12] The image of the *Grand Princess* held offshore, while possibly holding a slew of infected passengers, made international news and added to the sense of crisis building in California.

The day of the news conference announcing the stay-at-home order, the Newsom administration released an estimate that 56% of Californians—or 25.5 million people—could be infected by the coronavirus in just eight weeks. It was an alarming number especially given at the time the state had recorded just 23 deaths with fewer than 1,200 positive cases.[13]

Newsom's estimate of 25 million-plus infections, however, was based on the state doing absolutely nothing to stop the spread. Newsom's statewide order was a major play to "bend the curve"—a popular phrase used throughout spring and summer 2020 that effectively meant reducing the rate of infections to a level that would prevent hospitals from getting overrun. The governor appeared to recognize the monumental policy challenges before him and the tricky politics that would surely surround the order. He was fond (sometimes ad nauseam) of describing California as a "nation-state" that would require, on one hand, a forceful, universal response, while on the other hand, enough flexibility to meet the varying needs and conditions found in California's diverse array of communities. California, of course, is not a nation. Nevertheless, as a state with the world's fifth-largest economy and a population larger than 20 other states combined, it's hugely complex. Newsom argued the state's communities and people were "interdependent," thus necessitating the statewide stay-at-home order. Yet, he spoke of the desire to "meet the needs of our diverse communities."[14] In order to stop the spread and bend the curve, the state would need to coordinate precious, yet fractured, medical resources.

Newsom's plan required executing something of a high-wire act. By restricting the daily lives of millions of Californians and threatening the economic vitality of tens of thousands of small businesses, the plan to stop the spread and bend the curve called for securing medical resources and implementing a tough statewide stay-at-home order that restricted people's behavior. At the same time, Newsom promised to remain flexible to the diverse needs of Californians whose resistance to one-size-fits-all governance was legendary. A slip-up in either direction could lead to 1) a public health disaster; 2) a political disaster; or 3) a combination of public health and political disasters resulting from large numbers of infected Californians striking out at elected officials.

None of this was for the faint of heart. Yet Newsom's aggressive moves to deal with the growing public health crisis appeared to activate a "we're all in this together" communal spirit that often seems to be lacking in California's "turnstile society."[15] Some of California's biggest tech giants, including Google, Apple, and Tesla, all pledged to help by throwing ingenuity—that for which California's Silicon Valley companies were famous for—at the coronavirus problem. Silicon Valley-based Bloom Energy (a fuel cell generator company) made headlines when they modernized older-style ventilators to help meet the expected surge in demand.[16]

Newsom even seemed to set aside his raucous political disagreements with the Trump administration. Before the pandemic hit, Newsom and the President tangled frequently. In December 2019, President Trump called Newsom "incompetent" over Twitter and depicted California as "totally out of control" in his January State of the Union speech. Newsom in turn said California was the "most un-Trump state in America."[17]

The governor had reasons for lowering the political temperature. California, like many states, was desperate for support from the federal government. Newsom was successful in getting President Trump to issue a Major Disaster Declaration which brought more federal relief resources. He also got President Trump to send the naval hospital ship *Mercy* to Los Angeles to help increase the region's hospital bed and surgical capacity.

California's needs were far greater than a floating hospital, however. State officials estimated the state was short some 17,000 hospital beds; officials scrambled to secure more personal protective equipment (PPE), including gloves, swabs, and hundreds of millions of N95 masks needed for frontline medical personnel.[18] There was also a shortage of ventilators. The federal government managed to send 170 to Los Angeles County, but it turned out many had faulty batteries and components. They didn't work.

Perhaps the greatest challenge was tied to COVID-19 testing. Inadequate testing made it difficult for officials to track the virus and monitor and isolate infected people. Compared to South Korea or Germany—two countries that quickly became models for effective coronavirus testing—the United States' testing capacity was dreadfully slow to get off the ground.

In the early days of the pandemic the Centers for Disease Control and Prevention (CDC) decided to create its own coronavirus test. The agency then planned to distribute those tests to state and local public health agencies. But the CDC's test development procedures didn't manage to follow many of its own manufacturing protocols. The tests ended up contaminated and, when shipped to local officials, produced unreliable results. The CDC later farmed out test production to an outside firm to get the problems corrected.[19]

U.S. testing capacity was thus a far cry from what might be expected from a wealthy country and the world's lone "superpower." Yet the degree to which state governments were impacted by the testing shortage varied considerably. New York, which was fast becoming the epicenter of crisis by late March, had conducted more than 145,000 tests. By comparison, two weeks after Newsom issued the stay-at-home order, California had conducted only 88,000 tests.[20]

New York had received early approval of a state COVID-19 test, but that wasn't the case in California. This meant commercial labs' testing capacity went largely unused. Once California's commercial labs finally received testing authority they were then competing for supplies; labs in San Diego and Los Angeles competed with labs in northern California. County governments were also short on supplies. Madera County, for example, had a new state-of-the-art laboratory, but because they lacked other necessary testing supplies, technicians were forced to send tests to outside labs. Obtaining test results was thus painfully slow. By early April, thousands of tested Californians waited sometimes as many as 12 days for results, further hampering the state's capacity to test, trace, and isolate those infected.[21] Twelve days in the midst of a pandemic were an eternity. As a biomedical research expert explained, "In the grand scheme of things, the whole idea of this sheltering in place is to bring the number of new infections down, but if we don't know where we are on the infection curve, we're steering blind. . . . [T]esting is the key to know if we're having an effect with social distancing."[22]

Newsom's Early Political Support for COVID-19 Management

Initially, Californians gave Newsom wide latitude to manage the state's unparalleled public health crisis. Like a seasoned juggler, he coped with major testing challenges, confusion over which businesses and services were "essential" (and thus able to operate), widespread school closures, and more than 3 million Californians newly out of work. The governor was rewarded with largely good public reviews. A Public Policy Institute of California poll of registered voters in May 2020 showed Newsom with a 65% approval rating—a 12% *increase* from February. Nearly 70% of voters approved of Newsom's handling of the pandemic and a strong majority (59%) approved of his handling of jobs and the economy. Perhaps most importantly, the public expressed continued support for the stay-at-home orders. Only 28% of those surveyed said they wanted social physical distancing restrictions reduced in their local area.[23]

Newsom's aggressive actions and the public's general embrace of his decision making helped to raise his national profile. He jumped on national cable outlets to tout his leadership of the "nation-state" of California, where he emphasized logistics over politics. During an April 7 interview with MSNBC's Rachel Maddow, Newsom made a surprise announcement that he had entered into a $1 billion agreement to purchase 200 million masks (including 150 million of the highly effective N95 masks) to help protect frontline workers.[24] His unstated assertion was that he could succeed where President Trump could not. The mask delivery would later run into serious production delays (see Chapter 5) but the performance led to a #PresidentNewsom hashtag trending on Twitter.[25]

But as we'll see, much of the public goodwill towards Newsom didn't last. In fact if one looked closely, the political divisions that would later propel the recall movement were already evident in those early polls of the pandemic. A UC Berkeley Institute of Governmental Studies poll in April showed supporters of President Trump were far less likely to be concerned about spreading the virus to others. Nearly 78% of President Trump supporters said they were most concerned about the economic wreckage caused by keeping the stay-at-home order in place too long.[26] Only 22% expressed concern about the health effects of ending the order too soon. The cracks in Newsom's political pavement began to show.

Who Said Reopening the State Would Be Easy?

COVID-19 doesn't care about politics. It doesn't care about whether a state is blue or red or its victims are liberal or conservative. But that is not to say the virus hasn't shaped politics or that it has not *been* shaped by politics. The virus's human hosts have been perfectly willing to interpret it through a political lens and what the virus means for government, liberty, leadership, and a number of other hot-button culture war issues that have been waging for years. The virus is fundamentally "just biology" but what its arrival meant for society has had almost everything to do with ideology.

Indeed, as economically and politically difficult as it was to effectively shut the state down, Newsom's decisions about how and when to reopen the state proved to be far more difficult. By May, Newsom faced growing political pressure from sources both external and internal to the state to open up. Outside California, a narrative was building in conservative media that COVID-19 was a problem that plagued big cities in blue states, thus making restrictions in rural, more conservative areas burdensome and un-American.[27] Republicans could point to New York City as the case in point. Between March and May 2020, New York City had more than 203,000 confirmed cases of COVID-19 and more than 18,000 deaths.[28]

Research does suggest that urban, predominately Democratic-leaning areas suffered higher COVID-19 death rates in the early months of the pandemic, although less-populated conservative states saw relatively higher numbers as the pandemic wore on.[29] But for many conservatives, an ideology that mixes an affinity toward free market principles, distrust in government institutions, and a skepticism of science and expertise fueled their opposition.[30] COVID-19 restrictions were seen as an infringement on free market capitalism and individual liberty. Shutdowns, lockdowns, testing, tracing, isolation—the language and policies of the pandemic— were all seen as things dictated by untrustworthy "experts" working in the alphabet soup of federal agencies like the CDC, NIH, FDA, and HHS.

In late April 2020 Republican governors in Georgia, South Carolina, Tennessee, and Texas announced they would be rolling back COVID-19 restrictions—restrictions issued just three weeks prior. Georgia Republican Governor Brian Kemp was the first to fully open gyms, salons, restaurants, churches, and movie theaters despite not hitting many of the public health and testing-capability targets for reopening set by the White House a few days earlier.[31]

The "return to normal" steps by red-state governors blended nicely with President Trump's rose-colored-glasses approach to the pandemic. At a White House briefing on April 16, President Trump said America was winning the battle against the pandemic and that it was time "to open up . . . America wants to be open."[32] Yet, as many public health experts attested, the White House offered states only vague guidelines for reopening. Absent were a new national testing plan, a national tracing and isolation plan, and federally coordinated effort to deliver more PPE to PPE-starved states. Public health experts saw these as crucially needed steps to move safely to a second, more open, phase of the pandemic. Meanwhile, satisfied with his belief that the federal government had done all it could to defeat COVID-19, President Trump told the nation's governors, "You are going to call your own shots."[33] Public health experts were stunned at President Trump's dismissal of any additional federal role, given past federal responses to pandemic threats.[34]

With states now left to make their own choices, Newsom found himself in a political pickle. Conservative states were reopening, giving governors a platform by which they could appeal to business owners and Republican base voters highly skeptical of the deadly effects of COVID-19. The economy would hum while the coronavirus sort of lurked in the background. That was their idea anyway. Using the bully pulpit of the presidency, President Trump taunted states almost daily to open up.

Newsom was undoubtedly aware of the political traction that President Trump and Republicans might gain from this simple message. Political scientists have long documented that voters have little understanding of the complexities of public policymaking. The message—one that seemingly promised to shed the virus through sheer willpower alone—would certainly resonate with the Republican base but it might also appeal to a significant swath of independent "swing" voters who are typically the least engaged and least informed, and who make policy decisions on fairly flimsy grounds.[35]

Newsom, like most Democratic governors, placed health and safety first but critically also saw stopping the spread of the virus as the most fool-proof economic recovery plan. First, you needed to stop the spread; only then could you get people fully back to work and kids back in classrooms. This was obviously a more complicated argument than simply "opening up." At an April 15 press conference, he laid out six different criteria the state needed to meet before reopening: more testing, building hospital capacity, identifying promising treatments, developing physical distancing guidelines for businesses and schools, and creating an early warning data tracking system.[36] Notably, he couldn't say when these things would be accomplished but he reassured Californians that the stay-at-home order "can't be permanent state."[37]

But Newsom's detractors weren't satisfied. With California reasonably safe compared to other states, voices seeking an immediate reopening began to mobilize. The first demands originated from some of the most conservative pockets of California politics.

Perhaps the most vocal and arguably the most effective critic of the stay-at-home orders was Harmeet Dhillon, a civil rights attorney, a member of the Republican National Committee, a former vice chairwoman of the California Republican Party, and regular Fox News contributor. Just days following Newsom's press conference announcing the reopening criteria, Dhillon filed a lawsuit on behalf of churches who were forced to shut down religious services. The lawsuit argued that California's restrictions on places of worship violated the Constitution's First Amendment and individuals' freedom-of-religion rights.[38] Religious congregations were not alone in voicing their displeasure. Many business owners openly defied restrictions. Dozens of lawsuits were filed representing a whole range of interests: angry gun shop owners, couples who had their weddings canceled, barbers, manicurists, and musicians stuck playing live shows over Zoom.[39] There seemed to be a lawsuit for just about everyone.

From the beginning Newsom was wary of criminalizing violations of the stay-at-home order. He hoped for voluntary compliance and noted he'd only enlist law enforcement as a last resort. That's probably good because law enforcement officers passively resisted—or in some cases actively resisted—the order in many parts of the state.

Even some county governments got into the act. Opposition took root in California's northern, sparsely populated counties adjacent to the Oregon border which have long held disdain for rules and regulations emanating from Sacramento. On May 3, Modoc County (population 9,600) reopened its restaurants, bars, and churches.[40] Sutter and Yuba counties did the same three days later.

Open defiance wasn't just coming from rural counties with low case counts and a long history of sneering at Sacramento politicians. Conservatives in San Francisco, San Diego, Sacramento, and Huntington Beach organized demonstrations. At the Huntington Beach demonstration more than 3,000 packed in closely in direct violation of social distancing rules. Regardless of the location, protestors emphasized individual rights over governance.[41]

Six weeks into the stay-at-home order, statewide public polls still showed that a strong majority of Californians supported continuing the shelter-in-place order to help protect against the virus, but political pressure on Newsom began to grow.[42] More than 4 million Californians had filed for unemployment rates. Black and Latino residents lost their jobs to the pandemic or encountered problems with paying their rent or mortgage far more often than Whites. At the same time, racial and ethnic minorities were at the greatest risk of getting sick and dying given they made up a lopsided share of the state's essential workers.

The growing political and economic pressure caused Newsom to reshuffle his reopening timeline. But he yet again tried to thread a needle between reopening and getting the economy moving and protecting public health and safety, especially the health of the most vulnerable. "We're all impatient and we're deeply anxious and deeply desirous to start to turn the page and turn the corner," Newsom said at a press conference on May 1, opining on his thoughts about reopening. "We said 'weeks, not months,' four or five days ago. I now want to say 'many days, not weeks.' As long we continue to be prudent and thoughtful in certain recommendations, I think we'll be making some announcements."[43]

Reopening With a Local Flavor: A Recipe for Mass Confusion

Newsom's plan for a gradual reopening was rolled out on May 4, 2020. California, he announced, would be moving into the second stage of a four-part reopening plan. This second stage allowed some retailers selling non-essential goods (such as toy stores, florists, sporting goods retailers, etc.) to reopen for curbside pickup. Manufacturers and the supply companies who drive distribution chains could also operate. Stage 3, which Newsom said was still "months" away, would include the reopening of hair salons, gyms, religious services, and sports competitions (but with no fans). Stage 4 would be a full reopening with no restrictions on daily life. This, Newsom said, would not arrive until a vaccine could be developed and made widely available.[44]

Crucially, the plan gave county governments some flexibility. Counties who wanted to open up *more* of their local economy could do so but only if they met certain metrics. A county's COVID-19 case load could be no more than 1 in 10,000 persons over the previous two weeks and it could not have any COVID-related deaths over that same period. County hospitals needed the capability to meet a 35% surge of COVID-19 patients while also demonstrating the ability to meet a variety of testing and tracing targets.[45]

Newsom stressed that reopening would be guided by data. "Politics will not drive our decision-making. Protests won't drive our decision-making. Political pressure will not drive our decision-making," Newsom said. "We believe that the local public health data . . . should allow our counties to soon begin a science-based, thoughtful reopening of our economy, consistent with national guidelines, which would allow our residents to get back to work."[46]

County officials, especially those in conservative parts of the state, were enthusiastic about the "local control" part of the plan. Lisa Bartlett, an Orange County Supervisor and President of the California State Association of Counties told the *Los Angeles Times*, "Governor Newsom knows we have 58 counties and they are vastly different. Leaving it to local elected officials to work with their public health officers, I think is a great idea."[47] Indeed, a review of COVID-19 cases in mid-May helps illustrate the extreme variation found in the states' different regions. Among the less populated northern counties, only Humboldt had more than 50 cases. Los Angeles County, meanwhile, had more than 36,0000 cases—more than half of the state's total up to that point.[48]

By May 20, 2020, twenty-four counties, mostly smaller and more rural counties, had received approval to reopen faster than state guidelines allowed. But then Newsom quickly relaxed counties' reopening criteria further and by the end of the month—and notably less than three weeks after saying such changes would be "months" away—salons, gyms, and religious services were now open in large swaths of the state.[49]

Crucially, what was allowed or not allowed was still highly dependent on what county you were in. In some cases, even counties that shared a border did things quite differently, but for reasons that weren't always clear. Tesla's manufacturing plant in Alameda County was kept shuttered while its facilities in neighboring San Joaquin County, a county with a very similar COVID-19 death rate to Alameda's, were fully operational. In southern California, some beaches were open but not others. And where beaches were open you might be able to swim or surf but you couldn't lounge in the sand or play volleyball. In some counties you could play golf or tennis and get a haircut while in other places you could play golf and tennis but were forced to play shaggy because haircuts were banned.[50] Even the nine Bay Area counties, which for weeks had been in lockstep, began diverging over which businesses fell into "high risk" and "low risk" categories.[51]

By the end of June, Newsom was facing two major problems. Most importantly, COVID-19 cases were once again on the rise. As bars reopened and the public began socializing more, seeing friends and family and celebrating high school and college graduations, Father's Day, trips to the beach—the kinds of things millions of people do every day in normal times—cases crept upward. On June 18, Newsom issued an executive order requiring all Californians to wear face masks to help stop the spread. On June 22, the state reported a record high number of daily cases. It broke another record on June 23 and then again a few days later.[52] The total number of known infections topped 200,000 by June 30. On a day-to-day basis, California was recording as many cases as Florida or Texas—two large states governed by Republican governors who didn't take nearly as aggressive steps as Newsom to battle the virus. At the same time, defiance and opposition was growing at the local level: sheriffs in Fresno, Orange, Riverside, and Sacramento counties all said they wouldn't enforce the mask mandate—a clear signal that counties—although they are officially "administrative arms of the state government"—wouldn't always be willing partners in enforcing state law.[53]

Newsom thus faced growing skepticism about his political leadership. A new narrative was building: Newsom made decisions based on politics instead of science as he had promised. It was a theme—the idea that Newsom said one thing while he did another—that would dog him all through the recall campaign.

A Second Wave Wreaks Havoc

By early July it was clear that a new second COVID-19 wave was ravaging the state. Hospitalization rates climbed steadily; the number of people hospitalized with confirmed COVID-19 infections had climbed 50% since April when they had stabilized at least for a period. The Newsom administration began imposing new restrictions on the size of indoor gatherings in harder-hit counties just before the July Fourth holiday. Counties were placed on a new watchlist if they had three days of rising hospitalization rates, increasing community transmission, or declining hospital bed capacity.[54] Newsom used the metaphor of a "dimmer switch" to describe the watchlist; counties could make fine-tuned adjustments to restrictions as needed.

In reality, however, the watchlist brought more confusion, particularly when on July 13 Newsom announced a new round of closures, placing a stop on all indoor dining and closing bars, zoos, and museums. Even stricter regulations were placed on watchlist counties which once again underscored the patchwork of different rules and restrictions across the state. In the 29 counties on the watchlist in mid-July—a group covering about 80% of the state's population—gyms, nail and hair salons, shopping malls, churches, and offices with non-essential workers were all shuttered. In fact, in some watchlist counties, gyms and hair salons had reopened for just two days before Newsom's new orders shut them down again. One could be excused for complaining about whiplash. Nonetheless, Newsom explained that changing virus conditions demanded changing government responses.[55] But would the public be so rational?

By the end of July, more than 10,000 Californians had died from COVID-19; more than 5,000 Californians passed in July alone. COVID-19 continued to ravage some parts of the state more than others. Farm workers and meat packers in California's famed Central Valley, a disproportionate number of whom are Latino, who live in tight living quarters, share transportation to and from work, and often lack decent health care, were especially vulnerable. Workers' exposure was made worse when powerful agricultural and food packing companies skirted health and safety protocols, seemingly giving little care or thought to health and safety of their predominately migrant workforce.[56] Latinos compose 39% of the state's population, but by summer 2020 they were 56% of all confirmed COVID-19 cases and 46% of all deaths.[57]

With the new restrictions and continued masking requirements, cases and deaths once again started to decline by August offering weary Californians a glimmer of good news amidst all the hardship.[58] Progress against the virus wasn't good enough, however, to prevent disruption to a second school year. Los Angeles and San Diego Unified School Districts—the two largest districts in the state—announced in July that students would be forced to start the new school year online. Dozens of districts soon followed suit.[59]

In an effort to bring more coherence to the state's battle, Newsom scrapped the county watchlist program in favor of a color-coded tiered system (officially named the Blueprint for a Safer Economy framework) in August. This served as the latest guide for the types of business operations and activities that would be allowed in each county. This time each county's risk level was communicated through a four-color coding scheme. Purple indicated the most severe "widespread" risk level, followed by red, orange, and yellow in descending order. Counties' risk levels would be updated weekly; they could move to a less restrictive category if conditions improved. Under the purple tier most indoor businesses were closed but many, including hair salons, restaurants, and places of worship, could open outdoors with modifications. A move to a red tier, made possible if a county's COVID-19 case and positivity rates fell below a particular threshold, allowed many restaurants and businesses to open indoors at 25% capacity and schools could re-open for in-person instruction. Restrictions became even less burdensome as counties entered the orange and yellow tiers.[60]

By the early fall, public officials were gaining confidence that they could manage the pandemic. In late September 2020, COVID-19 test positivity rates and hospitalizations reached their lowest point since the pandemic. Death rates had declined more than 30% over the previous two weeks. New cases plateaued around 3,000 to 3,600 a day well into October. Los Angeles County, home to some 10 million residents, successfully moved from the purple to the red tier, allowing for the reopening of shopping malls, nail salons, and other businesses at 25% capacity. Breweries and card rooms moved operations outdoors. Playgrounds were reopened and schools could apply waivers to resume in-person instruction. Little did anyone know this would be the calm before the deadliest third wave arriving just in time for the holidays.

COVID-19's Third Wave

In the early days of the pandemic, when it looked as if California had escaped New York's COVID-19 disaster, public health experts gushed over the "California miracle," highlighting Governor Newsom's quick response and the willingness of most Californians to comply with social distancing, masking, and other safety protocols.[61]

When viewed through the fuller arc of the pandemic, any notions of a California miracle had largely vanished by summer 2020. And by December of that year, the miracle had turned into an utter nightmare: California was in the midst of a third wave that turned into what UCLA epidemiologist Dr. Robert Kim-Farley described as a "tsunami."[62] Newsom had once again tried to stop the spread by issuing another round of stay-at-home orders on November 19, imposing a month-long curfew of "non-essential" business and personal activity between 10 p.m. and 5 a.m. in counties in the purple tier. This covered about 94% of the state's population. Once again the governor met stiff resistance from law enforcement in certain parts of the state. In Riverside County, Sheriff Chad Bianco called the stay-at-home order "flat out ridiculous" and "dictatorial" and said he wouldn't enforce it.[63]

By Christmas Day, California had become the first state to record a 2 millionth infection; the state's ICU capacity hit zero percent for the first time.[64] Daily infection totals climbed above 50,000, and the daily number of deaths neared 400. More than 23,000 Californians had succumbed to the virus. Newsom once again sounded warning bells—the worst was yet to come if Californians didn't take precautions. "We're projecting that our hospital number will double in the next 30 days, and our projections have gotten much more solid," Newsom said. "I fear that, but we're not victims to that if we change our behaviors."[65] A group of ten Southern California local health departments joined in. They sent what they dubbed an urgent holiday message to the public: "Our systems are being overwhelmed, the virus is spreading everywhere. . . . [W]e cannot continue on our current path without facing serious consequences."[66]

Their concerns foreshadowed reality. By early January 2021, patients were lined up in stretchers in hospital hallways in the hardest-hit parts of Los Angeles County. There were no more ICU rooms available. In the Martin Luther King Jr. Community Hospital, patients were being treated in tents outside, in conference rooms, and even the chapel.[67] One in 16 people Los Angeles County had now tested positive for the virus. Latino hospitalization rates were nearly four times the rate of Whites.[68]

Once again, equipment issues developed. Treatment for the most ill, to the extent it was available, required intubation in order to oxygenate patients' organs. Some older hospitals with aging infrastructure lacked enough pressure to pump enough oxygen in the high volume of patients needing it. In the eastern areas in Los Angeles County and the San Fernando Valley, some hospitals declared an "internal disaster" as a way to divert ambulances bringing in new patients elsewhere.[69] To help conserve oxygen, the Los Angeles County Emergency Medical Services Agency (EMS) told ambulance crews not to bring patients to hospitals who had little chance of survival.[70] People's worst fears—a rationed health care system—was now a reality.

While a full account of factors behind the spread of the deadly third wave may be years away (for example, to what extent did weather, human behaviors beyond masking and indoor dining, or, quite simply, bad super-spreader luck play a role?), most initial accounts suggest the surge was caused by a collective change in Californians' behavior. Families gathered in larger numbers over the holidays. "Covid-exhaustion" grew with the constant shifting of rules and regulations. When cases dropped in September, the public may have been overconfident that the worst was now behind. Mobility data collected from cellphones demonstrated Californians traveled more and did less social distancing in October and November than at any time since the previous spring.[71] Growing cynicism and distrust of Newsom (and government more generally) likely played a part too since Newsom dined at the French Laundry in early November in direct violation of his own public health orders (see Chapter 6).

The grim news of climbing death toll—nearly 60,000 Californians were dead from COVID-19 by March 2021—was interrupted by hope brought by the long-awaited arrival of COVID-19 vaccines. The vaccine rollout in California, as detailed in Chapter 5, was plagued by early problems. Nonetheless, Newsom pinned his hopes on the idea that widespread inoculation by summer 2021 would not only save thousands of lives but would also help him fight for his own political life as the recall got fully underway. A vaccinated public would reduce the spread, get kids back in school, and put adults back to work, thereby making COVID-19 a distant memory. Newsom expressed confidence in the vaccines by announcing in April 2021 that the State of California would fully reopen June 15.[72] And to great fanfare, California did just that.

The Fourth Wave

Yet the virus fought back, obviously impervious to public health or Newsom's political needs. A more contagious Delta variant, which had originated in India, was slowly spreading throughout the United States in June and July 2021. Although California had above-average vaccination rates with more than 50% of its population fully vaccinated by the July Fourth holiday, millions were still left exposed to the extremely contagious variant. Los Angeles County where some 48% of population was still unvaccinated saw cases increase nearly 280% in the first two weeks of July. While the spike in cases was mostly attributable to the unvaccinated, evidence of (relatively rare) "breakthrough" infections occurring among the vaccinated led the Los Angeles County public health officials to impose a new universal indoor mask mandate on July 15.[73] Frustration spilled over into public view as the state, once again, seemed to be stepping backward, threatening to stoke tensions between the vaccinated and unvaccinated.[74]

Knowing that increasing the rate of vaccination still represented the clearest pathway out of the pandemic, Governor Newsom issued a new order requiring all state healthcare workers to get vaccinated by the fall. The order was the first of its kind in the nation.[75] Just a week later, on August 12, Newsom ordered all teachers to get vaccinated or undergo extensive testing. "We believe it's the right thing to do," Newsom said. "We think this is a sustainable way to keep our schools open . . . and doing everything in our power to keep our kids safe."[76]

Although the Delta variant was wreaking new havoc, case counts were far below the winter surge. This wasn't the case in Florida and Texas, however, where the Delta variant caused considerably higher spikes in cases, hospitalizations, and death. California's experience now looked quite favorable when compared to conservative states in the South where their governors went out of their way to avoid mask requirements and vaccination mandates. By mid-August 2021, California's positive case-load was half of Texas's and less than quarter of Florida's. One big question remained: what impact would all of this have on the voters?

Notes

1. Larry N. Gerston, Mary Currin-Percival, Garrick Percival and Terry Chris-tensen, *California Politics and Government: A Practical Approach* (Boston, MA: Cengage Press, 2021); Office of Governor Gavin Newsom, "Governor Newsom Announces Appointments," www.gov.ca.gov/2020/02/04/governor-newsom-announces-appointments-2-4-20/.
2. "San Jose woman is first known U.S. COVID-19 death," *San Jose Mercury News*, April 24, 2020.
3. Before officials linked Dowd's death to the coronavirus, the first recorded coronavirus deaths were believed to be in Washington State on February 26. Given the time needed from initial infection to death, public health officials believe Dowd was likely infected in early January. Crucially, Dowd, and two other Santa Clara County men who died from coronavirus complications on February 17 and March 6 had not traveled outside the country. This suggests community transmission was well underway in January. Public health officials had suspected this, but with no testing capacity at the time, they were left only guessing.
4. "The Chinese government's cover-up killed health care workers worldwide," *Foreign Policy*, March 18, 2021.
5. "China Identifies New Virus Causing Pneumonialike Illness," *New York Times*, January 8, 2020, www.nytimes.com/2020/01/08/health/china-pneumonia-outbreak-virus.html?referringSource=articleShare.
6. Ibid.
7. "The Chinese government's cover-up killed health care workers worldwide," *Foreign Policy*, March 18, 2021.
8. Viruses are named for their genetic structure. COVID-19 is an acronym for coronavirus 2019, given that the virus was detected at the end of 2019. The World Health Organization made an effort to give it a name that avoided social stigma. It thus has no reference to animals, humans, or country of

origin. See "The Illness Now Has a Name, COVID-19," www.nytimes.com/2020/02/11/world/asia/coronavirus-china.html?referringSource=articleShare.

9. "Trump's early travel 'bans' weren't early, weren't bans and didn't work," *Washington Post*, October 1, 2020, www.washingtonpost.com/outlook/2020/10/01/debate-early-travel-bans-china/.

10. "They ordered the Bay Area to shut down: Then came the hard part," *San Francisco Chronicle*, March 16, 2021, www.sfchronicle.com/health/article/A-year-after-Bay-Area-s-historic-stay-at-home-16028062.php.

11. "Newsom to Californians: Don't leave your homes," *San Francisco Chronicle*, March 20, 2020.

12. "Grand Princess cruise ship at center of coronavirus fight amid concerns about spread," *Los Angeles Times*.

13. "Is Newsom right? Will California see 25.5 million coronavirus cases in two months?," *Los Angeles Times*, March 20, 2020, www.latimes.com/california/story/2020-03-20/newsom-california-25-million-coronavirus-cases-two-months.

14. "Newsom to Californians: Don't leave your homes," *San Francisco Chronicle*, March 20, 2020.

15. Larry N. Gerston, *Not So Golden After All: The Rise and Fall of California* (Boca Raton, FL: CRC Press, 2012).

16. "California companies jump in to supply ventilators needed in coronavirus fight," *Los Angeles Times*, March 23, 2020, www.latimes.com/business/story/2020-03-23/coronavirus-california-companies-medical-supplies.

17. "Newsletter: Trump and Newsom's quiet cooperation, for now," *Los Angeles Times*, March 30, 2020.

18. "California lags in tests and hospital beds," *New York Times*, March 24, 2020.

19. "C.D.C. Labs Were Contaminated, Delaying Coronavirus Testing, Officials Say," *New York Times*, April 18, 2020.

20. "Testing in state is trailing New York," *San Francisco Chronicle*, March 28, 2020.

21. "Frustrated Gov. Newsom calls on task force to fix California's coronavirus testing shortfall," *CalMatters*, April 6, 2020.

22. "Coronavirus testing: New York has conducted 65% more tests than California. Here's why." *San Francisco Chronicle*, March 27, 2020.

23. Public Policy Institute of California, *Californians and Their Government*, 2020, www.ppic.org/publication/ppic-statewide-survey-californians-and-their-government-may-2020/.

24. "Newsom gave 'very little information' on $1-billion coronavirus mask purchase," *Los Angeles Times*, April 9, 2020, www.latimes.com/california/story/2020-04-09/gavin-newsom-coronavirus-masks-purchase-california-legislature.

25. "How the coronavirus crisis gave Gavin Newsom his leadership moment," www.theguardian.com/world/2020/apr/12/how-the-coronavirus-crisis-gave-gavin-newsom-his-leadership-moment.

26. University of California, Berkeley. Institute of Governmental Studies Poll. Release #2020–05.

27. "The coronavirus is deadliest where Democrats live," www.nytimes.com/2020/05/25/us/politics/coronavirus-red-blue-states.html?referringSource=articleShare.

28. Center for Disease Control and Prevention *COVID-19 Outbreak: New York City*, 2021. February 29–June 1, 2020, www.cdc.gov/mmwr/volumes/69/wr/mm6946a2.htm.

29. "Associations between governor political affiliation and COVID-19 cases, deaths, and testing in the U.S.," *American Journal of Preventive Medicine*, March 9, 2021, www.ajpmonline.org/article/S0749-3797(21)00135-5/fulltext.

30. Christopher Mooney, *The Republican War on Science* (New York, NY: Basic Books, 2005).

31. "Georgia's experiment in human sacrifice," *The Atlantic*, www.theatlantic.com/health/archive/2020/04/why-georgia-reopening-coronavirus-pandemic/610882/.

32. "Operation reopen America: Are we about to witness a second historic failure of leadership from Trump?," *The Guardian*, April 18, 2020, www.theguardian.com/us-news/2020/apr/18/operation-reopen-america-are-we-about-to-witness-a-second-historic-failure-of-leadership-from-trump.

33. Ibid.

34. See "How Obama's Handling of Ebola Compares with Trump's Handling of Coronavirus," *Boston Public Radio*, March 13, 2020, www.wgbh.org/news/politics/2020/03/13/how-obamas-handling-of-ebola-compares-with-trumps-handling-of-coronavirus; and "The US had a chance to learn from Anthrax, SARS, H1N1, and Ebola: So why is the federal coronavirus response so messy," *USA Today*, March 23, 2020, www.usatoday.com/story/news/nation/2020/03/23/coronavirus-shows-trump-administration-problems-with-biodefense-plan/2896252001/.

35. Jacob Hacker and Paul Pierson, *Winner-Take-All Politics* (New York, NY: Simon and Shuster Press, 2010).

36. "California's coronavirus reopening: Gavin Newsom's six-point plan will alter daily life." *San Francisco Chronicle*, April 14, 2021. https://www.sfchronicle.com/politics/article/California-s-coronavirus-reopening-Gov-Gavin-15200205.php

37. Ibid.

38. "S.F. attorney sues over California's coronavirus ban on religious gatherings," *San Francisco Chronicle*, www.sfchronicle.com/politics/article/SF-attorney-sues-over-California-s-coronavirus-15209188.php.

39 "Outraged parishioners, irked gun store owners, an angry bride: Courts flooded with anti-Newsom shutdown suits," *CalMatters*, https://calmatters.org/health/coronavirus/2020/05/california-shutdown-lawsuits-newsom-dhillon-coronavirus-shelter-in-place-executive-orders/#lawsuits.

40. "3 California counties are defying state orders on reopening businesses," *Vox.com*, www.vox.com/policy-and-politics/2020/5/2/21245163/california-counties-defying-state-stay-home-orders-reopening-businesses.

41. "Raucous protest in Huntington Beach demands beaches open, end of stay-at-home order," www.latimes.com/california/story/2020-05-01/protesters-in-huntington-beach-demand-california-reopen-slam-newsom-on-beach-closures.

42. "Poll: Most support shelter order," *San Jose Mercury News*, April 24, 2020.

43. "3 California counties are defying state orders on reopening businesses," *Vox.com*, www.vox.com/policy-and-politics/2020/5/2/21245163/california-counties-defying-state-stay-home-orders-reopening-businesses.

44. "Gov. Newsom says reopening California will begin this week amid coronavirus crisis," *Los Angeles Times*, May 4, 2020, www.latimes.com/california/story/2020-05-04/california-reopening-coronavirus-gavin-newsom-phases-begin-retail-pickup.

45. Ibid.

46. "Some California businesses could reopen within weeks as state fights coronavirus, Newsom says," *Los Angeles Times*, April 28, 2020, www.latimes.com/

california/story/2020-04-28/reopen-california-businesses-gavin-newsom-phases-stay-home-order-coronavirus.

47. Ibid.

48. "Once united, Bay Area counties take divergent paths toward reopening," *San Francisco Chronicle*, May 17, 2020, www.sfchronicle.com/bayarea/article/Once-united-Bay-Area-counties-take-divergent-15275526.php.

49. "Newsom faces growing concerns that he's reopening California too quickly," *Politico California*, www.politico.com/states/california/story/2020/05/27/newsom-faces-growing-concerns-that-hes-reopening-california-too-quickly-1288035.

50. "Mixed messages on reopening southern California create confusion, anger: Facebook town hall today," May 16, 2020, https://deadline.com/2020/05/southern-california-reopening-confusion-1202936517/.

51. "Once united, Bay Area counties take divergent paths toward reopening," *San Francisco Chronicle*, May 17, 2020, www.sfchronicle.com/bayarea/article/Once-united-Bay-Area-counties-take-divergent-15275526.php.

52. "Virus holds upper hand," *San Francisco Chronicle*, July 5, 2020.

53. "California's mask order tests the limits of Newsom's executive power," *Los Angeles Times*, June 18, 2020, www.latimes.com/california/story/2020-06-29/california-mask-order-gavin-newsom-powers-coronavirus.

54. "Newsom orders statewide reclosure of indoor dining, limits on church services, salons," *Los Angeles Times*, July 13, 2020, www.latimes.com/california/story/2020-07-13/newsom-california-county-rollback-reopening-coronavirus.

55. Ibid.

56. "State issues largest COVID-19 safety fine to Overhill Farms in Vernon," *Los Angeles Times*, September 10, 2020, www.latimes.com/california/story/2020-09-10/state-issues-largest-COVID-19-safety-fine-overhill-farms-vernon.

57. "Coronavirus ravages California's Central Valley, following cruel and familiar path," *Los Angeles Times*, June 28 2020, www.latimes.com/california/story/2020-07-28/coronavirus-ravages-californias-central-valley-following-a-cruel-and-familiar-path.

58. "Indoor haircuts are back as California tries reopening again," *CalMatters*, August 28, 2020, https://calmatters.org/economy/2020/08/california-reopen-hair-salons-indoor-haircuts/.

59. "Los Angeles and San Diego schools go online-only in the fall," *New York Times*, July 13, 2020, www.nytimes.com/2020/07/13/us/lausd-san-diego-school-reopening.html?referringSource=articleShare.

60. See California's Blueprint for a Safer Economy, https://emd.saccounty.net/EMD-COVID-19-Information/Documents/California-Color-Coded-Tier-System-en.pdf.

61. "How the 'California miracle' dissolved into a winter of coronavirus nightmare," *Los Angeles Times*, January 22, 2021.

62. Ibid.

63. "Riverside county sheriff calls stay-at-home order 'ridiculous,' says Newsom 'hypocritical'," *Desert Sun*, December 5, 2020, www.desertsun.com/story/news/2020/12/05/riverside-sheriff-newsom-hypocritical-stay-home-order-ridiculous/3844932001/.

64. "California COVID-19 update: Statewide available ICU capacity falls to 0% on Christmas Day," *Deadline*, December 25, 2020, https://deadline.com/2020/12/california-COVID-19-available-icu-capacity-falls-0-percent-1234661603/.

65. "California COVID-19: 2 million confirmed cases and counting," *Associated Press*, https://apnews.com/article/pandemics-los-angeles-california-coronavirus-pandemic-0a2c9ac75b6a8c05706289bace1b4024.
66. Ibid.
67. "Oxygen supply issue forced five Los Angeles-area hospitals to declare 'internal disaster,'" *Cnn.com*, www.cnn.com/2020/12/29/us/california-hospital-oxygen-covid/index.html.
68. "Tracking the coronavirus in California," *Los Angeles Times*, www.latimes.com/projects/california-coronavirus-cases-tracking-outbreak/.
69. Ibid.
70. "Los Angeles ambulance crews told not to transport patients who stand little chance of survival," *Cnn.com*, January 4, 2021, www.cnn.com/world/live-news/coronavirus-pandemic-vaccine-updates-01-04-21/h_4bd878281be24fc704169b9955041cee.
71. Institute for health metrics and evaluation, https://covid19.healthdata.org/united-states-of-america/california?view=mask-use&tab=trend.
72. "Governor aims to reopen California by mid-June, contingent on public health metrics," *npr.org*, www.npr.org/2021/04/06/984794054/governor-aims-to-reopen-california-by-mid-june-contingent-on-public-health-metri.
73. "Los Angeles County will require masks indoors as Delta variant spreads," *New York Times*, July 15, 2021.
74. "L.A. County will require masks to indoors amid alarming rise in coronavirus cases," *Los Angeles Times*, July 15, 2021, www.latimes.com/california/story/2021-07-15/l-a-county-will-require-masks-indoors-amid-covid-19-surge.
75. "California healthcare workers must be vaccinated by the end of September under new health order," *Los Angeles Times*, August 5, 2021.
76. Ibid.

Chapter 5

COVID-19 Scrambles California Governance

"*The buck stops here.*"

—*President Harry Truman*

It was President Harry Truman who popularized what is now an old saw: "The buck stops here." It's a phrase that has long created an expectation that executive leaders, by the nature of their position, carry final responsibility for the government's actions and outcomes, especially in times of public crises. There is a certain truth to this. Executives, whether a president, governor, or mayor, are singular figures. In moments of crisis, they can move more nimbly than larger legislative bodies. Through wars, natural disasters, financial shocks, crime waves, or other calamities, the public looks to executives to lead the way.

It should be no surprise that Governor Gavin Newsom became the face of California's response to the pandemic. As the state ping-ponged between shutdowns and re-openings, Newsom's face seemed to be everywhere as he spent press conference after press conference outlining the state's COVID-19 battle plans. As we document in this chapter, COVID-19 gave Newsom extraordinary powers. Like most executives in a time of crisis, he tried to remake the pandemic into something that could be controlled and managed. Yet COVID-19 unleashed a confluence of seemingly unrelenting challenges that exposed, and in many cases worsened, the state's long-standing structural and administrative problems, its simmering political divisions, and social and racial inequities. Far from managing the pandemic by "following the science," Newsom was, at several junctures, left reacting to emerging crises while explaining away his actions that looked self-serving or hypocritical to all but his most devoted supporters. Combined, these shaped what we describe in this chapter as Newsom's "problems in governance." They ultimately contributed to a damaging narrative that depicted Newsom as too powerful and self-serving while also in over his head.

DOI: 10.4324/9781003217954-5

Newsom's Challenges With the Legislature

We begin with the governor's problems with the legislature—an institution, lest we forget, dominated by his fellow co-partisans. The 2020 legislative session started out like most others. Newsom used his State of the State speech on February 19 to address the homelessness crisis and the expansion of childcare for working parents. Lawmakers readied the last of their nearly 3,000 laws they introduced that session. But less than a month later, on March 15, the same day the governor declared a statewide emergency, leaders of the State Senate and Assembly announced something remarkable: they were considering a legislative shutdown to stop the spread of disease. At the time, California had just 335 Covid cases.

The next day, the legislature passed a $1 billion emergency spending bill; $500 million from the state's general fund would be used to open two additional hospitals and buy additional ventilators and PPE in preparation for the expected onslaught of COVID patients. Another $500 million was authorized "for any purpose" related to Newsom's emergency declaration.[1] The legislature then announced it was going into recess. It wouldn't reopen for another 45 days.

Stepping into the void was Newsom. His newfound power was aided by the California Emergency Services Act, also known as CESA. Passed unanimously by the legislature and signed by Governor Ronald Reagan in 1970 with little fanfare, CESA granted the governor virtually unlimited powers during a declared "state of emergency." The law gave the governor power to "make, amend, or rescind" state regulations, to suspend state laws, to spend money from any fund legally available, and to commandeer state hospitals, hotels, and other private property.

Realizing the pandemic called for swift action and recognizing the expansive powers of CESA didn't mean everyone in the legislature was happy with the situation. Spending was a power granted to the legislative branch and the lawmakers were now on the sidelines. The tension between the legislature knowingly relinquishing power while trying to protect some semblance of its policy priorities and institutional standing would animate Newsom's roller-coaster ride with the institution as COVID-19 dug in over the next year.

This tension first revealed itself after Newsom's appearance on MSNBC's Rachel Maddow Show on April 7, 2020. There the governor announced a $1 billion deal to secure 200 million masks a month including 150 million of the higher quality N95 masks that filter airborne particles. "We're not waiting around any longer," Newsom said while mildly criticizing the federal government's inability to deliver adequate supplies of PPE.[2] The announcement created a lot of buzz: Maddow even noted, "I think you are going to make national news with this." Newsom certainly made news, but in the end, it may have done more political harm than good. It contributed to a storyline that the governor's big policy announcements were full of splash and pizazz but on closer inspection weren't all they were cracked up to be.

Indeed, upon implementation, the mask deal created immediate political headaches for Newsom. Legislative leaders were angry they didn't know of the purchase until a mere 45 minutes before Newsom went on air. The vice-chair of the Joint Legislative Budget Committee, Democrat Phil Ting, learned about the deal only after he read a story about the Maddow interview in the *Los Angeles Times* the next day. "Since the recess, communication between the administration and the legislature has been poor," Ting said. "We really haven't received information in a timely manner."[3]

To secure the deal Newsom said he needed the legislature to approve a $495 million check in the next 48 hours.[4] But he failed to give lawmakers copies of the contract, any details about the cost per mask, quality control, or his plans to get the materials where they needed to go.[5] At one point Newsom even said that giving more details would prevent the masks from getting delivered. "I care more about producing a big result. Others again are going to consume themselves around process," he said. Emphasizing outcomes over process, even if it meant angering key legislative allies, was becoming Newsom's COVID modus operandi. Assembly Speaker Anthony Rendon grew frustrated. "The problem that my members have is lack of time. They feel like they are being told just before the public is told, but without enough time to provide any meaningful feedback."[6]

The contract, it turned out, was with BYD ("Build Your Dreams"), a Chinese electric vehicle manufacturer with a subsidiary based in Los Angeles. It was an odd choice except that BYD had a record of hiring lobbyists to secure no-bid contracts with public agencies.[7] The company had no previous experience making personal protective equipment. Only when the coronavirus hit did BYD switch its manufacturing to mask making. This was appealing to Newsom since the company promised to produce masks at a scale California needed. Its previous work came with a spotty track record; BYD was perhaps best known to officials for delivering electric buses to Los Angeles County which had a slew of mechanical problems.[8] At the federal level, Congress had recently banned BYD from receiving federal contracts over concerns about the company's ties to the Chinese government.[9]

Legislature leaders repeatedly asked the Newsom administration for contract details. Though government contracts are supposed to be made public under state law, the legislature was repeatedly rebuffed.[10] Newsom finally released the details in early May. The state had agreed to pay $3.30 per N95 mask; a rate far above what Los Angeles paid to an

American manufacturer around the same time. Newsom defended the cost, negotiations citing a worldwide shortage of masks when the state entered contract and BYD's promise of speedy work.[11]

But soon there would be another problem. Federal inspectors twice denied certification of BYD's N95 masks, forcing the company to refund half the state's down payment causing it to miss its original April 30 delivery target.[12] Newsom extended the deadline but by the end of May, and with N95s still not delivered, Newsom was forced to extend the agreement a second time. BYD didn't obtain final certification until June 8. The N95 masks didn't arrive until July—a full *three months* after Newsom's splashy announcement on national television.[13]

Newson's tensions with the legislature over spending and oversight would continue into the all-important battle over the 2020–2021 state budget. Drafting the yearly budget is the most important thing the legislature does. Only this time COVID-19 scrambled the whole process. The legislature was out through much of March and all of April—a crucial period when lawmakers would normally hold budget hearings and settle on spending levels. But on March 25 the governor made an alarming announcement: COVID-19, he estimated, was going to blow a massive hole in the state budget. Income, corporate, and sales tax revenues were all predicted to decline from the turmoil in financial markets and the spike in unemployment. Health care costs to the state were also expected to soar.

The governor announced California would need to dive into its "rainy day" fund—extra savings approved by voters in 2014 for use in tough economic times.[14] And these were tough times indeed. By May, and with the legislature just now returning, Newsom estimated California's deficit would climb to a "jaw dropping" $54 billion—a deficit larger than the state experienced during the Great Recession which itself had been billed as the worst economic recession since the Great Depression. While pleading for additional federal financial support, Newsom prepared lawmakers and the public for bad times ahead. Deep cuts to schools, social services, local governments, and a variety of other public programs were all on the horizon.[15] For Newsom, this was another critical test of leadership. In his first budget, pre-COVID-19, the main challenge for him and the legislature was how to divvy up a big budget surplus. That was a dream scenario for a figure like Newsom given his vision for strong, activist state government. Of course Newsom was not ideologically inclined to cut spending, but now the budget crisis amidst a pandemic offered him another opportunity to prove his leadership mettle.

The governor pledged to work collaboratively with the legislature. What he was selling, however, didn't go over well with most Democratic lawmakers. Most notable was the governor's plan to cut some $15 billion in state spending, most of it from education and health and human services.[16] In total his proposals would cut funding from some 89 different state programs. Newsom also proposed a painful 10% pay cut for most state workers, a move he estimated would save nearly $3 billion.[17] And in a show of solidarity with state workers—most of whom were unionized and some of Newsom's biggest political supporters—Newsom pledged to cut his own salary by the same amount.

The legislature countered with their own plan which included a far rosier view of the California COVID-19 economy than Newsom portrayed. This more optimistic forecast (in essence the legislature was telling the governor they didn't think the COVID-19 economy was going to be as bad as he said it would be), along with some spending deferrals, a plan to use about half the state's "rainy day" reserves, and other accounting maneuvers allowed the legislature to propose far fewer cuts.

On June 22, 2020, Newsom and the legislature came to a budget agreement that was far closer to what Democrats in the legislature wanted. Spending on K-12 education was kept in place; the budget avoided some of the deepest cuts to social services that would disproportionately harm the already vulnerable. Additional dollars were given to local governments to cope with the pandemic and rising homelessness. There were some real cuts, however. Higher education spending was slashed as was money for the state court system, and money for low- and middle-income family housing.[18] State employees were also forced to take their unwanted pay cut.

What didn't get cut was Newsom's *own* salary. Employee pay data from the State Controller's Office revealed Newsom received his full $17,479 salary for July, the same month when other state employees had experienced cuts in their paycheck. Newsom's office blamed it on an "oversight" by the Controller's office. To save face, Newsom wrote a letter to the Controller's office asking for his pay to be cut retroactively.[19] Union leaders stood by him but the incident once again made it easier for Newsom's opponents to paint him as a politician who said one thing while something else actually happened.

Upon passing the state budget, the legislature again adjourned for a short recess because of additional member infections from the virus. This time, the body was supposed to reassemble after July 4, but with more members becoming ill, business at the Capitol did not resume until August 17, only to end its activity for the entire year on August 31. Left without attention were hundreds of bills on housing production, homelessness, criminal justice, climate change, labor rules, taxes, and additional remedies to help fill the expected budget deficit. No one could blame the state legislature for shuttering once again as infections entered the chamber, but for long with so much pending legislation on the line? Democratic leaders in the Senate. Assembly disagreed over the legalities of remote voting leaving the legislature at an impasse. Not until August 2020 did both chambers operate via remote voting. In the meantime,

Speaker Rendon estimated the virus-caused assembly shutdown would force lawmakers to reduce the number of bills under consideration to 600 or 700 from the nearly 3,000 that had been introduced.[20] The irony is that the five-month deadlock was not between Republicans and Democrats but entirely within the Democratic leadership in the two chambers. As a result, Newsom operated with only limited accountability to the legislative branch through much of this period.

This might partly explain Newsom's poor communication with the legislature as the calendar turned to 2021. He once again irked the legislature when he announced the end to stay-at-home orders in late January over social media instead of alerting lawmakers. In response, Laura Friedman, a Democratic Assemblywoman from Burbank, tweeted, "If you think state legislators were blindsided by, and confused about, the shifting and confusing public health directives, you'd be correct. If you think we have been quiet about it in Sacramento, you'd be wrong."[21] So much for intra-party comity.

As pandemic wore on, it became clear the legislature was more right about the budget forecast than Newsom was. In what might have seemed to some in Sacramento like a divine budget miracle, the state budget made a 180-degree turn by spring 2021. Newsom's prediction of a massive state revenue shortfall never materialized. Instead, the 2021–2022 budget—now the second budget of the pandemic—showed a $76 billion surplus.[22]

This massive surplus—the largest in state history—was not, of course, a result of divine intervention. It was a byproduct of the two very different economies that have long operated in California but diverged even further during the pandemic. The first, filled with low-skill, low- wage jobs, hit lower and working-class family incomes hard as unemployment spiked. But the second economy—the playground of the wealthiest Californians whose income (and tax payments) is tied to stock portfolios and capital gains—roared on. Wealthy Californians pay the lion's share of state income taxes; when the stock market proved impervious to the devastation and human suffering of the pandemic, revenue flowed into state coffers in surprising amounts.[23] Tens of billions of dollars in federal financial aid to cope with the pandemic were additionally helpful. For the governor, the budget surplus couldn't have come at a better time. It was a drop of good news amidst a lot of bad. As we'll document in Chapter 6, it meant the state could send tax rebate checks of up to $1,100 for millions of Californians—right before the recall election.

The Legislature Quarrels With Newsom Over Executive Orders

While Newsom was haggling over the budget, there were also disagreements with the legislature over his use of executive orders. Between March

2020 and May 2021, the governor issued no less than 60 executive orders dealing with the effects of COVID-19.[24] Some of these, like his extension on licensing deadlines for real estate developers and ambulance drivers, were technical and didn't generate much discussion or controversy. Others did, however. On April 16, 2020, Newsom ordered paid sick leave to all food-sector workers at large employers affected by the virus. This move angered Republicans who saw it as a government interference in companies' affairs.[25] So too did his earlier rule that gun dealers were "non-essential" businesses and must be closed during the stay-at-home order.

One that generated a long-running conflict (and lawsuits) was the governor's executive order issued on May 8, 2020. The order required county elections officials to send vote-by-mail ballots for the 2020 general elections to all registered voters in state—some 22 million people in total. Newsom said his powers to change election protocols rested in the California Emergency Services Act, and thus framed the decision around his desire to keep voters safe. "Elections and the right to vote are foundational to our democracy," Newsom said. "No Californian should be forced to risk their health in order to exercise their right to vote."[26]

Republicans saw it through an entirely different lens. Using much of the same rhetoric as President Trump—who had regularly attacked mail-in-voting as "dangerous" and "rigged"—California Republicans called the order a "brazen power grab" that would lead to voter fraud.[27] "Democrats continue to use this pandemic as a ploy to implement their partisan election agenda, and Governor Newsom's executive order is the latest direct assault on the integrity of our elections," said Ronna McDaniel, Chairwoman of the Republican National Committee.[28] Research shows election fraud using vote-by-mail is extraordinarily rare and that at least traditionally it hasn't favored one party over the other.[29] This didn't stop Republicans from suing to stop it. The lawsuit filed in federal district on May 24 referenced "fraud" more than 14 times.[30] It alleged Newsom illegally usurped legislative authority to "set the time, place, and manner" of the election. A second lawsuit was then filed in state court by Republican members of the State Assembly, James Gallagher and Kevin Riley (Riley himself would become a candidate for governor during the recall election). That lawsuit focused less on fraud and more on the argument that Newsom overstepped his authority under the state constitution. "The governor changed and amended state statute, which he is not authorized to do. That is a legislative power," Gallagher said.[31]

Just a few weeks later, on June 18, the Democratic-controlled legislature put into law the same all-vote-by-mail process that Newsom originally ordered. In other words, the legislature reaffirmed Newsom's order, only this time via the regular legislative process.[32] Now seeing their case as moot (given that the law superseded Newsom's order) Republicans dropped their lawsuit in federal court. But the state lawsuit carried on. It found a sympathetic ear of a Sutter County Superior Court judge—a county that would later vote in favor of recalling Newsom by a 2:1 margin—who ruled that Newsom had overstepped his authority by requiring the distribution of millions of vote-by-mail ballots. The Emergency Services Act, the judge ruled, allows the governor power "to suspend certain statutes, not *amend* any statutes or create *new* ones [emphasis added]." Gallagher and Riley called the decision a victory for "separation of powers."[33]

Though the ruling came just days before the 2020 presidential election, it did nothing to interfere with the election itself. The legislature, after all, had passed legislation requiring a vote-by-mail election the previous June. And later, the Sutter County ruling was overturned. Citing the governor's broad "police powers" under CESA, a state appellate court in May 2021 ruled Newsom had indeed complied with both the law and the California Constitution. But more than anything, the saga over vote-by-mail was a clear indication—one of many that would reveal themselves over the pandemic—of the political divisions roiling across and within state government. From Republicans in the legislature to the courthouse, a clear message was building: Newsom was usurping his legal authority and needed to be stopped.

Crisis Unfolds in California's Public Health Bureaucracy

While the governor managed tensions with the legislature and dogged opposition from conservatives over his aggressive use of executive orders, a simmering crisis was brewing elsewhere in the state's public health bureaucracy. State and local public health officials were under enormous stress as COVID-19 cases and deaths rose. The state's director of public health resigned in August 2020 after an accounting glitch revealed that the results of 250,000 COVID-19 tests had been temporarily misplaced, leading to an undercount of infected individuals and questions of accuracy when accuracy was terribly needed.[34] All told, three high-level California public health officials resigned in the early months of the pandemic.

The greatest bureaucratic damage took place at the local level. By March 2021, at least 18 key local public health officials in 13 California counties had resigned, including three in Orange County alone. Some departures occurred as a result of intimidation by local citizens, others because of the loss of support from local elected officials, and in a few instances, pressure from both sources. In Placer County, the public health officer resigned after the Board of Supervisors abruptly ended a local health emergency order and embraced a "herd immunity" strategy rejected by almost every qualified immunology specialist.[35] In Orange

County, the public health director resigned after protests outside her home and a sign at a local public meeting depicting her as a Nazi.[36] In Riverside County, the County Board of Supervisors fired the public health director because he cancelled two large annual festivals and required residents to wear masks when in public.[37] Uniform consistency on dealing with the pandemic, to the extent there ever was any, went by the wayside; it was every county for itself.

Early on, state leaders attempted to confront the pandemic through "contact tracing," detective-like research designed to locate individuals infected with COVID-19 as a means to find others who might be infected. Contact tracing efforts at the local level foreshadowed implementation inconsistencies of state COVID-19 policies downstream. Experts estimated that the nation would need an army of as many as 300,000 people to successfully quash the pandemic. Less than two months into fighting the pandemic, Governor Newsom pledged to organize 10,000 tracers to interact with local governments, a number much less than would be expected given that California housed 12% of the nation's population. Referencing the state's previous management of epidemics such as measles and tuberculosis, he said, "We have been contact tracing for years and years, decades in California."[38] For Newsom, it seemed that dealing with the pandemic was simply the latest chapter typical in disease containment.

But this pandemic required much more than a "typical" state intervention with conventional resources. To begin with, the disease was spreading faster than public officials could act. As such, the state was unable to mobilize even a 10,000-person contact-tracing unit. A report by the state Auditor General in April 2021 found that only 2,200 state employees had been assigned to contact tracing, and even these were not well trained.[39] In a sense, neither number mattered; the California Department of Public Health estimated that controlling the spread of the pandemic would require at least 31,400 contact tracers. An unfortunate tragedy followed. Without ample state support, local health officials were able to contact only a fraction of the infected population. Several counties didn't even try to contact those with COVID-19 because they just didn't have the necessary resources.[40] Without contact tracing, containment of the virus was nearly impossible.

Whether through newspaper ads, social media, or in-person threats, local public health officials faced unprecedented intimidation. The lack of support, confusing state and local directives, and a depressing work setting led to a drain of expertise when it was needed the most, and at a great cost. Said the CEO of the National Association of County and City Health Officials, "We're moving at breakneck speed here to stop a pandemic, and you can't afford to hit the pause button and say, 'We're going to change the leadership around here and we'll get back to you after we hire somebody.'"[41] The environment for public officials became so threatened that in September 2020, Governor Newsom issued an executive order allowing local governments to withhold addresses and other information of key personnel from public view.

As local government officials struggled over how to handle the pandemic and whom to blame, life for the frontline doctors and nurses, never particularly easy, became unbearable. A study by Blue Shield toward the end of 2020 found that two thirds of California physicians, nurses, and supporting health care professionals felt "emotionally drained, frustrated, overworked, and burned out."[42] And fairly or not, they looked to Gavin Newsom as the source of their misery. As one health foundation newsletter put it, "For much of the pandemic, Gov. Gavin Newsom has pushed the responsibility—and blame—of reopening largely onto counties and . . . local health officers, who have worked for months without days off, giving up time with their families to attack this crisis head-on."[43] From elected local officials to providers to sizable segments of the state, California's health care system no longer seemed to work.

Trouble With the Vaccine Rollout

Public health matters for the governor didn't improve much with the COVID-19 vaccine rollout, at least at first. During the summer and fall of 2020, state public health employees spent months preparing an 84-page vaccine management plan that covered every aspect of a product launch including provider recruitment, storage and handling, and, of course, vaccination professionals, the actual injection process, and sites.[44] All they needed was the vaccine, the first batch of which arrived in California on December 14, 2020.

Yet, despite the promise of state "preparedness," movement of the vaccine from delivery to injections stammered badly. Three weeks after vaccine arrival to designated locations, California had administered only 453,000 injections of its 1.3-million-dose supply.[45] In early January 2021, Newsom promised inoculations of at least one million doses of the vaccine within the next ten days, yet after a dozen days there were no indications that the new goal had been met.[46] The state's ineptitude persisted. One month after receiving vaccine shipments, California ranked 44th among the 50 states in the percentages of vaccine doses administered to an anxious public.[47]

Californians weren't happy. A Berkeley IGS poll taken in late January 2021 found a substantial drop in Newsom's job approval to 46% from 64% in September 2020. On managing the pandemic, less than a third of the public gave the governor good or excellent grades, and on overseeing distribution of the vaccine, only 22% approved of the governor's effort.[48] By late April 2021, California improved to 25th in vaccine distribution,[49] but the state's early vaccination history became a source of anger among recall proponents. You know that story about "first impressions . . ." Worse yet, Newsom caught flak from supporters as well as enemies. Said long-time ally and former Newsom strategist Garry South about the rollout, "I don't think Californians can understand why we have hundreds of thousands of doses sitting there, and they're not being administered." A conservative radio host was predictably more blunt: "Look, all we heard—all year long—from Gavin Newsom was that once we have the vaccine, all problems will be solved, the lockdowns will end and we can get back to normal life here in California. And that's not the case."[50] Fair or not, the governor was now facing criticism from just about every direction.

What exactly was the hold-up? The state's vaccination plan was largely dependent upon a software system known as PrepMod, a network for connecting patient waitlists with vaccine inventory. Providers throughout the state complained the management tool failed to accurately coordinate the two components. Other complaints centered on COVIDReadi, a registration site for providers. In addition, the two software problems interfered with CalReadi, California's virus testing program. Combined, the tools for managing vaccination simply didn't work as planned.[51] How ironic that the state known for technological wizardry couldn't seem to get the job done.

Pummeled by criticism from local governments and the medical establishment, Governor Newsom went in a different direction for vaccine distribution. In late January 2021, he announced that the state would contract with health care insurance provider Blue Shield to run the state's beleaguered vaccination program. Once again Newsom entered into a no-bid contract that included a $15 million administrative fee for Blue Shield to manage distribution of COVID-19 vaccines to the state's 58 counties.

Turning to the private sector in itself wasn't a particularly unpredictable move for Newsom, given his attitude toward the coordinating issues between the state and local governments. In his book, *Citizenville: How to Take the Town Square Digital and Reinvent Government*, Newsom wrote that when government can't solve problems, "We simply have to make it possible for people *outside* government to help us fix the problem."[52] More controversial was the circumstance under which the state turned to the private sector. A no-bid contract from the California Department of Public Health was given to a health insurance entity that contributed more than one million dollars to Newsom's 2018 gubernatorial campaign and $20 million more to the Newsom-proposed California Access to Housing and Services fund for homeless people just one week before the contract announcement.[53] A coincidence? Perhaps. However, for critics already suspicious of Newsom's motives, the no-bid contract only added more fuel to the COVID-19 management fire.

As it turns out, the Blue Shield outsourcing was only one of many examples of no-bid contracts in the health sector. State Health and Human Services Director Mark Ghaly praised the process because it allowed private sector companies to fill important needs during the pandemic. Nevertheless, one analysis found that during the first 14 months of the pandemic, the state outsourced at least 30 no-bid contracts to tech and health care companies worth $113 million, much of which went to Newsom supporters. Former state Department of Public Health epidemiologist Flojaune Cofer had a different take, saying, "This outsourcing . . . [and] lack of public investment in our public health system is weakening us," and that the companies are not accountable the way public agencies would be.[54] For many, "transparency," a behavior critical to public confidence in the governmental process, was becoming a rare commodity in the governance of California.

The potential conflict of interest notwithstanding, successful rollout of the vaccine eventually emerged. By early April 2021, Blue Shield had organized a network of 2,400 sites throughout the state capable of vaccinating 6 million people per week. But, critics still wondered, would the vaccine be distributed equitably? That was the next challenge.

Equity Problems

As COVID-19 vaccines became increasingly available, there remained a lingering question of pent-up demand versus limited supply. From the beginning, experts worried that some groups, particularly people of color and the poor, would not receive vaccinations proportionately to the rest of California residents. Worse yet, those concerned about distribution feared the problem was likely to persist until the supply equaled or exceeded demand. As we documented in the previous chapter, this hindrance was exacerbated by the unenviable fact that people of color contracted and died from COVID-19 at higher rates than Whites. Another problem concerned addressing the vaccination needs of educators as well as the ventilation and space needs of their facilities. Still, at least in the initial stages of injections, doling out vaccines to first responders, health care providers, and the elderly made sense to most people. But what about vaccines for the rest of the state, and in what would they be distributed?

Newsom attempted to address the issue in early February 2021. From the previous December on, the governor had encouraged schools to re-open as soon as possible; such action would represent a major step toward returning the state to some form of normalcy. It would also go a long way toward relieving pressure from parents, especially those who were pressed into hiring babysitters, temporary home-schooling assistance, or both. After all, too many working parents, particularly women, had found themselves in the no-win situation of returning to their jobs with their young children at home alone or staying home with their kids and foregoing work.

But there was another problem: the California Teachers Association (CTA), representing more than 300,000 educators, had vehemently opposed resuming in-class instruction because of safety concerns for teachers, other school personnel, and students. This in itself was awkward, given that the CTA had been a staunch Newsom ally and major gubernatorial campaign contributor.

Hope for breaking the impasse came in February 2021, when the governor announced that the state would set aside 10% of California's weekly vaccine allotments for educators, beginning in March. A CTA representative called the new designated allocation "an important step to ensuring teachers and school staff to get the vaccine before opening schools . . . for in-person instruction."[55] That earmark, along with a multi-billion-dollar school facilities improvement plan enacted by the legislature, offered hope for resolving the educators' concerns.

Settling the stalemate with teachers was only a beginning down the equity path. A much larger issue centered on vaccine delivery to the poorest and most vulnerable residents, including racial and ethnic minorities. A report by the Centers for Disease Control covering the period of December 14, 2020 through March 1, 2021, ranked California 45th of 49 states (Hawaii was not included) in distributing COVID-19 vaccines to the most susceptible areas of the state.[56] The report confirmed complaints from low-income county clinics of inadequate vaccine supplies for their populations. Most low-income residents and people of color were long-time components of the Democratic Party, and therefore, part of Newsom's coalition. Another problem.

Thus, in early March, under Newsom's direction, the state elected to dedicate 40% of its vaccine doses to the 446 zip codes thought to have the most vulnerable populations (out of 1,746 zip codes). According to state officials, most of the exposed population pockets were in southern California and the Central Valley. That set off complaints in the Bay Area, where spokespersons argued that the allotment system ignored largely impoverished Latino areas in northern California.[57] After considerable complaining, the zip code formula was altered to include predominately Latino neighborhoods in the Bay Area. Still, the supply-versus-demand problem continued, only now with racial and ethnic overtones. It was something that would be resolved only through enough vaccines and a massive targeted campaign, and that situation wouldn't occur until late spring.

Back to School Problems

When Governor Newsom shut down the state in mid-March 2020, he hoped the disruption of public education would last no more than a month. Yet, almost immediately, he realized that the state's new-found public health crisis would extend much longer than he and others had expected. At a news conference on March 17, 2020, the governor warned of a long-term statewide closure: "Don't anticipate schools are going to open up in a week [or] in a few weeks. . . . Few, if any, will open before the summer break."[58] Newsom's depressing prediction was on the mark. And so, the first of several explosive pandemic reality checks for California set in, and with it the new reality of distance learning, an education method whereby teachers would work with their students remotely via laptops, tablets, or similar electronic devices.

You would think that high-tech-oriented California would be well equipped to address the sudden shift in education pedagogy, but it was not the case. A comprehensive analysis by the Boston Consulting Group in June 2020 found that 17% of California students were without electronic devices; worse yet, 25%, or about 1.5 million students, had no access to high-speed connections—this, three months after the shutdown. In another sign of the scale challenges in the education sector, some 8% of public school teachers were without high-speed internet connections.[59] These conditions existed to various degrees between the March 2020 school shutdown and the end of the 2020–2021 school year.

The networking and equipment problems were slow to leave. With the pandemic only worsening, California public schools did not re-open as they traditionally do in late August and early September 2020. In fact, as the new academic year began, much of the distance learning deficiencies remained. As of October 2020, State Superintendent of Public Instruction Tony Thurmond, the state's highest elected K-12 education official, estimated that up to one million of California's 6.1 million K-12 students still lacked either computers, internet access, or both elements necessary for distance learning.[60] A poll of parents in fall 2020 found that a discouraging 82% believed that distance learning during the previous spring was either "not too effective" (55%) or "not effective at all" (27%). Nor were the parents very happy about managing distance learning for their kids during the new academic year; 58% anticipated that managing their kids' distance learning would be "difficult," compared with 39% who expected the new method to be "easy."[61]

Then there were issues related to the public school facilities that did not meet the health safety standards prescribed by the Centers of Disease Control and Prevention (CDC). One reputable study estimated that 38% of the state's schools required repairs or renovation for ventilation, heating, and air conditioning needs.[62] The state had put together a small fund of $600 million, but that wouldn't go very far in addressing the structural problems of nearly 4,000 of the state's 11,000 public schools. In addition, new CDC-recommended six-foot space requirements between students virtually guaranteed schools would be not able to accommodate all students or have to accept them all but on split schedules, potentially adding to instructional costs. On July 17, 2020, Governor Newsom issued an executive order limiting attendance—should there be any—to no more than 10% of a school's population. Given those conditions, few schools opened in the fall. Distance learning would remain for the time being, although no one knew how long that would be.

The longer students were required to remain home for distance learning because of COVID-19, the longer that untold numbers of parents had to choose between staying at home for their kids or returning to work, which presented serious financial concerns. Also, with little structure, students were less likely to adapt to the new education format. One study found that during the 2020–2021 academic year, student enrollment in public schools declined by 155,000 students, five times the declines of recent years.[63] With the start of the 2020–2021 academic year offering no relief, "normal" seemed to be a concept of the past. Things did not look good for students, teachers, parents, and most of all, Governor Gavin Newsom.

Problems in the Employment Development Department (EDD)

If the problems with the public health bureaucracy and California's schools weren't already enough, COVID-19 was placing new strain on the state's Employment Development Department (EDD), known to most as the state's unemployment agency. The EDD's woes began long before Gavin Newsom's ascendance to the governor's office. The state unemployment agency's ineptitude can be traced at least back to the 1980s. It has a history of staffing and technology ills which repeatedly have been addressed with Band-Aids instead of major surgery.[64] Judging from the agency's difficulties in managing unemployment claims and distributing payment, little has changed. For years, some applicants had been wrongly denied benefits, others had suffered interminably long delays on their requests, and others still given wrong payments.

The latest EDD fiasco began during the late spring of 2020. Earlier in the year, Congress passed the $2.2 trillion Coronavirus Aid, Relief, and Economic Security Act (known as CARES), the first major COVID-19 relief package. A major component of the legislation provided $600 per week in federal unemployment benefits for people who had become unemployed by the shutdown and received state unemployment benefits. The new funds would be bundled with the state unemployment checks.

The federal COVID-19 relief legislation couldn't have been more timely, given that California's unemployment rate soared to 15.5% in April 2020 from 5.5% during the previous March. Over that period alone, the state EDD processed 3.2 million claims; meanwhile, another 800,000 unemployment claims remained in limbo because of antiquated processing equipment and insufficient personnel.[65] Still, the wheels of the EDD vehicle couldn't get started. For example, 32 days passed before the EDD began distributing federal funds to those who hadn't previously qualified for unemployment (officially known as the Pandemic Unemployment Assistance Program). In addition, an astounding 61 days elapsed before the EDD began implementing the Pandemic Unemployment Compensation program, which distributed funds to those who had exhausted state benefits but were still unemployed.[66] These lengthy delays posed an incredible burden for millions of Californians.

The demands on the agency were of epic proportions—more than double the claims administered during the Great Recession of 2009, and the state's resources weren't up to meeting the needs. Compounding the slow response were the furloughs of several EDD employees because of the governor's budget cutbacks. In an attempt to alleviate the growing backlog, the agency processed unemployment applications without interviewing applicants. That invited further complications. By August 2020, agency had processed 9.7 million claims from people who had lost their jobs or hours at work since March; worse yet, the number grew to 22 million by May 2021. Yet, the EDD just couldn't keep up with soaring demand. By October 2020, the EDD had accumulated a backlog of at least 1.6 million unemployment claims that the agency did not expect to manage until the following January at the earliest.[67] At one point, 6 million unemployed Californians waited for checks as daily needs accrued and bills went unpaid.

Sometimes, one problem begets another. That became a common theme in California governance during the pandemic. As the EDD struggled to deliver checks to applicants, the agency found itself losing quality control, which, as we noted, was never an agency high point to begin with. By November 2020, independent audits discovered that the EDD had paid as much as one billion dollars in fraudulent claims by 35,000 prisoners. But there was more. The dollar value of bad claims in total jumped $11 billion by the end of January 2021, with eventual fears that as much as $30 billion could have been erroneously dispensed.[68] For Newsom, another mismanagement issue was dropped in his political lap, and he was running out of room.

Crisis in California's Prisons

California's prison system, notorious for its malign neglect of inmates' health even in the best of times, was also experiencing major COVID-19 outbreaks. San Quentin Prison, the state's oldest facility, led the way early on with 600 inmate infections in June 2020 alone. The outbreak had been entirely preventable. State prisons had transferred more than 100 inmates to San Quentin from an overcrowded facility in southern California.

Somehow prison officials didn't think to test the inmates before their arrival. COVID-19 quickly spread through the facility.[69]

COVID-19 would continue to wreak havoc in the state's sprawling prison system in which inmates, confined in tight overcrowded spaces with poor ventilation, were some of the most vulnerable citizens to the virus.

In July Newsom issued an executive order making some 8,000 inmates eligible for early release.[70] Weeks later, California's prison population, which had once peaked at 173,000 inmates in 2007—more than double the system's designed capacity—had plummeted to less than 100,000—a number not seen since the 1990s.[71] By December 2020 more than 18,000 inmates had received early release under different state prison reform and pandemic-specific relief programs. All signs point to Newsom being judicious in the implementation of his decision, saying, "I simply will not en masse release people without looking individual by individual."[72] Still, that didn't keep Newsom's opponents from attacking the governor for being easy on criminals and soft on crime.

Meanwhile, prison infections roared on. The case rate of COVID-19, 390 per 1,000 people, was more than six times the state average and increasing by the month. By summer 2021, the prison system had recorded nearly 50,000 cases of COVID-19 and almost 250 inmates had died.[73]

Newsom's Problems in Governance

Governor Newsom's problems with governance hit him from multiple directions. It was relentless as COVID-19 stressed institutions already under pressure. In his effort to contain and manage so many simultaneous crises, Newsom and the state's pandemic response activated and reinvigorated a conservative-led fight that accused Newsom as a figure too powerful and over his head in managing a disaster. The result, as they saw it, was a Newsom-led government too overreaching and incompetent, if not corrupt. For many other Californians, including Democrats and Independents, those not inclined to wage ideological warfare against the governor, they were left with feelings of frustration, exhaustion, and confusion. Fair or not, many voters weren't willing or able to distinguish lines of responsibility, leaving Newsom accountable for just about everything that went wrong during this period. As head of the executive branch, even Newsom appeared to think so. "The buck stops with me," he said at one point, channeling his best Harry Truman. It seemed like one of those cases of needing to "be careful of what you wish for."

To be fair, every governor stumbled in dealing with the pandemic in one way or another. Even New York's Governor Andrew Cuomo, exalted in the early going for what was then viewed as incredibly sensitive and attentive leadership, found himself in a heap of trouble as the pandemic raged on. But neither Cuomo nor any other state governor faced the threat of a recall election that could lead to dismissal from office.[74] For that reason, virtually every story of government mismanagement or a Newsom misstep took on an extra measure of gravity as time wore on. Time, as we'll show, was definitely not on the governor's side. How the recall went from longshot to reality is the part of the story we turn to next.

Notes

1. "Legislature passes $1.1 billion in emergency coronavirus funding: Then leaves the Capitol," *CalMatters*, March 16, 2020, https://calmatters.org/health/coronavirus/2020/03/california-coronavirus-emergency-response-1-billion-dollar-bill/.
2. "Newsom gave 'very little' information on $1 billion coronavirus purchase, lawmakers say," *Los Angeles Times*, April 9, 2020, www.latimes.com/california/story/2020-04-09/gavin-newsom-coronavirus-masks-purchase-california-legislature.
3. "Many California Lawmakers First Learned of Billion Dollar Mask Deal on 'Rachel Maddow'," *CapRadio*, www.capradio.org/articles/2020/04/09/many-california-lawmakers-first-learned-of-governors-billion-dollar-mask-deal-on-rachel-maddow/.
4. When the legislature passed the $1-billion emergency COVID-19 spending bill, it required the governor and his advisors to give a 72-hour notice before authorizing new spending. In this case, Newsom argued an even tighter timeline was needed.
5. "Does Gavin Newsom have the grit to take on the coronavirus?," *New York Times*, April 19, 2020, www.nytimes.com/2020/04/19/opinion/gavin-newsom-california-coronavirus.html.
6. "Criticism grows over Gov. Newsom's management of the coronavirus crisis," *Los Angeles Times*, April 29, 2020, www.latimes.com/california/story/2020-04-29/gavin-newsom-coronavirus-response-criticism-nonprofits-legislators.
7. "Stalls, stops, and breakdowns: Problems plague push for electric buses," *Los Angeles Times*, May 20, 2018, https://www.latimes.com/local/lanow/la-me-electric-buses-20180520-story.html.
8. Ibid.
9. "Newsom's mask deal shows tendency for big plans, few details," *Associated Press*, April 15, 2020, www.thestar.com/news/world/us/2020/04/15/newsoms-mask-deal-shows-tendency-for-big-plans-few-details.html.
10. "Newsom administration refuses to divulge nearly $1 billion contract for coronavirus masks," *Los Angeles Times*, May 4, 2020, www.latimes.com/california/story/2020-05-04/gavin-newsom-will-not-release-california-coronavirus-masks-byd-contract.
11. "New cost details emerge in California's secretive coronavirus masks deal with Chinese company," *Los Angeles Times*, May 6, 2020, www.latimes.com/california/story/2020-05-06/california-coronavirus-mask-price-byd-coronavirus.
12. "Newsom extends California's medical mask deal with BYD," *San Francisco Chronicle*, July 22, 2020, www.sfchronicle.com/politics/article/Newsom-extends-California-s-medical-mask-deal-15426955.php.
13. Ibid.

14. "Coronavirus threatens to wipe out California's $21 billion surplus. And it could get worse," *Los Angeles Times*, March 25, 2020.
15. "Here's how a $54 billion budget deficit will hurt Californians," *CalMatters*, May 7, 2020, https://calmatters.org/economy/2020/05/california-budget-deficit-severe-cuts-ahead-recession/.
16. "California's coronavirus budget crisis leaves Newsom and lawmakers at odds," *Los Angeles Times*, May 28, 2020, www.latimes.com/california/story/2020-05-28/coronavirus-crisis-spending-cuts-california-legislature-gavin-newsom.
17. "California state workers took a pay cut, Gavin Newsom didn't," *Sacramento Bee*, August 20, 2020.
18. Ibid.
19. Ibid.
20. "'Hella connected': How California lawmakers are governing from home," *CalMatters*, April 6, 2020, www.capradio.org/articles/2020/04/06/hella-connected-how-california-lawmakers-are-governing-from-home/.
21. "Lawmakers Vent After Being 'Blindsided' by Newsom," *KQED.org*, January 27, 2021, www.kqed.org/news/11857197/lawmakers-vent-after-being-blindsided-by-newsom.
22. "California is award in cash, thanks to booming market," *New York Times*, April 28, 2021, www.nytimes.com/2021/04/28/business/california-budget-stock-market.html.
23. Ibid.
24. "State appeals court upholds Gov. Newsom's emergency powers during pandemic," *Los Angeles Times*, May 5, 2021, www.latimes.com/california/story/2021-05-05/appeals-court-upholds-newsoms-emergency-powers-during-pandemic.
25. "Newsom executive orders test constitutional bounds: And legislative goodwill," *Politico California*, April 22, 2020.
26. "Governor Newsom Issues Executive Order to Protect Public Health by Mailing Every Registered Voter a Ballot Ahead of the November Election," *Office of Governor Gavin Newsom*, www.gov.ca.gov/2020/05/08/governor-newsom-issues-executive-order-to-protect-public-health-by-mailing-every-registered-voter-a-ballot-ahead-of-the-november-general-election/.
27. "Republicans sue Newsom over vote-by-mail order for November election," *Los Angeles Times*, May 24, 2020, www.latimes.com/california/story/2020-05-24/republicans-sue-newsom-over-vote-by-mail-order-for-november-election.
28. "Republicans sue to block California Gov. Newsom from mailing ballots to all voters," *USA Today*, May 25, 2020, www.usatoday.com/story/news/politics/elections/2020/05/25/coronavirus-republicans-sue-to-stop-gavin-newsomes-california-vote-by-mail-order/5254867002/.
29. "Miniscule number of potentially fraudulent ballots in states with universal mail voting undercuts Trump claim about election risks," *Washington Post*, June 8, 2020, https://www.washingtonpost.com/politics/miniscule-number-of-potentially-fraudulent-ballots-in-states-with-universal-mail-voting-undercuts-trump-claims-about-election-risks/2020/06/08/1e78aa26-a5c5-11ea-bb20-ebf0921f3bbd_story.html.
30. Republican National Committee; National Republican Congressional Committee; and California Republican Party vs. Newsom. Filed May 24, 2020, https://s3.documentcloud.org/documents/6927648/RNCvNewsom.pdf.
31. "Appeals Court to Decide if Newsom Overstepped His Authority With Mail-In-Ballots," *Courthouse News Service*, April 20, 2021, www.courthousenews.

com/appeals-court-to-decide-if-newsom-overstepped-his-authority-with-mail-in-ballots/.

32. The California State Legislature first provided a major boost to vote-by-mail when it adopted the Voter's Choice Act in 2016. That law required that all registered voters be granted opportunities to vote by mail by 2024. By reaffirming Newsom's order, the legislature was, in effect, speeding up its own vote-by-mail timeline set forth in the Voter's Choice Act. See Larry N. Gerston, Mary Currin-Percival, Garrick Percival and Terry Christensen, *California Politics and Government: A Practical Approach* (Boston, MA: Cengage Press, 2021).

33. "Gov. Newsom rebuked by Sutter County court for use of executive power amid COVID-19 pandemic," *Los Angeles Times*, November 2, 2020.

34. "Amid pressures of pandemic, Newsom quickly accepts health officer's resignation," *CalMatters*, August 10, 2020, https://calmatters.org/health/coronavirus/2020/08/newsom-quickly-accepts-public-health-officer-resignation/.

35. "Pandemic Backlash Jeopardizes Public Health Powers, Leaders," *Kaiser Health News*, December 15, 2020, https://khn.org/news/article/pandemic-backlash-jeopardizes-public-health-powers-leaders/.

36. "Amid death threats and anger, 7 Calif. Health officials have quit since pandemic began," *SFGate*, June 16, 2020, www.sfgate.com/bayarea/article/CA-health-directors-quit-amid-death-threats-15343863.php.

37. "Supervisors appoint new public health officer; Kaiser 'no longer employed' by Riverside County," *Desert Sun*, March 23, 2021, www.desertsun.com/story/news/health/2021/03/23/riverside-county-supervisors-appoint-new-public-health-officer/6972360002/.

38. "How California's contact tracing army could serve as model for nation's reopening," *Politico*, April 27, 2020, www.politico.com/states/california/story/2020/04/27/how-californias-contact-tracing-army-could-serve-as-model-for-nations-reopening-1280023.

39. "Public Health Is Exceeding Its Testing Targets, but Contact Tracing Efforts Statewide Are Lagging," www.auditor.ca.gov/reports/2020-612/auditresults.html#:~:text=Public%20Health%20Is%20Exceeding%20Its,Tracing%20Efforts%20Statewide%20Are%20Lagging&text=Consistently%20fast%20turnaround%20times%20are,the%20spread%20of%20the%20disease.

40. "So you think your California county is tracing contacts of sick people? Maybe not," *CalMatters*, August 10, 2020, https://calmatters.org/health/2020/07/california-contact-tracing-coronavirus/.

41. "Public health leaders in California, nationwide leaving jobs amid pandemic pressures," *Orange County Register*, August 13, 2020, www.ocregister.com/2020/08/13/public-health-leaders-in-california-nationwide-leaving-jobs-amid-pandemic-pressures/.

42. "As COVID-19 surges in California, healthcare workers, ICUs and providers struggle to cope," *Blue Shield California News Center*, December 18, 2020, https://news.blueshieldca.com/2020/12/18/as-COVID-19-surges-in-california-healthcare-workers-icus-and-providers-struggle-to-cope.

43. "Public health officials are our COVID-19 commanders: Treat them with respect," *California Health Care Foundation*, September 1, 2020, https://californiahealthline.org/news/public-health-officials-are-our-covid-commanders-treat-them-with-respect/.

44. "COVID-19 vaccination plan," *State of California*, October 16, 2020, www.cdph.ca.gov/Programs/CID/DCDC/CDPH%20Document%20Library/COVID-19/COVID-19-Vaccination-Plan-California-Interim-Draft_V1.0.

pdf?_cldee=Y2Jha2VyQGNhbGGhvc3BpdGFsLm9yZw%3d%3d&recipienti
d=contact-a44bb655054aea11a812000d3a3b70c9-d3b1f5fdf153475aa1e6
98a39640f95b&esid=8767241f-2213-eb11-a813–000d3a3abdcf.

45. "Why has CA only used 35% of its vaccine doses?," *CalMatters*, January 5, 2021, https://calmatters.org/newsletters/whatmatters/2021/01/california-used-vaccine-doses/.

46. "Newsom promised 1 million COVID-19 vaccinations. California can't tell if he hit his goal," *Los Angeles Times*, January 21, 2021, www.latimes.com/california/story/2021-01-21/california-data-collection-issues-COVID-19-vaccinations-in-10-days-gavin-newsom-promise.

47. "California planning to make big changes to vaccination plan: After feds direct states to do so," *San Francisco Chronicle*, January 12, 2021, www.google.com/search?q=California+planning+to+make+big+changes+to+vaccination+plan–afrer+feds+direct+states+to+do+so&rlz=1C5CHFA_enUS773US773&oq=California+planning+to+make+big+changes+to+vaccination+plan–afrer+feds+direct+states+to+do+so&aqs=chrome.69i57.26939j0j7&sourceid=chrome&ie=UTF-8.

48. "Voters now much more critical of Governor Newsom's performance," *Berkeley IGS Poll*, February 2, 2021, www.igs.berkeley.edu/sites/default/files/release_2021-01_governor_newsom.pdf.

49. www.beckershospitalreview.com/public-health/states-ranked-by-percentage-of-COVID-19-vaccines-administered.html.

50. "'It's all fallen apart,' Newsom scrambles to save California: And his career," *Politico*, January 11, 2021, www.politico.com/news/2021/01/11/gavin-newsom-california-scramble-fallen-apart-456665.

51. See "California COVID-19 vaccine rollout hit with software system problems," *Los Angeles Times*, January 8, 2021, www.latimes.com/california/story/2021-01-08/COVID-19-vaccine-rollout-hit-with-software-system-snag.

52. Gavin Newsom and Lisa Dickey, *Citizenville: How to Take the Town Square Digital and Reinvent Government* (New York, NY: Penguin Books, 2013), p. 81.

53. See "Track the millions flowing to California's race for governor," *Los Angeles Times*, November 6, 2018, www.latimes.com/projects/la-pol-ca-california-governor-2018-money/; "Blue shield of California commits $20 million to support Gov. Newsom's initiative to tackle homelessness, behavioral health services," https://news.blueshieldca.com/2020/01/17/newsom-homeless; and "Why blue shield for California's vaccine effort? Gavin Newsom's administration says little," *San Francisco Chronicle*, January 29, 2021, www.sfchronicle.com/politics/article/Why-Blue-Shield-for-California-s-COVID-vaccine-15909689.php.

54. "Critics hit Newsom's reliance on tech," *San Francisco Chronicle*, May 9, 2021, www.sfchronicle.com/news/article/Newsom-s-reliance-on-Big-Tech-in-pandemic-16161367.php.

55. "California will earmark 10% of weekly COVID-19 vaccine supply for teachers," *Los Angeles Times*, February 19, 2021, www.latimes.com/california/story/2021-02-19/gavin-newsom-10-percent-COVID-19-vaccines-educators-california-schools-open.

56. "County-level COVID-19 vaccination coverage and social vulnerability: United States," December 14, 2020–March 1, 2021," *Centers for Disease Control and Prevention*, March 26, 2021, www.cdc.gov/mmwr/volumes/70/wr/mm7012e1.htm.

57. "Bay Area lawmakers pressure Newsom administration after vaccine talks hit 'standoff'," *San Francisco Chronicle*, March 12, 2021, www.sfchronicle. com/politics/article/Bay-Area-lawmakers-pressure-Newsom-administration-16021946.php.

58. Quoted in "Newsom: Coronavirus likely to close California schools for rest of the year," *CalMatters*, March 17, 2020, https://calmatters.org/health/coronavirus/2020/03/california-schools-likely-closed-rest-of-year-coronavirus/.

59. "Closing the K-12 digital divide in the age of distance learning," *Boston Consulting Group*, June 2020, www.commonsensemedia.org/sites/default/files/uploads/pdfs/common_sense_media_report_final_6_26_7.38am_web_updated.pdf.

60. "Up to 1 million California students may still lack connectivity during distance learning," *EdSource*, October 15, 2020, https://edsource.org/2020/california-still-lacks-connectivity-for-more-than-300000-students-during-distance-learning/641537.

61. "California voters, including parents, have deep concerns about distance learning," *EdSource*, October 8, 2020, https://edsource.org/2020/california-voters-including-parents-have-deep-concerns-about-distance-learning/640685.

62. "To safely reopen schools, we have to talk about indoor air quality and ventilation," *Edsource*, October 15, 2020, https://edsource.org/2020/to-safely-reopen-schools-we-have-to-talk-about-indoor-air-quality-and-ventilation/640701.

63. "California public schools suffer record enrollment drop," *CalMatters*, January 26, 2021, https://calmatters.org/education/2021/01/california-schools-record-enrollment-drop/.

64. For a brief discussion of the EDD's history, see "It's 'chaos': California's unemployment agency hired thousands, but didn't fix core problems," *The Sacramento Bee*, September 30, 2020, www.sacbee.com/news/politics-government/capitol-alert/article246088615.html. Also see "California's EDD unemployment system disaster: Predictable fiasco?," *IEEE Spectrum*, October 17, 2013, https://spectrum.ieee.org/riskfactor/computing/it/californias-edd-unemployment-system-disaster-predicted-fiasco.

65. "Californians battling unemployment amid coronavirus are stymied by state agency's issues," *Los Angeles Times*, April 27, 2020, www.latimes.com/california/story/2020-04-27/coronavirus-california-unemployment-insurance-claims-technology-issues-edd.

66. "Report chronicles missteps by state unemployment agencies that left millions on the lurch," *Los Angeles Times*, June 2, 2021, www.latimes.com/politics/story/2021-06-02/state-unemployment-departments-struggled-to-meet-demand-during-pandemic-report-finds.

67. "Furloughed EDD workers could have processed thousands more California unemployment claims," *The Sacramento Bee*, October 6, 2020, www.sacbee.com/news/politics-government/the-state-worker/article246186705.html.

68. See "Latest unemployment scandal: State paid inmates $1B in fraudulent claims," *CalMatters*, November 25, 2000, https://calmatters.org/newsletters/whatmatters/2020/11/california-edd-fraud-claims-inmates/, "Millions in California coronavirus jobless benefits sent to out-of-state prisoners," *Los Angeles Times*, January 5, 2021, www.latimes.com/california/story/2021-01-05/how-california-covid-benefits-went-out-of-state-prisoners, "State's failures hurt unemployed," *San Francisco Chronicle*, January 29, 2021, and "EDD provides updates on unemployment benefit fraud and fraud prevention efforts,"

Employment Development Department, State of California, January 25, 2021, https://edd.ca.gov/about_edd/pdf/news-21-05.pdf.

69. "'Shocking, heartbreaking,' coronavirus outbreak in Calif. prison alarms health experts," *National Public Radio*, www.npr.org/2020/06/27/884149444/shocking-heartbreaking-coronavirus-outbreak-in-ca-prison-alarms-health-officials.

70. In March 2020, the state had already expedited the release of 3,500 inmates due to concerns about the spread of COVID-19. Officials described this as a "decompression" of the prison system. See "California to release 8,000 prisoners in hopes of easing coronavirus crisis," *Los Angeles Times*, July 10, 2021, www.latimes.com/california/story/2020-07-10/california-release-8000-prisoners-coronavirus-crisis-newsom.

71. "California prison population drops below 100,000 for first time in 30 years," *San Francisco Chronicle*, July 30, 2020, www.sfchronicle.com/crime/article/California-prison-population-drops-below-100-000-15448043.php.

72. "'People are terrified': A coronavirus surge across California's prisons renews calls for releases," *The Guardian*, December 29, 2020, www.theguardian.com/us-news/2020/dec/29/california-coronavirus-cases-prison-system.

73. Los Angeles Times, "Tracking the coronavirus in California," www.latimes.com/projects/california-coronavirus-cases-tracking-outbreak/ Accessed August 7, 2021.

74. Governor Andrew Cuomo resigned from office on August 23, 2021 after a New York State Attorney General report concluded he had sexually harassed nearly a dozen women.

Chapter 6

The Newsom Recall
Movement Grows

If the people have the right, the ability and intelligence to elect,
they have as well the right, ability and intelligence to reject or to recall.
—Hiram Johnson

Few people have been as influential on California government and politics as Hiram Johnson. He didn't start out that way, to be sure. As a
deputy district attorney in San Francisco, Johnson successfully prosecuted
a 1906 corruption case of a city employee who acted illegally on behalf
of the Southern Pacific Railroad. Dubbed "the Octopus"[1] for its ability
to penetrate and rule over every important political and economic aspect
of the state, the Southern Pacific's first political loss came at the hands of
the little-known Johnson.

From there, Johnson's new-found fame catapulted him to the leadership of the Progressive movement, a crusade dedicated to restoring rule
by the people in place of dictatorship by unelected powerful interests.
After he was elected governor in 1910, Johnson proposed three changes
to the state's political arrangement in the name of "Direct Democracy":
the initiative, the referendum, and the recall. But of these three governing
mechanisms, only the recall focuses on the possible removal of elected
officials all the way from statewide office holders to local school board
members.

When the measures were presented to the voters as proposed constitutional amendments in 1911, the initiative and referendum proposal
barely gained the required simple majority. Meanwhile, the recall sailed
through by a three-to-one margin. Whatever else, the voters were determined to keep their elected officials on a short leash, and they have to
this day. Although voters have been offered numerous opportunities to
recall the governor over time, they have rarely followed through with it.
The Newsom effort was just the second time a gubernatorial recall had
reached the ballot in California, thus making it a pivotal moment in the
state's history.

DOI: 10.4324/9781003217954-6

For months Newsom and his team officially all but ignored the growing recall effort, viewing it more like an unworthy nuisance than a serious challenge. After all, five previous efforts failed to gain traction and quickly died for lack of petition interest. Why should this attempt have been any different?

But the sixth effort was different, although few observers realized it at first. Not until March 2021, nine months after the recall effort began, did Newsom officially acknowledge the growing effort to remove him from office, saying "I'm not going to take this recall effort attempt lying down."[2] The question was, could Newsom recover and beat back what, for many, had become a serious movement to end his governorship?

In this chapter, we first discuss the challenges of recall petition signature-gathering in California. Included is the request by the recall team to a court for additional time because of the COVID-19 pandemic, a bid that, if approved, could become a tipping point in the election long before the actual voting took place.

Next, we discuss the California version of the recall process in detail. Although 19 states employ this aspect of direct democracy, each has its own set of rules. The California approach is particularly unique for its low qualification threshold for the ballot and ease of candidacies getting on the ballot.

From there, we turn to the events that led to the recall petitioning process. Let's remember that recall elections of state governors are rare events—only four in the nation's history and two of those in California. For that reason, the Newsom recall campaign assumed great significance in the state. Moreover, the campaign gained national prominence. And for good reason. Throughout the country, protests emerged against state and local pandemic rules, many of them proclaimed throughout California. Organized rallies and marches had occurred in at least six other states, with Michigan antagonists at one time actually entering the state capitol with firearms.[3] Clearly, other governors were on the hot seat over similar pandemic-related issues and voter concerns. Trouble in California could mean trouble for them as well.

Following the critical junctures prior to qualification, we focus on the recall petition campaign and its major actors. Unlike the Davis recall effort, the Newsom recall effort began on a shoestring without election professionals or much money. Yet, after a slow start, the pro-recall forces gathered momentum and ultimately proved to be worthy adversaries for Newsom and his team. A couple of key moments were particularly valuable for the challengers.

Lastly, we turn to the governor, officially a disinterested party but unofficially very concerned about the growing recall storm. What was the phantom Newsom network doing to thwart the assault as the petition process gathered steam? What did they do, or fail to do, that might have thrown the pro-recall efforts off course? What events helped or harmed the governor's efforts, particularly in terms of his activities and use of his office? The answers to these questions could foretell the kind of campaign yet to come.

Signature Gathering: Slow Start and Strong Finish

Every political campaign needs resources, including experienced leadership and financing. The sixth effort to depose California Governor Gavin Newsom had neither. Orrin Heatlie, a retired sheriff's sergeant-turned-grassroots-activist led the signature campaign. Of note is that Heatlie had little political experience, other than a superficial last-minute involvement with the first Newsom recall attempt that failed to qualify along with the next four attempts. Nevertheless, his disenchantment grew over time. Heatlie grew increasingly irritated with several Newsom policies, but none more disgraceful than the Governor's recommendation that undocumented immigrants shouldn't answer the door to authorities without a warrant. That offended the former law enforcement officer.[4] Such an approach to governance led Heatlie and two others to begin a new attempt to wrestle Newsom from his job. Starting with an initial budget of $1,000, he launched the signature-gathering effort from an aluminum Airstream trailer parked in his Folsom, California driveway.

The three recall leaders launched their recall mission outside traditional Republican circles. Why? Because they considered Republican politicians almost as politically corrupt as Democrats.[5] Rather than embracing the trappings of a professionally organized undertaking, the pro-recall leaders viewed their commitment as a mission for the people on behalf of the people. This, they reasoned, is why Californians have the recall: "It's a policymaking capability that lies with the voters," reasoned *Recall-Gavin2020.com* strategist Michael Netter, one of the three initial principals.[6] Referencing the voters' decision to reject a 2020 state ballot proposition (Proposition 16) that had asked voters to reverse California's ban on affirmative action, they believed the electorate was a lot more conservative than the state's ultra-left leaders.

For their part, the national Republican Party kept its distance from the recall campaign, believing that it would implode. Only when it was certain that the recall petition would qualify did the national party "gallantly" jump in.[7] Even at that, most leading Republicans in the state remained remarkably quiet.[8] There was no reason to waste precious resources on a fruitless endeavor. Still, although the recall effort began with a Libertarian nonpartisan theme, it quickly assumed a largely Republican character.

On June 10, 2020, the California Patriot Coalition, the official name for *RecallGavin2020.com*, was given the go-ahead by the California Secretary of State to begin collecting signatures from registered voters over a period lasting no longer than 160 days, or to November 17, 2020. Under California election law for statewide officers, petitioners must acquire signatures equal to 12% of the vote in the previous gubernatorial election or, in this case, about 1,495,000 registered voters. Although 12% may seem like a lot of signatures, the California requirement is the second lowest of the 19 recall states.

Still, the recall petitioners had a challenge. Petition-gathering for a recall election is a labor-intense effort that depends on voter signatures. Because the COVID-19-caused statewide shutdown kept most people at home for several months during the signature-gathering period, recall proponents had great difficulty taking their case to the voters. In fact, over the first 143 days of the effort, recall proponents were able to gather only 55,565 signatures,[9] some of which, no doubt, would be invalid. With a November 17 deadline approaching, *RecallGavin2020.com* needed a miracle. They got one.

On October 27, recall proponents went to court, asking for permission to extend the signature deadline 120 days because of the pandemic-caused stay-at-home executive order issued by Governor Newsom.[10] After reviewing the request, Superior Court Judge James Arguelles asked Alex Padilla, the then-Democratic Secretary of State, or his representative, to appear at a November 6 court hearing along with the recall proponents. On the day of the hearing, representatives from the Secretary of State's office *failed to appear!* With no input from the state, Judge Arguelles granted the recall petitioners the full 120 days, extending the petition-gathering deadline to March 29, 2021.

The *RecallGavin2020.com* representatives were astounded by the outcome. "One hundred twenty days was an outlier number for us," said an exulted Michael Netter. "We had hoped for 90 [days] and figured that the most we'd get would be 60 or maybe 75, but getting everything was an incredible moment for the campaign," he added.[11]

Netter was right. Those 120 extra days were key to the pro-recall signature effort. Imagine if the California Secretary of State or a designated official had appeared at the hearing with arguments to deny the request. Perhaps the judge would forge an extension compromise less than the 120-day request but certainly more than zero. Given the small number of signatures gathered before the November 6 hearing, a shorter extension may well have ended the recall effort altogether. But with no opposition to make the state's case, the judge granted the petitioners' request.

From that point, good things happened for the recall-Newsom campaign. Beginning with the French Laundry incident on November 6 (ironically, the same day as the judge's ruling!), inconsistent management of the pandemic by the governor, and an increasingly unhappy public, the signature collection effort took off. By the new deadline, recall petitioners had collected 2.1 million signatures, more than 1.6 million of which were valid, according to the Secretary of State. Thus, the petitioners qualified a recall election of the Governor.

Events That Led to the Sixth Recall Effort

And so began what appeared to many as the quixotic political journey to depose the state of its highest-ranking elected official. What the organizers lacked in experience and resources they made up for with gumption and volunteers. But more than energy and enthusiasm would be required. Ultimately, the petition qualified for a recall election largely because of extraordinary passion, the governor's response to the COVID-19 pandemic, and the perception of Newsom as being out of touch with what the petitioners believed were California's core political values.

In politics, rarely does a single issue change the course of an election campaign. Instead, different voter groups coalesce around several themes to the point that a majority is forged. The effort to turn away California's governor began on such a note. Other than an overarching shared conservative discontent with all things "government" in an otherwise blue state, the early organizers had little in common other than contempt for Gavin Newsom.

Downstream, toward the end of the petition-gathering process, COVID-19 became a rallying cry for the recall movement. But long before that moment, there were major grievances about the state's conditions that increasing numbers of Californians believed could only be alleviated by replacing the state's top leader. Among the many early issues were immigration mismanagement, rural discontent, homelessness, and Newsom's demeanor.

Claims of Abused Immigration Practices

Concern of an overly protective immigration policy was a starting point for many. For years, California's Democratic establishment had provided a host of benefits for undocumented immigrants ranging from driver's licenses to in-state college tuition to declaring California a "sanctuary state" dedicated to protecting the group from what supporters believed to be illegal federal interference.[12] For those upset with the changing racial and ethnic composition of the state, such policies were perceived as sending California in the wrong direction.

But Newsom added insult to injury. Within a few months of taking office, the state legislature passed and the governor signed a law extending the state-subsidized health benefits for children to young adults 25 years old and younger.[13] There was more. When the federal government excluded undocumented immigrants from receiving COVID-19 stimulus checks, Newsom created a program to provide unemployed undocumented residents one-time relief checks of $500.[14] Anti-immigrant groups were filled with anger.

For the petitioners, California was quickly losing its attraction to hard-working folks. Nowhere was the demographic shift more palpable than in Orange County, once proudly the cornerstone of political conservatism. In the words of a local pollster assessing the change of public opinion, "Our generation is dying. There's an increase in Hispanics, Vietnamese and other Asians. White 60-year-old males are dying or retiring and going to Phoenix."[15] Many of these people viewed Newsom as the source of an immigration problem out of control. And it wasn't only in Orange County. While most Californians approved the state's pro-undocumented immigrant policies,[16] an outspoken conservative-oriented minority felt different and ignored. Accordingly, passage of the recall was a long-overdue opportunity for California to restore core values.

Rural Discontent

There was a time when rural values were the framework of California politics. Land and water were plentiful, allowing ranchers, farmers, and town folk to enjoy the fruits of life. Their collective existence wasn't per-fect, to be sure. Discrimination, poverty, and lawlessness existed along with other failings, but for most members of rural society, life at least seemed manageable. Because California's constitution provided dispro-portionate representation of rural counties in the state legislature, rural values dominated the policymaking process even as large urban areas came to overshadow pastoral sectors. Then came a series of U.S. Supreme Court decisions during the 1960s which required state legislatures to be organized along the lines of "one man, one vote."[17] Shortly thereafter, rural populations in California and elsewhere lost control of state poli-cies. Since then, the values divide between rural and urban California (as well as most states with large cities) has increasingly become difficult to reconcile.

Fast forward to the twenty-first century and the cultural chasm is deeper than ever. From the perspective of many rural dwellers, the prevalence of a liberal governor and one-sided Democratic legislature seemingly year after year and decade after decade have left non-urban Californians second-class citizens. They rejected Gavin Newsom's embrace of same-sex marriage, strict gun control, high taxes, and statewide closures of businesses and schools when no COVID-19 problems existed where they lived.[18]

Thus, when the possibility of removing Gavin Newsom from his job emerged, large numbers of rural Californians seized the opportunity. In Amador County, 19.1% of the eligible voters signed recall petitions, fol-lowed by 18.2% in Lassen County and Calaveras County. In fact, in 30 of California's 58 counties, 10% or more of the eligible voters signed recall petitions. Compare those percentages with San Francisco's 1.8% and Los Angeles County's 4.6% and you get the idea. Yes, Orange County and San Diego County had healthy percentages, but nowhere proportionately near the counties at the top. There are two other points to consider: most of the high signature counties voted heavily for Republican Donald Trump in the 2020 presidential election and had relatively few incidences of COVID-19 early on.[19] Simply put, relatively rural, unpopulated areas became sources of recall support.

Homelessness

There's nothing new about homelessness in California. If anything, the issue has become more pronounced over time. Perhaps that's because as of 2019, with 12% of the nation's population, California had 28% of the nation's homeless population.[20] As noted earlier (see Chapter 2), in 2002 then-San Francisco Supervisor Gavin Newsom proposed and the voters passed a ballot initiative known as "Care Not Cash," which used welfare grant money for housing instead of cash grants. Shortly after he became mayor later in the year, Newsom implemented the program. Newsom declared the program a success; the long-term data proved otherwise.[21]

That was the Newsom *then*. One year after assuming the governorship, Newsom did a complete reversal in the homeless issue, declaring, "The state of California can no longer treat homelessness and housing insecurity as someone else's problem, buried below other priorities which are easier to win or better suited for soundbites."[22] At the time, Newsom proposed spending $1.5 billion in state funds on the issue.

Fast forward to spring 2021, when the governor proposed a new four-year, $12 billion plan to end homelessness. That's a far cry from Newsom's homelessness objectives as mayor. With 9 agencies and 47 programs at the state level, the commitment to solving homelessness was clear, but for many, success was not, especially considering Newsom's record in San Francisco.

Meanwhile, voters seemed more cautious about the homelessness question than Newsom. A February 2020 statewide survey on voter attitudes toward the issue found that 87.5% of the respondents were "very adamant about careful control of spending on homelessness."[23] Moreover, in some cities, frustration had boiled to the point that "citizen patrols [had] been organized, vigilante style, to walk the street and push [the homeless] out."[24] Clearly, the governor seemed to be heading in one direction—more and more spending on the controversial issue—while large numbers of voters seemed to be heading in another. For pro-recall supporters, spending on homelessness had hit a huge nerve, and they were no longer willing to wait for action.

Questionable Decision Making and Political Fallout

In the earliest moments of the pandemic, Governor Newsom spoke with authority, spouting out statistics of success and commending Californians for rallying against COVID-19. Perhaps taking a cue from the successful press conferences of New York Governor Andrew Cuomo who, for a period of time, had become something of an anti-Trump celebrity, Newsom tried to assure Californians that the state had bent the curve to the point of minimizing serious damage.

But as the Newsom administration began to see the multi-faceted gravity of the COVID-19 pandemic, press conferences and announcements took on an air of uncertainty and hesitation. Worse yet, some local leaders increasingly viewed Newsom's COVID-19 policies as erratic bureaucratic responses to the crisis rather than the science-directed answers based on the data. It seemed a moment of panic rather than leadership. No sooner were state documents and guidelines printed than they were dropped for updated documents.

Advocates for seniors, non-profits, or small businesses hung on every Newsom press conference, never sure whether his remarks on an issue would remain or change at the next press conference. For example, the legal director of a disability rights organization complained of repeatedly reaching out to Newsom administration personnel for policy clarification on vaccination priorities, only to receive no response. In another instance, the chief executive of the California Association of Nonprofits grumbled over "not getting answers to what we need [to know]." The complaints of mixed messages also came from the medical community.[25]

Frustration for some stakeholders reached a boiling point in March 2021. After yet another revision in Newsom's effort to re-open the state, Santa Clara County Chief Administrator Jeff Smith, also a physician, complained, "He [Newsom] is changing the blueprint rules without any logical reason. Our futures are in the hands of a governor trying to stop a recall. He has already killed tens of thousands by opening too soon in May [2020]. Now he wants to do it again."[26] Considering the dependence of residents on local public health specialists, such criticisms were not likely to be viewed as constructive building blocks of public support.

Newsom the Elitist

Repeatedly, the governor asked for patience from the public, stressing a "we're all in this together" approach of shared sacrifice as the key to overcoming the COVID-19 pandemic. For many Californians, his words struck a sincere tone. Then, on November 6, 2020, a critically important date, Governor Newsom ignored his own executive stay-at-home mandate as he dined indoors *sans* mask with lobbyist friends at the French

Laundry, one of the most exclusive restaurants in the state located in Napa Valley. Suddenly, it seemed that "we're all in this together" was replaced by "do as I say, not as I do." More important, Newsom's dining engagement became a fundamental rallying moment of what had been a stalled recall signature collection effort. The press was particularly critical of the governor, as exemplified by comments in a *Sacramento Bee* editorial: "Nothing will launder the stain of stupidity from [Newsom's] reputation after this ill-conceived outing."[27] Newsom apologized, but his actions spoke louder than his words.

But for some, Newsom's behavior was more than stupid: he projected arrogance. As Newsom consultant Garry South put it, "That was the damaging thing about the French Laundry thing: it crystalized this notion of Newsom as breathing rarefied air in Pacific Heights—as San Francisco royalty."[28] And royalty was the last thing California needed in a moment of profound despair and deep anxiety.

The remarkable confluence of events—the dinner and the recall petition extension on the same day!—became a lightning rod to new signature gathering. A recall effort that had collected only 55,000 signatures over five months gathered another 500,000 signatures during the following month alone. Suddenly, a moribund effort sprang to life.

Had Newsom's French Laundry faux pas been his sole misstep, he might have escaped a significant loss of public support, but other questionable events encircled the exclusive restaurant fiasco. One of these dealt with COVID-19 federal assistance for Gavin Newson's businesses. Since 1992, Newsom had been a partner in PlumpJack, an assortment of more than four dozen wineries, bars, restaurants, hotels, and liquor stores. By 2018, the year of his election as governor, Newsom's income had grown to $1.2 million, much of which had come from these enterprises. To his credit, before he assumed his new elected position, Newsom gave up his management role at PlumpJack, transferring title and control into a blind trust administered by a friend. From that point on, PlumpJack was out of the political picture—or so it seemed at the time.

Things changed in 2020 when it was learned that PlumpJack received $2.9 million in COVID-19 relief through the Small Business Administration's Paycheck Protection Program (PPP). Under the terms of the program, 60% of the money was required to be used for employee salaries. PlumpJack had 358 employees, who would have averaged $4,800 each in PPP payments had the funds been evenly divided. So far, so good. But it turns out that the money was not divided evenly, and that $918,000 went to one unit of PlumpJack consisting of only 14 employees, or an average of nearly $160,000 per employee.[29] Once public, the government loan caused a stir. In the words of a senior policy analyst at the nonpartisan, nonprofit Project on Government Oversight, "It [PlumpJack] seems to be a small business, but it got a lot of money. I'm not sure how the company justifies taking that much money when there are a lot of companies looking to get assistance."[30] More questions were raised.

To be clear, Newsom had no role in the Small Business Administration-PlumpJack Paycheck Protection Program loan arrangement, but he had a long history with the company and retained an ownership stake. Nevertheless, in light of the other activities involving Newsom, the conditions of the PlumpJack arrangement took on a larger dimension than what might have been with another person, and gave critics reason to criticize the loan and its circumstances as well as the governor.[31]

As Newsom's managerial problems multiplied, his administration changed gears. Chief of Staff Ann O'Leary departed and was replaced by Sacramento insider Jim DeBoo. The new key aide brought opportunities in some respects and potential liabilities in others. The opportunity came from DeBoo's previous employment as a senior aide in the state legislature, which offered the possibility for Newsom to work closer with the legislative branch. The potential liability came with DeBoo's most recent employment as a lobbyist, which for some reinforced the lobbyist connection which had been so public in the French Laundry episode.

A bad decision and a questionable federal loan to a company where he no longer worked combined to reinforce a gray cloud over Governor Gavin Newsom and his administration. The timing couldn't have been worse, given a raging pandemic and stumbling state leadership.

Media Criticism

In politics, it almost always helps policymakers to have the media on his or her side when managing particularly controversial governmental programs. That's because people rely on the media to acquire factual information about issues and events directed by public officials.[32] With something as overwhelming as the COVID-19 pandemic—a once-in-a-century public health menace—every step taken by government authorities was sure to be examined through a political microscope in the name of the press. As with any ongoing major story, media views of Newsom's pandemic management played a major role in framing public discussion.

At first, press reviews indicated support for Newsom's COVID-19 stewardship. The *Los Angeles Times*, considered by many to be the most influential newspaper in California, praised Newsom for acting quickly and decisively with his early shutdown order of the state. "As a result," a May 2020 editorial opined, "California is faring much better than states where governors were slow to take pandemic precautions."[33] Admiration for the California governor came from national sources as well. Writing in April 2020 just weeks after Newsom's statewide shutdown order, Todd Purdum of the *Atlantic* observed, "California is ascendant and its governor, Gavin

Newsom, knows it. His state is having dramatic success in containing the coronavirus pandemic, and Newsom is so bullish about California as if it were one of the world's most powerful nations, not merely the largest state."[34] Added the *Guardian* about the same time, "[A]mid the federal government's faltering response to the coronavirus crisis, Newsom is getting both local and national recognition for stepping into a leadership vacuum."[35] Yes, there was plenty of praise for the California governor in the early going of fighting the pandemic, but it didn't last for long.

In May 2020, Governor Newsom announced that the state would ease the restrictions connected with the shutdown. Protests had emerged in Orange County and Sacramento, resulting in arrests. In addition, 1,200 religious leaders announced that they would defiantly resume in-person services irrespective of the shutdown mandate. Numerous local governments elected either to ignore the mandate or view it as a "recommendation" rather than an order. Shortly after that, more than 600 COVID-19 infections broke out in San Quentin prison, leading the state to release thousands of prisoners. Then in the following July, with soaring numbers of new cases, Newsom once again tightened the shutdown. But for many, Newsom's actions were too little, too late.

Again, the press weighed in. In June 2020, *California Healthline*, an independent daily newspaper dedicated to healthcare issues, expressed concern about Governor Newsom's lack of follow through. Referring to unfulfilled promises to obtain enough masks, provide shelter for homeless people infected with the virus, and produce adequate COVID-19 testing, the *California Healthline* pronounced that the pandemic "exposed [Newsom's] penchant for making ambitious, showy announcements that aren't necessarily ready for prime time. His plans regularly lack detail and, in some cases, follow-through."[36] In early July 2020, the *Mercury News* complained about Newsom's lack of consistency: "He has sent conflicting and mixed messages about what constitutes compliance. He has teeter-tottered between warnings about the dangers of the virus and declarations of the urgent need to reopen the state's economy."[37] Later in the month, the *Sacramento Bee* grumbled about the failure of Newsom's contact tracing program, which the governor had declared essential to reopening the state.[38] By August, it was clear that the Newsom administration's glow had lost its glimmer. And all this was *before* the infamous French Laundry episode.

The California Recall Version Compared With Other States

Each state with the recall instrument has its own idiosyncrasies; in other words, there is no template. Among the 19 recall states, California's system is considered to have one of the most liberal rules for initiating the recall and removing the incumbent. To begin with, unlike most other states, no reason is necessary for recall proponents to seek removal of an elected incumbent. Also, the recall process can occur at any time during the office holder's stay in office—in Newsom's case, 14 months before the next regularly scheduled election. Lastly, candidate signature requirements are minimal as is the percentage of signatures to authorize a recall election.

Of the 19 recall states where the elected official is removed by majority vote, only 6, including California, present the voters with a list of replacement candidates simultaneously at the time of the recall election. Of the remaining 13, 9 choose a successor in a separate election, and 5 use an appointment process for a temporary successor until the next regularly scheduled election. Thus, with the California version, change can be swift and dramatic.

Consider the case of California Governor Gray Davis: he was elected to a second term on November 5, 2002 and was sworn in on January 6, 2003. Within two months of Davis's having taken the oath for his new term, the Secretary of State certified a recall petition for circulation. On October 7, 2003, Davis became the second governor in the nation's history (and first in California) to be recalled from office. You might ask, if there was so much antipathy against Davis, how could he have been re-elected just a few months earlier? Such are the vagaries of California politics.

The vagaries in 2021 were much different from 2003. Yes, California Democrats outnumbered by 46% to 24%, a nearly two-to-one margin. But while Republicans represented the core of the opposition, they were joined by a sizable chunk of Independents and even a slice of Democrats. The Newsom recall effort seemed to be about more than Republicans versus Democrats; it had the tone of general fatigue that overwhelmed much of the state's population.

Uncertain during the buildup to the election, however, was whether the voters thought a change in governance through a recall of Gavin Newsom would make matters better or worse.

Explaining the Recall Process, California Style

On April 26, 2021, Shirley Weber, California's new Secretary of State, announced that the Newsom recall campaign exceeded the constitutional threshold to trigger a special election. Proponents had accumulated more than 1,495,000 valid petition signatures from registered voters, thereby fulfilling the state constitutional requirement of at least 12% of the voters in the 2018 gubernatorial contest. A precise election date would be determined after various state officials sequentially completed a series of recall election obligations, including

- estimated election costs from the state's 58 counties,
- a 30-day window to allow recall petitioners to withdraw their signatures (decided by only 43 signatories, which left no effect on the recall),
- a separate election cost analysis provided by the California Department of Finance within a 30-day period, and
- as many as 30 calendar days for the Joint State Legislature Budget Committee to determine the commitment of state funds to cover local government costs.

Explaining the Ballot

As for the California recall election ballot, the voters are asked to answer two questions. The first question asks the voter to respond "yes" or "no" on whether to remove (recall) the governor from office. The second question asks the voter to select the new governor from the list of replacement candidates. The process sounds simple enough, but there are some important caveats. For example, while the election participants answer the first question about the governor's future, simultaneously they also have the opportunity to select a replacement candidate as the next governor, should the incumbent be recalled. Of course, the outcome of the replacement candidates contest is important only if the governor is removed. But no one knows that on election day, which is why the voters are asked to reply to the second question.

Another oddity lies with the vote requirements to remove and replace the governor. In a recall election, a simple majority is required to remove the governor from office; however, in the replacement election, the candidate with the most votes wins. Thus, with a field of 46 candidates in the Newsom recall, a replacement candidate with a small percentage of the vote, a plurality, could prevail. In other words, it's a lot easier for a replacement candidate to win the governorship through the recall than through a general election. That quirk raises the issue of fairness. Why doesn't the process require the same threshold to replace the governor as it requires to remove the governor?

Last-Minute Change in the Recall Rules

Per state election law, the recall election review process moved along, but not fast enough, the Newsom team felt. With the pandemic abating and lots of state and federal aid in hand, recall opponents felt that the election should be called as soon as possible. But how, given all of the stops for various reviews and projections? One day before its adjournment, allies in the Democratic-controlled state legislature passed a law eliminating the 30-day period for the Joint State Legislature Budget Committee to review local government election management costs.

The impact of the change in recall law reduced the review time by as much as 30 days. Legislative Republicans cried foul. Said Republican Assemblyman Vince Fong, the sudden change in the rules "is an attempt to put a thumb on the scale, to try to obtain a partisan outcome for one side."[39] The Newsom campaign team said nothing; with the governor's popularity now improving, they wanted the election over as soon as possible. But as we now know, the reappearance of the COVID-19 pandemic in the form of the Delta variant presented a serious threat both to the state's recovery and Governor Newsom's political survival in the recall election.

Governor Newsom's Stealth Non-Campaign Campaign

The Newsom campaign didn't wait for an official start date to organize its counter-recall efforts. All along the governor had communicated with Californians regularly by using the attributes of his office through press conferences and official announcements. Being governor gave Newsom a potentially powerful and expansive outreach platform unequalled by everyone else. Especially in the early days of the pandemic, Newsom held almost daily news conferences with the latest "dashboard" data on critical data points such as COVID tests and positivity rates, hospital bed availability, vaccine delivery percentages, and percentage of those who had been vaccinated. He would go about the state and visit vaccination centers, medical research facilities, and just about any place where the combination of the backdrop and his encouragement might give reason for people to become vaccinated against COVID-19.

On March 9, 2021, on the verge of announcing the third reopening date, Newsom delivered his COVID-19-delayed annual State of the State address at an empty Los Angeles Dodger Stadium. As he spoke, the governor noted that the 54,000-seat facility had about as many seats as COVID-19 deaths in California at the time. The mere backdrop silently reminded his audience of just how much life in the Golden State had been altered. But, oh, how his perspective of state capabilities had changed.

At the time of COVID-19's introduction to the nation, a confident Newsom boasted that massive vaccination campaigns were old news in California and that the state was more than ready to comfortably slay the monster disease. Fourteen months later, the once-beleaguered governor stated that California's public health community "entered this pandemic with a care economy suffering from decades of underinvestment."[40] Nevertheless, Newsom proudly noted, Californians were winning the COVID-19 battle—again.

But much more than pronouncements would have to happen for Newsom to prevail. Both his immediate position as governor and long-term future as a possible candidate for even higher office were at stake more than ever. Fending off the disease and his recall opponents were now connected and Newsom knew it, even if he didn't publicly acknowledge as much. A recall rejection would also require the cooperation and success from state and local public health agencies, incredible amounts of money to make his case. Success would also necessitate a large dose of political discipline, which had abandoned Newsom and his administration while responding to the pandemic in the early days of the public health disaster.

Faced with the growing reality that the recall petition would qualify for an election, Gavin Newsom began to organize financial resources. On March 15, six weeks before the Secretary of State announced the petitioners had reached their signature goal, Newsom announced creation of a campaign committee. As the incumbent, he enjoyed a critical advantage over his would-be recall challengers: no dollar limit on campaign donations. California law has an individual donor limit of $32,400 per election campaign, but the incumbent is exempt from any such constraint. That allowed Newsom to gear up for an expensive campaign quickly.

And the dollars came in big bunches. Within three short months, he amassed more than $16 million, plus another $9 million for a re-election campaign, more than twice the amount of money raised by the entire field of challengers who faced the donor limit.[41] Moreover, the dollars flowed from a broad swath of the state's population, ranging from progressive to business interests. The official campaign wouldn't begin until June; the Newsom financial juggernaut was neither waiting nor taking any chances.

Ready, Set, Go!

With the various reviews completed, it fell to Lieutenant Governor Eleni Kounalakis, to establish a recall election date which, according to the state constitution, must be within 60 to 80 days of the time the lieutenant governor receives the compiled information. The rules also stipulated that all recall candidacy paperwork must be completed 59 days before the election. On July 2, Kounalakis selected September 14 as the election date, leaving would-be candidates 11 days to turn in all recall filing papers.

Recall proponents were outraged over the short campaign period, lessened by the decision of Joint State Legislature Budget Committee to refrain from using any of the 30 allotted days to review petition materials.

But, in fact, the pro-recall element had been campaigning for more than a year. The force was driven initially by ideologically-fueled anger over non-COVID-19 issues. With even more the anguish stemming from the virus, momentum for Newsom's removal only seemed to grow.

Notes

1. Frank Norris used this title to explain the reach of the Southern Pacific Railroad in his novel, *The Octopus*, Doubleday & Company, 1901.
2. "Newsom won't 'take this recall attempt lying down' as Democrats launch defense," *Los Angeles Times*, March 16, 2021, www.latimes.com/california/story/2021-03-15/gavin-newsom-denounces-republican-california-recall-covid-19.
3. "Protests are popping up across the U.S. over stay-at-home restrictions," *CNN*, April 17, 2020, www.cnn.com/2020/04/16/us/protests-coronavirus-stay-home-orders/index.html.
4. "The three men who could take down Gavin Newsom," *Politico Magazine*, March 19, 2021, www.politico.com/news/magazine/2021/03/19/gavin-newsom-recall-476746.
5. Interview with Michael Netter, campaign strategist, *Recall Gavin 2020*, July 7, 2021.
6. Ibid.
7. Mark Z. Barabak, "National Republicans have gone in on the Newsom recall: They're doing him a big favor," *Los Angeles Times*, March 25, 2021, https://news.yahoo.com/column-national-republicans-gone-newsom-130009214.html.
8. "Some of the biggest names in state GOP silent on Newsom recall," *The Sacramento Bee*, April 22, 2021, www.sacbee.com/article250793854.html.
9. Source: Ballotpedia, https://ballotpedia.org/Gavin_Newsom_recall,_Governor_of_California_(2019–2021).
10. Interview with Michael Netter, campaign strategist, *Recall Gavin 2020*, July 8, 2021.
11. Interview with Michael Netter, campaign strategist, *Recall Gavin 2020*, July 7, 2021.
12. "California gives immigrants here illegally unprecedented rights, benefits, petitions," *Los Angeles Times*, August 11, 2015, www.latimes.com/local/california/la-me-california-immigrant-rights-20150811-story.html.
13. "California is 1st state to offer health benefits to adult undocumented immigrants," *NPR*, July 10, 2019, www.npr.org/2019/07/10/740147546/california-first-state-to-offer-health-benefits-to-adult-undocumented-immigrants.
14. "Governor Newsom announces new initiatives to support California workers impacted by COVID-19," *Office of the Governor*, April 15, 2020, www.gov.ca.gov/2020/04/15/governor-newsom-announces-new-initiatives-to-support-california-workers-impacted-by-covid-19/.
15. "Column: The Newsom recall effort has a big problem: Orange County," *Los Angeles Times*, March 4, 2021, www.latimes.com/california/story/2021-03-04/skelton-orange-county-republicans-democrats-california-governor-newsom-recall-chances.
16. For a recent survey, see "Californians at their government, public policy institute of California," March 2021, www.ppic.org/publication/ppic-statewide-survey-californians-and-their-government-march-2021/.

17. The major cases impacting states legislatures were *Baker v. Carr*, 1962, which mandated the districts of state legislature lower chambers to have approximately the same populations; and *Reynolds v. Sims*, 1964, which mandated that the districts of state legislature upper chambers to have approximately the same populations. No doubt, today's U.S. Supreme Court would have used the term, "one person, one vote."

18. "Petitions to recall Newsom illustrate split state," *San Francisco Chronicle*, March 28, 2021, www.pressreader.com/usa/san-francisco-chronicle-late-edition-sunday/20210328/281509343973249.

19. See "So who wants to recall Gov. Newsom? Signatures point to Trump's California," *Los Angeles Times*, April 29, 2021, www.latimes.com/projects/newsom-recall-election-signatures-how-many-californians-signed/.

20. "The 2020 Annual Homeless Assessment Report (AHAR) to Congress," *U.S. Department of Housing and Urban Development*, January 2021, www.huduser.gov/portal/sites/default/files/pdf/2020-AHAR-Part-1.pdf.

21. See "A decade of homelessness: Thousands in S.F. remain in crisis," *San Francisco Chronicle*, June 27, 2014, www.sfchronicle.com/archive/item/A-decade-of-homelessness-Thousands-in-S-F-30431.php and "The truth about care not cash," *Street Spirit*, published by "The American Friends Service Committee," March 2005, www.thestreetspirit.org/March2005/care.htm.

22. "Governor Newsom delivers state of the state address on homelessness," *Office of the Governor*, February 19, 2020.

23. "New USC poll reveals likely California voters' sentiments on homelessness ahead of March 3 primary," *USC Schwarzenegger Poll*, February 13, 2020.

24. "As homelessness surges in California, so does a backlash," *The New York Times*, October 21, 2019, www.nytimes.com/2019/10/21/us/california-homeless-backlash.html.

25. These examples were all cited in "Criticism grows over Gov. Gavin Newsom's management of the coronavirus crisis," *Los Angeles Times*, April 29, 2020, www.latimes.com/california/story/2020-04-29/gavin-newsom-coronavirus-response-criticism-nonprofits.-legislators.

26. "California to accelerate reopening while directing more vaccines to hard-hit communities," March 3, 2021, www.politico.com/states/california/story/2021/03/04/california-to-accelerate-reopening-while-directing-more-vaccines-to-hard-hit-communities-1366752.

27. "Gavin Newsom's hypocritical French Laundry fiasco harms California's COVID-19 efforts," *The Sacramento Bee*, November 13, 2020, www.sacbee.com/opinion/editorials/article247181176.html.

28. Quoted in *Los Angeles Magazine*, February 23, 2021, www.lamag.com/mag-features/gavin-newsom-recall/.

29. "New Newsom scandal: Gavin's companies got $3 million in PPP loans," *SFist*, December 10, 2020, https://sfist.com/2020/12/10/new-newsom-scandal-gavins-companies-got-3-million-in-ppp-loans/.

30. "Gavin Newsom's companies received Nearly $3 million in COVID relief loans," *Newsweek*, December 10, 2020, www.newsweek.com/gavin-newsom-companies-3-million-covid-relief-loans-1553826.

31. "Small business owners react after companies founded by Gov. Newsom receive nearly $3 million in PPP loans," *ABC7*, San Francisco, December 9, 2020, https://abc7news.com/plumpjack-management-group-llc-gov-newsom-winery-sba-releases-detailed-ppp-data-what-business-does-gavin-own/8653462/.

32. Shanto Iyengar and Jennifer A. McGrady, *Media Politics: A Citizen's Guide*, 4th edition (New York, NY: W.W. Norton, 2019), p. 251.

33. "Editorial: Gavin Newsom has been the leader California needs during coronavirus: But he can do better," *Los Angeles Times*, May 10, 2020, www.latimes.com/opinion/story/2020-05-10/gov-newsom-pretty-good-pandemic-leader-but-can-do-better.
34. "Gavin Newsom's nation-state," *The Atlantic*, www.theatlantic.com/politics/archive/2020/04/coronavirus-california-gavin-newsom/610006/.
35. "How the coronavirus gave Gavin Newsom his leadership moment," *The Guardian*, www.theguardian.com/world/2020/apr/12/how-the-coronavirus-crisis-gave-gavin-newsom-his-leadership-moment.
36. "Newsom likes to 'go big' but doesn't always deliver," *California Healthline*, June 4, 2020, https://californiahealthline.org/news/newsom-likes-to-go-big-but-doesnt-always-deliver/.
37. "Editorial: Governor Newsom's coronavirus leadership falls, woefully short," *Mercury News*, July 4, 2020, www.mercurynews.com/2020/07/04/editorial-newsom-coronavirus-leadership-falls-woefully-short/.
38. "California's coronavirus strategy failed: Should Gov. Newsom impose another shutdown," *The Sacramento Bee*, July 23, 2020, www.sacbee.com/opinion/editorials/article244411497.html.
39. "GOP cries foul as California Oks new governor recall rules," *Associated Press*, June 28, 2021, article/california-business-laws-government-and-politics-32edadc9729979a91b45555ebe6bbe4c.
40. Governor Gavin Newsom, "State of the union," *Address*, March 9, 2021, www.gov.ca.gov/2021/03/09/governor-newsom-delivers-state-of-the-state-address-charting-californias-path-to-a-brighter-future/.
41. "Newsom's recall fundraising edge becomes a charm with union, tribal, tech money," *San Francisco Chronicle*, June 17, 2021, www.sfchronicle.com/politics/article/Newsom-s-recall-fundraising-edge-becomes-a-16256317.php.

Chapter 7

The Recall Campaign

"Every election is determined by the people who show up."
—Larry Sabato, political analyst and
University of Virginia professor

In traditionally blue California, Democrats enjoy a nearly two-to-one advantage over Republicans. As a result, we might tend to interpret Sabato's statement as irrelevant in a place like California. Certainly the political deck was stacked in a way that would seem to leave Newsom safe from a recall. Indeed, less than three years earlier, Newsom had obliterated Republican nominee John Cox (the same John Cox who remerged as a recall replacement candidate) by 24 points. Yet, the only people who count in elections *are* those who cast their votes. All the public opinion polls, focus groups, anecdotal accounts, candidate debates, and wonky data analyses might provide insight and fodder for predictions, but they never substitute for those who actually participate in the election.

This is a particularly important insight within the context of a special election, a voting opportunity that usually has only a single topic for the voters and occurs at a time different from that of regularly scheduled elections. Because they take place at odd times and with narrow agendas, special elections tend to draw few voters. And generally, the fewer the voters, the less certain that the end result will reflect the overall sentiment of the entire electorate. Such a possible condition framed the political environment of the Newsom recall election, making the outcome anything but predictable.

In this chapter, we dig into to the official campaign to unseat Governor Gavin Newsom. As we'll document, what began as a longshot effort by political outsiders picked up incredible momentum after the French Laundry debacle and Newsom's challenges in managing the pandemic. We delve into the list of grievances that recall supporters held against Newsom and introduce readers to the major contenders hoping to replace him. Recall proponents, we'll show, were convinced that

DOI: 10.4324/9781003217954-7

Newsom's COVID-19 policies and related misadventures would be their ticket to a recall victory.[1] The recall effort took on the look and feel of roller coaster ride. The movement gathered strength during the winter of 2020–2021, only to fade during spring 2021 when COVID-19 waned. It then seemingly gathered strength again later that summer as the Delta variant surged. It was enough to make even a seasoned political observer's head spin.

We then turn to examine Newsom's campaign against the recall, how the governor eventually framed the meaning of the election and how he labeled his opponents. Contrary to the Newsom camp's insistence that the recall effort was Trump-inspired, there was no direct evidence of this. Money from the national Republican Party didn't come until well into the campaign, and even then, national party spending wasn't all that much. Finally, we take a closer look at how Newsom eventually beat back the most serious threat to his political career he had ever faced.

The Recall Newsom Campaign

As we noted in the previous chapter, the official recall campaign was a conservative-led effort, but it began, and mostly operated outside, traditional Republican circles. The dissimilar groups that composed the effort had little in common other than their antipathy for "Big Government" and the commitment to removing Newsom who epitomized senseless government and a state bureaucracy run amok. At the center of the campaign was a longstanding list of grievances. Supporters were upset with the state's liberal tilt which had led to relatively high taxes and accommodations to undocumented immigrants. Added to that were concerns about burgeoning homeless population, poorly managed water policies that caused havoc to the agricultural community, endless wildfires and displaced populations, a shaky electricity grid, and piled-up trash along California's once-pristine highway system.

For activists in the recall campaign these were linked by one thing in common: a governor who thought more about himself than the state. One person—Gavin Newsom—was responsible for the state's despair. And not surprisingly, this central idea helped create a sense of urgency among activists that the governor had to go. The argument resonated in pockets of Orange and San Diego counties and the Inland Empire as well as the Central Valley. But it was particularly popular in the extreme northern parts of California, whose residents had long complained about being ignored by the state's Democratic political establishment.[2]

These original complaints became augmented with Gavin Newsom's stewardship of the battle against COVID-19 which added a whole new set of grievances including mask mandates, school closures, and waste of the taxpayers' dollars.[3] There was also anger over the way Newsom distributed the huge $75 billion state surplus courtesy of federal COVID-19 funds; recall election proponents saw his allocations as little more than payoffs to likely supporter groups. In the words of Orrin Heatlie, "He's [Newsom] running like a mafia don passing out money to his loyal followers to try and win them over or maintain their loyalty."[4] Heatlie's characterization of Newsom went along with a general perception of the governor by recall proponents as an out-of-touch elitist. U.C. Berkeley pollster Mark DiCamillo summed up the antipathy, noting that Newsom's detractors viewed him "as higher up in the social strata than other Californians."[5] Translation: his rules are for others, not himself! The recall campaign didn't start with COVID-19, but in a bizarre way the pandemic was a gift to petitioners and a potential weapon with which to politically bludgeon Newsom.

With respect to the *Recall Gavin 2020* campaign strategy, the approach became simple enough: attack Governor Newsom for poor leadership, bad priorities, terrible COVID-19 management, and most of all being an arrogant elitist who refused to follow his own rules.[6] Living with COVID-19 created an array of problems from shuttered schools to closed businesses. Opening and shutting down the state to various degrees over 18 months only added to the population's stress. Anger toward mandated masking—what many conservatives saw as an affront to individual liberty—grew with every surge of the virus that led to tighter masking requirements.

Worrying about replacement candidates was secondary to removing Newsom from office. Typically, in recall elections with several potential replacement candidates, political party leaders often attempt to mobilize support behind a single candidate so as to increase the party's chance of victory. However, the Newsom team strongly discouraged any well-known Democrat from entering the race because of concerns that such presence might give Newsom supporters to vote "no" and choose the Democrat on the replacement ballot. Since no Democrat of notoriety appeared on the replacement ballot, Republican leaders actually encouraged a big field of conservative candidates, thinking that if large enough numbers of Republican voters would come out, they would be able to offset the Democratic numerical advantage. That was the thinking of former California Republican Party Chair Tom Del Becarro, organizer of *RescueCalifornia.org*, another recall group: "You have these candidates from some of the largest cities in California pulling in constituents, you knit it all (sic) together, and it makes a 'yes' vote very possible."[7]

Once the deadline for replacement candidates passed, a debate ensued among Republican candidates and leaders over whether the state Republican Party should officially endorse at the next Republican Party state convention in August. Given that an official endorsement required 60% of the convention delegates, meeting or surpassing the threshold with 24 Republican candidates in the race was virtually impossible. But the deliberation did temporarily suck out badly needed oxygen from party leaders and candidates whose time would have been better spent focusing on Governor Newsom.

The short recall campaign time frame, range of grievances, and paucity of funds led proponents to disproportionately rely on social media to deliver their messages. Ads on Facebook and other social media sites were tailored for specific populations by area and issue. For example, water-deprived Central California voters received Facebook ads on Newsom's mismanagement of the drought, while conservative voters in Orange County saw recall ads focusing on the escalating homeless problem. Political consultant Dan Schnur described the phenomenon as "political micro-targeting," a process for matching narrow messages with targeted voter populations.[8] Given the disparate assortment of potential pro-recall voters, social media was the best—and cheapest—method to deliver information to so many different audiences.[9]

What was not a major factor was the Republican Party apparatus. In fact, Republican leaders in general were a sore point for the grassroots-based *RecallGavin2020.com* organization because of what its leadership viewed as Johnnies-come-lately to the party. Commenting on the late entry of Republican leaders as the signature-collecting period was ending, *RecallGavin2020.com* campaign strategist Michael Netter grumbled, "Instead of uniting a campaign with direct [financial] aid, groups like Reform California (a conservative California Republican organization) and the Republican Party are jumping on the bandwagon now with their alleged 'strategy.' In fact, the [financial] burden of the recall has fallen on us 100%."[10]

On the stump, Republican replacement candidates went to the areas with the greatest voter potential such as the Central Valley and the most northern parts of the state. Evangelical churches became rich targets of opportunity because of their huge audiences and generally conservative approaches to government, right-to-life concerns, and gay rights, and their anger with Newsom over his attempts to close access to religious institutions during COVID-19 lockdown periods.[11]

The Replacement Candidates

For recall proponents, removing Newsom from office was only half the battle because of the second question that asked voters to select a replacement. Of course, the issue would be moot if Newsom prevailed, but that outcome was increasingly uncertain over time. With that, we turn to the candidates.

The Cast

More than 80 individuals, some prominent—many not, publicly expressed their intentions to run as replacement candidates in the Newsom campaign. To move from interest to candidacy, they had to submit a check of about $4,200 along with at least 65 signatures from registered voters. And that's about it. By July 16, the end of the sign-up period, 46 individuals had fulfilled the requirements: 24 Republicans, 9 Democrats, 2 Greens, 1 Libertarian, and 10 individuals with no political party preference. Most of the candidates weren't seasoned politicians, but that really didn't matter; they would be legitimate candidates for the state's highest office, should Newsom falter with the first question on the ballot. And inasmuch as many recall proponents considered seasoned politicians responsible for and out of touch with the state's issues, a cast of largely nonpolitical amateurs suited them just fine.

Larry Elder, 69

Although a last-minute entry as a recall replacement candidate, Elder quickly became a front-runner. He raised $5 million by early August, quickly exceeding every Republican candidate including the largely self-funded John Cox, and just as quickly became the replacement candidate front runner. An Emerson College poll released in early August found that Elder topped all replacement candidates with 23% of the vote, more than three times any other challenger.[12] Successive polls placed Elder way ahead of the others through the rest of the campaign.

Elder brought an unusual set of credentials. As a longtime conservative and nationally syndicated radio talk show host, Elder had a wider reach than his competitors. His three-hour talk show was broadcast daily in Los Angeles, San Diego, San Francisco, and Sacramento as well as dozens of small cities throughout California. The Los Angeles native had 2.5 million followers on social media and a national radio audience of 1.5 million, who could become sources of campaign contributions.[13] He opposed any pandemic-related mandates, including vaccines; described *Roe v. Wade* as one of the worst decisions ever handed down by the U.S. Supreme Court; dissented from any form of gun control; disputed any need for affirmative action; disputed that there should be any minimum wage; and argued that the costs of fighting climate change weren't worth the effort.[14]

An African American, Elder claimed he had never experienced racism. Toward the end of the campaign, he was heavily criticized for remarks he had made disparaging women. He also flipflopped on the 2020 presidential election, ultimately embracing President Trump's accusation of rigged results even before the votes had been cast. After saying that Biden won a few months earlier, he reversed himself and claimed that President Trump had been denied the win because of "shenanigans." He also expressed the fear that the recall election would be similarly filled with fraud.[15] Sound familiar? Still, Elder's radio show allowed him to reach conservative voters along with slices of independents and Democrats who had issues with Newsom.

John Cox, 66

Describing himself as a businessperson, not a politician, Cox had considerable unsuccessful experience in the latter category. Six times previously, Cox sought a series of state and national elective offices, including a defeated campaign for governor against Gavin Newsom in 2018. As we noted earlier, Cox lost that race by 24 points. But that didn't keep him from emerging as the first major recall replacement candidate. And he had money, lots of it. In June 2021 alone, Cox purchased $5 million of television ads; by the election's end, his campaign raised $10 million (most of it his own).

Cox campaigned as a conservative Republican for school choice (charter schools, vouchers), a 25% state income tax cut, and less government. And he had props, too! At first, he traversed the state with a live (yes, live!) 1,000-pound Kodiak bear, claiming that it would take a beast to overpower Newsom and his crony lobbyists; toward the end, he toured with a *Monopoly*-like board he called "Gavinopoly," with each square signifying a bad Newsom decision or policy. His political PR antics notwithstanding, Cox fell behind Elder once the radio host entered the race.

Kevin Faulconer, 54

A former mayor from San Diego, the second most-populated city in California, Faulconer presented a solid political base and history as something of a policy wonk. As mayor, the moderate Republican created a new City of San Diego department, the Office of Race and Equity to deal with systemic racism. At the same time, Faulconer had a consistent record of supporting increased funding for the San Diego Police Department.

Unlike most of the other Republicans in the race, historically Faulconer had been able to attract support from Democrats and Independents—not an easy task for Republican candidates in California. Aside from criticizing Newsom's COVID-19 management, Faulconer, a self-proclaimed policy wonk, took aim at the governor's approach to homelessness and crime. He promised to make cities clean up homeless camps and increase penalties for violent crimes. Faulconer had a respectable campaign war chest in the neighborhood of $5 million, yet he was unable to translate his themes to the voters even though he was by far the most experienced candidate.

Caitlyn Jenner, 71

In some ways, Jenner differentiated herself from the others. As a former Olympic decathlon gold winner, participant in reality TV, and transgender spokesperson, Jenner was the closest of the candidates to celebrity status similar to that of 2003 replacement candidate Arnold Schwarzenegger. However, Schwarzenegger had promoted a statewide ballot proposition establishing funding for afterschool sports prior to the Gray Davis recall, thereby presenting a modicum of political credentials as a candidate.

For her part, Jenner had virtually no political experience and exhibited little knowledge about key issues beyond topic sentences during the recall campaign. Despite her notoriety, Jenner was never able to generate much campaign buzz or raise campaign funds. Still, Jenner had 11.1 million followers on Instagram and 3.4 million followers on Twitter. And while these numbers were national, Californians no doubt represented a sizable chunk.

Kevin Kiley, 36

As a third-term state assemblymember from Placer County, Kiley's rural northern California residence was a key stomping ground for the recall Newsom movement. Well before the recall petition qualified for a vote, Kiley wrote a book about Newsom in which he attacked the governor for taking self-government away from the people and abusing his executive power.[16] He may have been among the earliest Newsom antagonists, but Kiley was never able to expand his small local base.

Doug Ose, 66

With six years as a member of the House of Representatives under his belt between 1999 and 2005, Ose embraced traditional conservative causes. On his recall candidate platform, Ose called for school vouchers, protective custody of homeless people suffering from addiction, and the re-incarceration of prisoners released by Governor Newsom because of federal court orders related to overcrowding. With his base in rural northern California, Ose had little reach into the more populated parts of the state. He dropped out of the running on August 16 after suffering a heart attack, although his name remained on the ballot.

Ted Gaines, 63

Of all the recall replacement candidates, Gaines had the most political experience. He served on the State Board of Equalization, a statewide political body but one with little public attention. Previous offices included the State Senate, State Assembly, and Placer County Board of

Supervisors. Gaines opposed tax increases, California's sanctuary state status, and high-speed rail. He espoused tougher treatment for criminals and bolstered public safety. Like Kiley, Gaines lived in "Recall Country," otherwise known as rural northern California where the passion against Newsom was the highest but where the population was small.

Kevin Paffrath, 29

Prior to the recall campaign, Democrat Kevin Paffrath was a political unknown. However, he gained notoriety through a prominent presence on social media, where the real estate investor had about 1.7 million subscribers on his "Meet Kevin" YouTube channel. The previously unknown Democrat offered a blend of conservative and liberal approaches to governance. On the right, he wanted to make it illegal for any homeless people to sleep on city sidewalks and give more rights to gun owners. On the left, he supported a guaranteed minimum income and alternative energy development.[17] Paffrath ridiculed the Newsom team for discouraging voters from selecting a replacement candidate, saying, "The governor is gambling with the lives of Californians for his own personal gain."[18] He was briefly a hit in a *SurveyUSA* poll of recall replacement candidates with 27%, followed by 23% for Republican Larry Elder,[19] but that poll became an outlier over time.

The remaining candidates entered the recall replacement ballot with a variety of backgrounds. They included actors, pastors, educators, business owners, current and former law enforcement personnel, attorneys, a suspended physician, entertainers, community volunteers, a software engineer, an aircraft mechanic, a musician, and a college student. For almost all, the Newsom recall election was their first attempt at elected office. Nothing like starting a political career at the top!

The Newsom Response

On April 6, 2021, Newsom announced that California would reopen (for the third time) on June 15. "Reopen" didn't necessarily entail returning to normal, however. Mask requirements would continue for the future along with a few other rules. Newsom would also continue several executive orders just in case he had to adjust the delicate reopening process. Some medical leaders critically wondered why the governor would announce a reopening more than two months out, but Newsom had an election to consider. The sooner the state returned to normal, the sooner Newsom would have the political weight of the pandemic off his back.[20] It was a gamble, but a gamble the governor had to make. His political future and resolution of the public health menace were one.

By the June 15, 2021 reopening, the governor seemed to find his stride. COVID-19 was on the run, unemployment was heading down, and the state was moving on the vaccination program, ranking 18th among the 50 states with 50% of the state's population vaccinated and seemingly no longer threatened by the pandemic's grasp.[21] Newsom even eased off the mask requirement for those who had been vaccinated; those without vaccinations were required to wear masks indoors, relying on the "honor" system. Still, the pandemic seemed on the run, the economy was beginning to sizzle, and the upcoming school year looked promising. Defeat of the recall seemed so likely that Newsom's Democratic allies in the state legislature changed an aspect of the recall law to speed up the recall election to September 14.

Just as the state showed signs of recovery, it was hit yet again by COVID-19, this time in the form of the Delta variant. In the first four weeks after the June 15 reopening, the number of daily cases statewide rocketed by 347%, from 700 to more than 3,000.[22] In Sacramento, the state legislature ordered all visitors coming into the building to wear masks because of an outbreak there.

The resurrected pandemic played no favorites. In Los Angeles County, the nation's most populated county, new COVID-19 cases increased by a staggering 500% within a month of the June 15 reopening, leading the Department of Public Health to require resumed masking indoors by everyone regardless of vaccination status.[23] In Alameda County, home to 1.7 million residents, between early June and early July, the number of cases soared by 357%.[24] By the end of July, counties representing 50% of the state's population reinstituted requirements to wear masks. Perhaps remembering the anger over masks earlier in the pandemic, Newsom refrained from issuing a statewide order—at least before September 14.

All of this meant the pandemic was once again at the top of people's minds. Already, many residents were grumbling over a statewide mandate issued by the California Department of Health and Human Services in July for all K-12 public education students to wear masks upon return to school in August.[25] As with other instances of rejection, parent groups sued state Public Health Officer, Dr. Tomas Aragon, over the requirement.[26]

The Newsom campaign received a shock in late July when an Institute of Governmental Studies out of U.C. Berkeley found likely voters evenly split over the recall. That was bad enough. Then, in early August, a *SurveyUSA* poll found 51% of the respondents voting "Yes" to recall and 40% voting "No."[27] With the election now only five weeks away, the Newsom campaign was panicked, so they kicked the campaign into overdrive. During the month of August alone, the Newsom team pumped $36 million into television commercials, warning of the disaster that would strike if Newsom was recalled and a conservative Republican like Larry Elder became governor. Then came the great poll shock of the race: three weeks after its early August poll, *SurveyUSA* announced it had made serious methodological errors in the previous release. The polling organization now found voters *rejecting* the recall by double digits.[28] Still, the Newsom campaign got the message, even if it was in error.

Beyond the potential recall of Newsom, Democrats around this time began to view the state election in national terms. If a Republican replacement candidate won and California's 88-year-old U.S. Senator Dianne Feinstein left office, control of that legislative body would certainly switch to the Republicans. Then again, there was an even wider picture to consider: how much would a Newsom defeat in California embolden Republicans in recall states with Democratic governors like Michigan's Gretchen Witmer and Wisconsin's Tony Evers? Could the California recall become a backdoor entry for national Republicans to improve their 2024 presidential hopes by installing Republican governors? Newsom, himself, wondered aloud in mid-August whether national Democrats understood the urgency. From his perspective, a Republican becoming governor "would have profound consequences nationwide, and go to not just politics, but to policy and policymaking."[29]

In addition, the poll's findings pointed to a questionable future for the governor: 58% agreed that regardless of the recall, California should elect a different governor in 2022, the time of the next statewide election; only 42% said they would vote to re-elect Newsom.[30] Of course, polls are only snapshots of how respondents feel at the moment they're asked the questions. Still, given the recall momentum building a few weeks before the September 14 recall election, Newsom's hold on his job seemed tenuous at best.

The campaign thus left nothing to chance. And this time as COVID cases mounted, Newsom was better prepared as well. In late July, Governor Newsom upped the ante by becoming the first state chief executive to require COVID-19 vaccinations for all 246,000 state employees as well as two million healthcare employees in both the public and private sectors. San Francisco issued the same requirement for its 35,000 government employees, followed by other cities. Soon after, the California Department of Health mandated vaccinations for all two million healthcare workers. And in August, Newsom ordered all school employees to get vaccinated or be tested at least once weekly.[31] The last thing anyone needed was for the schools to be closed again. That same month, the two major state university systems required all students to be vaccinated by the start of the fall semester.

Once again, the compliance issue came into play. For example, almost immediately after Los Angeles County issued a new mask mandate, Sheriff Alex Villanueva announced that his department would not enforce it, repeating the statement made by the sheriff when Governor Newsom ordered the statewide shutdown the previous December.[32] In addition, elected officials from several cities within the county stated their local governments would not abide by the new mandate.[33] The resistance to the renewed mandates lessened the likelihood of citizen cooperation, thereby increasing the likelihood of a longer struggle to regain control of the pandemic. Moreover, it also proved yet again the difficulties of attempting to make state policy amidst uncooperative local governments.

Campaign Themes

As the campaign wore on, the Newsom team emphasized two major topics: that the recall proponents were little more than outlier shills for former President Donald Trump, and that under Newsom California was roaring back as a leader among the states.

Regarding the first strategy, early on Newsom supporters sought to connect rightwing extremists, anti-vaxxers, and supporters of former President Donald Trump into one evil cabal out to harm California. One campaign ad wrote, "Who is behind the recall? A partisan, Republican coalition of national Republicans, anti-vaxxers, Q-Anon conspiracy theorists, and anti-immigrant supporters." Newsom's ballot language went even further, claiming that the election was an attempt "by national Republicans and Trump supporters . . . to force an election and grab power in California."[34] The approach made sense, given that Californians voted heavily against President Trump in the 2020 presidential election and the deep level of party polarization in American politics. But while it's true that some outlier groups signed petitions in the early days and supported the effort, there was no overtly powerful evidence that such interests had a major role in the pro-recall leadership or campaign.[35] The problem was that President Trump had been amazingly mum; it was hard to persuade voters about a boogey man if the boogey man wasn't there. No matter. Newsom invoked the Trump name again, and again. For some it was a reach too far.

But then Newsom caught a break with the ascent of Republican Larry Elder in the polls. Bearing in mind Elder's values and that only 34% of the California electorate voted for Donald Trump in the 2020 presidential election, Newsom found a way to attack Elder and Trump simultaneously. He attacked Elder as being to the right of Trump, warning that if elected, Elder would undo the state's approaches to immigration, the minimum wage, abortion, and climate change, as other longstanding California nationally recognized policies.[36] Newsom's focus on one candidate— the front-runner in most replacement polls—helped to draw a clear line between what Californians had (Newsom) and what they could get (Elder) if the governor were recalled.

As the days wound down to the September 14 close of the election, Elder out-Trumped President Trump. He spoke of ceasing Newsom's increasingly ambitious vaccination efforts and reversing the governor's mask mandates "before my first cup of tea," should Newsom be recalled and Elder prevail in the replacement phase of the recall election.[37] But then, Elder upped the ante. A week before the election's end, Elder played the rigged election card, saying, "[T]here might very well be shenanigans, as there were in the 2020 election." President Trump then jumped in, asking, "Does anybody really believe the California recall election isn't rigged?"[38] Now the Trump-Elder connection was palpable.

Newsom wasted little time with his counterattack. "It's just an extension of the big lie . . . 'stop the steal,'" he pounced. "The election hasn't even happened, and now they're all feigning that the upcoming vote is 'rigged.'"[39] Not only did Newsom redouble his attacks on the Elder-Trump axis, but Republicans helped the governor make his case. Former California Republican Party Chair Ron Nehring lamented, "How someone can assert that they know the results of the election before the polls have closed is truly bizarre."[40] Even Orrin Heatlie, chief organizer of the *RecallGavin2020.com* movement that collected 1.6 million petition signatures, expressed concern that Elder's "rigged election" claim could hurt the goal of removing Newsom: "If people feel their vote won't count, they won't vote."[41] Of course, the irony was that those who rejected the vote as rigged hurt their own objective—removal of Newsom from office. Whether he knew it or not, Elder's campaign remarks were manna from Heaven for the Newsom campaign.

The second part of Newsom's strategy to beat back the recall centered on the re-emergence of California's economy. Upon his reopening announcement in April, the governor had proclaimed, "California is roaring back." A campaign ad that began with those words continued, "Newsom is delivering money to your pocket. Plus, an extra 500 bucks for families with kids—$4 billion straight to small businesses through the nation's largest grant program—cleaning up our streets and getting 65,000 Californians into housing—and free pre-K for every California child, regardless of income."

But that wasn't all. The governor proposed and the legislature approved $5.2 billion in rent relief for tenants and landlords; $2 billion to help Californians with overdue water and utility bills; a four-year, $12 billion homeless relief plan; and even $600 "rebate" checks to Californians earning less than $75,000 annually, assisting two out of three state residents. In all, state officials estimated that 15.2 million households would benefit from the portfolio of COVID-19 relief programs.[42] The timing of the latest refund round couldn't be better—checks began flowing in late August, just three weeks before the September 14 recall election date.[43]

Meanwhile, people were pleased with the changing economic complexion of the state. Customers were shopping and traveling, and jammed freeways never looked so good. And shouldn't they have felt positive? Even in June, as the new Delta variant hit the state, California added 73,000 jobs, and in July another 114,500 jobs.[44] Yes, the state had regained only 58% of jobs lost during the pandemic, but California was moving forward. In July, a statewide consumer confidence index found that public satisfaction with the economy had soared to heights that hadn't been seen since March 2019.[45] Maybe the state was finally on the roll that Newsom had promised in May.[46]

However, it wasn't quite that simple. Lost in the excitement was the fact that a large share of the funding for these programs and others came from $75 billion that had been bestowed upon the state by the Congress to relieve Californians from the many stresses associated with the COVID-19 pandemic. This raised the question, how on earth could such commitments be sustained in the future? They couldn't, according to former California governor and fellow Democrat Jerry Brown. In describing the state's current economic condition as "artificially pumped up" by temporary funds, Brown predicted that without prudent stewardship, "within two years we'll see fiscal stress."[47] Such concerns may have been worthwhile to those thinking into the future, but their impact on the recall campaign was likely to be insignificant. Newsom had a pot of gold at his disposal and he distributed it accordingly.

By late August, Newsom was also promoting California's relatively strong performance battling the Delta variant. The aggressive response by Newsom and the state's public health agencies yielded positive results. A comparison of California with Texas and Florida, the nation's second and third largest states, showed that while California was below the national average of new COVID-19 cases, Texas and Florida were well above the national average.[48] And by September, California had the lowest COVID-19 infection rate in the nation. It helped that by that time 82% of the state's eligible residents had at least one dose of the vaccine.[49]

The Newsom approach paid off with the state's voters. In a Public Policy Institute of California poll of likely voters released in early September 2021, the voters' approval of Newsom's management of the state dropped from 53% to 39%; belief that matters in California would get worse if Newsom was recalled from office, 41% to 33%; and, most importantly said they would vote against the recall by a margin of 58% to 39%.[50] The economy and COVID-19 were codependent and the voters saw that the former would improve with the latter. Finally, the Newsom team saw daylight.

Generating Campaign Funds

Despite not publicly recognizing any legitimacy of the recall undertaking through the winter months, Newsom allies went to work with an ambitious funding program. At the time of Secretary of State Weber's announcement of the election, the pro-recall forces had amassed $5.45 million, slightly more than Newsom's allies, who had raised $4.56 million.[51] But the moment the contest was declared, the governor's campaign went on the offensive financially as well as politically. By mid-September, the anti-recall Newsom collective had amassed $83 million, nearly double the $45 million raised by pro-recall and replacement candidate forces.[52] At the campaign's end, Newsom had raised more money than for his race for governor in 2018.

And it came in big chunks. Among the Newsom supporters, the Service Employees International Union (SEIU) led the charge with $4 million. Netflix CEO Reed Hastings chipped in $3.1 million. Close behind, the California Democratic Party and California Teachers Associations each contributed $2 million. Additional donations of $1 million or more came from 12 other individuals or groups. Clearly, big money and big organizations wanted the governor to remain in office. Healthcare, education, and organized labor groups were particularly active supporters of Newsom as well. Money alone generally is not the only factor producing an election victory; just ask Meg Whitman, the Republican gubernatorial candidate in 2010 who outspent Democrat Jerry Brown $177 million to $36 million, and *lost*![53] Still, as the saying goes, it doesn't hurt.

Leaving Out His Party Preference

But it wasn't all roses for the Newsom campaign. An unfortunate wrinkle occurred as the recall review process ended. Recall rules allow the target and challengers to place their political party affiliation next to their names on the ballot when they send their material to Shirley Weber, the Secretary of State. Weber, a former assemblymember, was appointed by the governor less than six months earlier to fill the vacancy created after Newsom appointed Alex Padilla, the Secretary of State at the time, to the U.S. Senate seat vacated by newly elected Vice President Kamala Harris. Inasmuch as Democrats outnumber Republicans in the state, it was a no-brainer for Newsom to select another Democrat. For those voters who are not as politically engaged yet looking for a reason to vote one way or the other, the political party preference listing of a candidate could make a difference, even for Newsom.

In late June Newsom's designated campaign personnel discovered that they had failed to include the governor's political party preference when they filed the paperwork in February 2020, responding to the recall petition. Seeking to correct what they described as an "oversight," the Newsom team asked Weber to include his political party status, but she refused on the grounds that his request conflicted with state law. Talk about awkward. Newsom then sued his Secretary of State over the rejection, with the court ultimately concluding that Weber had acted appropriately. The lawsuit made the news with election law expert Jessica Levinson describing the misstep as "the continuing clown car of this recall."[54]

Yet, at the end of the day, the absence of Newsom's political party designation had little, if any impact on the outcome. Part of Newsom's buoyancy stemmed from the strong support he enjoyed from state Democratic Party leaders. Although his political party designation would not appear next to his name, every major Democratic elected official in the state opposed the recall. By the campaign's end, President Joe Biden and Vice President Kamala Harris also stumped in the state for Newsom. Even former President Barack Obama campaigned for Newsom via a taped message. Most voters knew Newsom was a Democrat. And in any case, the election was turning into one more focused on the dangers of Elder than any foibles connected to Newsom.

With party squabbles out of the picture, concern focused on turnout— a worry that continued throughout the short campaign. After all, what good was party unity if the masses failed to turn out?

Unforeseen Developments

All election campaigns, even brief ones, occur on a foundation of uncertainty. Candidates can try to frame the issues, get the word out, successfully raise a bundle, and collect endless endorsements, but those are knowns. Of just as much concern are the unforeseen events—the unexpected occurrences that may cast a pall on all the careful work done to control the narrative from beginning to end. Few campaigns can avoid these sudden problems entirely and strategists do their best to anticipate potential obstacles, especially those that pop up at the last minute. With this in mind, we turn to two potential hotspots that could have affected the election outcome: Newsom gaffes and voter turnout.

Haunted by Gaffes

The Newsom political affiliation omission joined the growing list of times that the governor had drawn precisely the wrong kind of attention to himself. The much-publicized French Laundry incident wasn't the only example of bad judgment. Not reducing his salary at the same time Newsom sliced the salaries of all state workers was another unforced error.

Then there was the issue of Newsom's company, PlumpJack, receiving several million dollars from the federal government for COVID-19 assistance while so many small businesses in the state starved for funds to stay alive. Yes, Newsom had removed himself from the company's management, but how many people really cared, given that he still benefited financially? And how about Newsom's inconsistent messages on important issues like whether masks would be required for kids returning to school in the fall? For some people, these and similar incidents were innocent mistakes; for others, they exposed patterns ranging from arrogance to incompetence.

Yet another issue emerged in late July, this time focusing on two of Newsom's children. An anti-school reopening group posted a picture of the governor's kids maskless at a basketball camp, despite the fact that the state required all summer camps to require mask-wearing for children ages 2–11 at all times. Recall replacement candidate Republican Assemblyman Kevin Kiley quickly jumped on the violation, tweeting, "When you have a political class that consistently breaks its own rules, that's a good sign both the politicians and the rules need to go."[55] Of course, Kiley spoke as a candidate with his own agenda. Still, to the extent that voters connected the camp blunders with other Newsom errors in judgment, the latest gaffe could reinforce the others.

Uncertain Voter Turnout

Despite the Newsom campaign's public posture of inevitability, at least one major unknown variable remained in the closing weeks of the campaign: would the voters turn out and if they did, for whom, and even more so, in what proportions? Yes, by election time Newsom was comfortably ahead in the polls, but polls don't vote, people do. The recall was a "special election," and historically they have produced relatively low turnouts with Democrats voting even less than Republicans.[56] Bearing in mind a nearly two-to-one margin of registered Democrats to registered Republicans, the Newsom campaign attempted to frame the election as an attack by former Republican President Trump and his allies, making political party affiliation a key element in the discussion.[57]

From the very beginning of the contest, Newsom's campaign advisors had trouble estimating who exactly was going to turn out to participate in the election. On the one hand, most polls of registered voters taken in the spring showed a majority of voters opposed the recall. Polls broken down by party showed the schism was clear. Among Republicans, 85% supported the recall; among Democrats, 75% opposed the recall. But since California Democrats outnumbered Republicans by an overwhelming margin, Newsom's future seemed secure. But there was a hitch. Whatever the merits of keeping him in office, Newsom's supporters appeared anemic in their intention to actually vote against the recall, compared to the opposition. A Berkeley IGS poll taken in late April 2021 found that 75% of the state's Republican voters had a high interest in the recall election versus only 36% of Democratic voters.[58] Clearly, Republicans were much more determined to vote than Democrats.

Little changed over the next three months. Another IGS poll released in late July found 87% of Republicans with high interest in the recall election, compared with 58% of Democrats. The enthusiasm gap largely remained. Registered voters still rejected the recall by a comfortable margin of 51% to 36%. However, among those most likely to participate in the recall election, 47% committed to voting yes and 50% declared opposition.[59]

So, what did all of this mean? Between the enthusiasm gap favoring Republicans and a nearly two-to-one Democratic registration margin, the election could be a real squeaker. With the Newsom campaign initially viewing an early recall election date as an asset, some observers began to speculate whether the Newsom team would have enough time to whip up a solid voter turnout. Others in the Newsom camp began to question the use of resources, suggestion that they needed to spend more money on face-to-face canvassing instead of TV ads.[60] Even the governor seemed to sense the changing "Big Picture:" "Usually someone in my position would say the methodology of these polls is bunk. But the reality is this is close and it all comes down to one fundamental thing: Polls don't vote, people vote," Newsom acknowledged.[61] And the numbers began to suggest that there might not be enough voters on his side.

Still, the Newsom campaign believed that they had an ace in the hole in the form of a reorganized election voting process. For the past few elections, California had been gravitating toward statewide mailed-in election ballots instead of traditional precinct voting centers. As discussed in Chapter 5, when the pandemic forced the state to shut down, Governor Newsom issued an executive order (later affirmed by the legislature in June 2020) mandating that ballots be mailed to every registered voter for the November 2020 election. With the new system, voters were given the option of returning the ballots in person either to a designated voting site, a special drop box, or by mail. Then, in February 2021, the state legislature passed and Newsom signed a bill extending the vote-by-mail concept to any statewide election held in that year. Translation: the recall election would provide ballots for all registered voters.

The Recall Campaign Ends

As August ended and September began, the Newsom team began to see the fruits of their labor. A fresh round of public opinion polls showed the pro-recall effort losing strength and a renewed voter confidence in the governor. There were reasons for the change. To begin with, new state and local government mandates required vaccinations of various groups; large businesses also required their employees to be vaccinated. Clearly, the days of cajoling were over. Given the tightened requirements, the vaccination rates went up. The Delta variant led to a surge of new virus cases at first but then began to wane as the state and local governments strengthened their grips.

The new effort paid off. Whereas the Delta variant had caused California's COVID-19 positivity rate to reach 7.0% on August 2, the rate dipped to 4.1% on September 7, well below the national average of 9.9%.[62] In fact, among the 50 states, California now had the 5th lowest positivity rate in the nation.[63] For Newsom, the timing couldn't be better.

Changing Public Opinion

As the state began to regain control of the pandemic, public opinion about the recall election changed as well. To begin with, the enthusiasm gap about the event between Democrats Republicans changed markedly. By September 6, a PPIC poll not only found that the Republican enthusiasm advantage had disappeared, but that a slight advantage was found with Democrats. Now 75% of Democrats viewed the outcome of the recall election as "very important," compared with 70% of Republicans.[64]

All this was reinforced with a slew of six recall election polls released during the first week in September, each of which revealed Newsom defeating the recall effort by margins ranging from 7 points to 19 points. If Newsom, the pandemic, and the recall were conflated in the eyes of the voters, they were certainly seeing a different picture in September than they did in July or August.

In late August, 22 million ballots were mailed to the state's voters. By September 13, the day before the end of the campaign period, 7.5 million voters had participated at a rate of 80% of the turnout during the same period of the 2020 presidential election. That in itself was impressive, given the low turnout conundrum with special elections. But more importantly, early voting data revealed that Democrats overperformed during the period; that is, they voted in higher proportions than their percentage of the electorate.[65] By the deadline, 12.8 million voters had participated, resulting in a respectable turnout of 58%, three points below the 2003 recall vote turnout for the Gray Davis recall election.

Alignment of Newsom, COVID-19 Management, and the Voters

The recall attempt against Governor Gavin Newsom was defeated on September 14 by an overwhelming margin of 61.9% to 38.1%, exactly identical to Newsom's margin over Republican challenger John Cox in the 2018 gubernatorial election. President-Trump acolyte Larry Elder won the meaningless second question with 48% of the vote, which meant little other than a reflection on the woeful condition of the shrinking California Republican Party.

The overwhelming "get tough" Newsom-led statewide response to the latest virus surge seemed to be welcomed by the voters, and Newsom was given the credit. According to a CNN exit poll, 58% of the recall election voters agreed that Newsom's COVID-19 management was either about right or not strict enough. Regarding COVID-19 vaccinations, 64% viewed the pandemic protocol as a public health responsibility versus 36% who considered it a personal responsibility. And with respect to the controversial question of whether masks should be required in schools, 75% said "yes" compared with 25% who said "no." Perhaps most significantly, by a 3-to-2 margin, respondents said the COVID-19 conditions were getting better in California. Simply put, Newsom's aggressive response to the virus met with public approval and they voted accordingly.

What began as a grassroots grievance against the governor for mismanagement of myriad issues, many of which were out of his control, ended with validation of the governor's management of the worst virus to strike in one hundred years. Whether Newsom could catapult his recall to success to re-election 14 months later would be a story for another day.

Notes

1. "Gavin Newsom and the coronavirus-driven California recall effort," U.S. News and World Report, www.usnews.com/news/elections/articles/2021-02-19/gavin-newsom-and-the-coronavirus-driven-california-recall-effort.
2. See "In recall campaign against Newsom, rural California finds its movement," Los Angeles Times, March 12, 2021, www.latimes.com/california/story/2021-03-12/la-me-newsom-recall-northern-california and "Who wants to recall Gov. Newsom? Signatures point to Trump's California," Los Angeles Times, April 29, 2021, www.latimes.com/projects/newsom-recall-election-signatures-how-many-californians-signed/.
3. For a complete list of grievances, see Recall Gavin Newsom, https://recallgavin2020.com/.
4. "Bearing gifts instead of bad news, Newsom's political fortunes rise as California reopens," Los Angeles Times, June 16, 2021, www.latimes.com/california/story/2021-06-16/newsom-california-reopening-political-fortunes.
5. Quoted in "Is Gavin Newsom an out-of-touch elite? Why recall supporters can't stand him," The Sacramento Bee, March 11, 2021, www.sacbee.com/news/politics-government/capitol-alert/article249818418.html.
6. "Is Gavin Newsom an out-of-touch elite? Why recall supporters can't stand him," The Sacramento Bee, March 11, 2021, www.sacbee.com/news/politics-government/capitol-alert/article249818418.html.
7. "Why Republicans want to pack the California recall ballot," Politico, July 13, 2021, https://www.politico.com/states/california/story/2021/07/13/why-republicans-want-to-pack-the-california-recall-ballot-1388263.
8. "'Total recall' election of '03 gives way to niche-focused ground war of '21," Orange County Register, August 22, 2021, www.ocregister.com/2021/08/22/total-recall-election-of-03-gives-way-to-niche-focused-ground-war-in-21/.
9. "Inside the social media war that could turn the California recall," Los Angeles Times, September 1, 2021, www.latimes.com/california/story/2021-09-01/how-social-media-impacts-newsom-california-recall-election.
10. Interview with Mike Netter, RecallGavin2020.com strategist, July 7, 2021.

11. "Prayer and politicking: Churches become a center of the California recall campaign," *Los Angeles Times*, September 2021, www.latimes.com/california/story/2021-09-07/churches-become-a-center-of-california-recall-campaign.

12. "Newsom clings to lead in recall while crime becomes a top issue," *Emerson College Polling*, August 2, 2021, https://emersonpolling.reportablenews.com/pr/newsom-clings-to-lead-in-recall-while-crime-becomes-a-top-issue-for-ca-voters.

13. George Skelton, "Column: Does Larry Elder have a path to the governor's office? Maybe if Democrats don't turn out," *Los Angeles Times*, July 15, 2021, www.latimes.com/california/story/2021-07-15/skelton-recall-republicans-conservatives-turnout-newsom-california.

14. "He opposes gun control, the minimum wage—and could be California's next governor," *Politico*, August 17, 2021, www.politico.com/news/2021/08/17/ca-recall-election-larry-elder-505735.

15. "Elder warns of 'shenanigans' in California recall election," *The Hill*, September 8, 2021, https://thehill.com/homenews/campaign/571427-elder-warns-of-shenanigans-in-california-recall-election.

16. Kevin Kiley, *Recall Newsom: The Case against America's Most Corrupt Governor*, Portand, OR: Bookbaby (2021).

17. "Who the heck is Kevin Paffrath? Recall could make him governor," *San Jose Mercury News*, August 9, 2021, www.mercurynews.com/2021/08/07/who-the-heck-is-kevin-paffrath-recall-might-make-him-governor/.

18. "Who is Kevin Paffrath? Democrat emerges as one of Gavin Newsom's top recall challengers," *Newsweek*, August 17, 2021, www.newsweek.com/who-kevin-paffrath-democrat-emerges-one-gavin-newsoms-top-recall-challengers-1620237.

19. "Statewide: Majority of CA voters back Newsom recall: YouTube's 'Meet Kevin' Paffrath, radio's Larry Elder lead pack of potential replacements," *SurveyUSA Election Poll #26046*, August 4, 2021, www.surveyusa.com/client/PollReport.aspx?g=25e1dad6-a844-4525-b80e-d32f904acbb2.

20. "Newsom states his political future on beating the pandemic by June," *San Francisco Chronicle*, April 7, 2021, www.sfchronicle.com/politics/article/Newsom-stakes-his-political-future-on-beating-the-16081556.php.

21. "States ranked by percentage of population fully vaccinated: July 2," *Becker's Hospital Review*, www.beckershospitalreview.com/public-health/states-ranked-by-percentage-of-population-vaccinated-march-15.html.

22. "COVID cases surging in California a month after reopening," *CalMatters*, July 15, 2021, https://calmatters.org/health/coronavirus/2021/07/california-covid-cases-surging/.

23. See "Los Angeles covid cases up 500% over past month: Test positivity rises near 700% as delta variant takes hold, deadline," July 13, 2021, https://deadline.com/2021/07/los-angeles-covid-cases-up-500-percent-1234792465/ and.

24. "Alameda County's COVID: Cases spike among the unvaccinated after June reopening," *San Jose Mercury News*, July 9, 2021, www.mercurynews.com/2021/07/09/alameda-countys-covid-cases-spike-among-the-unvaccinated-after-june-reopening/.

25. "California parent groups sue Gavin Newsom over COVID mask mandate for schools," *The Sacramento Bee*, July 22, 2021, www.sacbee.com/news/politics-government/capitol-alert/article252967063.html.

26. "San Diego parent group seeking to end school mask mandate sues state," *San Diego Union-Tribune*, July 27, 2021, www.latimes.com/california/story/2021-07-27/san-diego-group-sues-state-to-end-school-mask-mandate#:~:

text=A%20San%20Diego%2Dbased%20parent,for%20families%2C%20
not%20a%20requirement.
27. SurveyUSA Election Poll, 26046, August 4, 2021, www.surveyusa.com/client/
PollReport.aspx?g=f054d152-ceac-48dc-a422-2f22c7a00521.
28. SurveyUSA Election Poll 26076, August 31, 2021, www.surveyusa.com/
client/PollReport.aspx?g=f054d152-ceac-48dc-a422-2f22c7a00521/.
29. "Volatile California governor recall has Democrats nervous about Feinstein
seat," *CNN*, August 13, 2021, www.cnn.com/2021/08/13/politics/gavin-newsom-
recall-dianne-feinstein/index.html.
30. "California voters split on recalling Governor Newsom," *Emerson College/
Nextstar Media Poll*, July 24, 2021, https://emersonpolling.reportablenews.
com/pr/california-voters-split-on-recalling-governor-newsom.
31. "Gov. Newsom orders school employees to get vaccinated or be tested regularly," *Los Angeles Times*, August 10, 2021, www.latimes.com/world-nation/
newsletter/2021-08-12/newsletter-gov-newsom-orders-school-employees-to-
get-vaccinated-or-be-tested-regularly-todays-headlines.
32. Los Angeles County's sheriff declines to enforce the mask mandate about
to resume," *New York Times*, July 17, 2021, www.nytimes.com/2021/07/17/
world/los-angeles-sheriff-mask.html.
33. "California cities are defying new mask mandates," *The Hill*, July 23, 2021,
www.google.com/search?q=los+angeles+county+mask+mandate&rlz=1C5C
HFA_enUS773US773&oq=los+angeles+county+mask+mandate&aqs=chro
me.69i57j0i512l9.8240j0j7&sourceid=chrome&ie=UTF-8.
34. Quoted in "Newsom's claim that recall is 'power grab' allowed, for now,"
San Francisco Chronicle, August 5, 2021, www.sfchronicle.com/bayarea/
article/Newsom-can-keep-power-grab-language-in-16363906.php.
35. See "Far-right movements including QAnon, virus skeptics linked to Newsom recall," *Los Angeles Times*, January 23, 2021, www.latimes.com/califor-
nia/story/2021-01-23/recall-newsom-effort-qanon-antivaxxer-extremist-ties
and "Facebook banned leader of Newsom recall during 2020 crackdown,"
San Francisco Chronicle, www.sfchronicle.com/politics/article/Facebook-
banned-Gavin-Newsom-recall-organizer-16113017.php.
36. "Gavin Newsom warns: GOP recall challenger Larry Elder 'is to the right of
Donald Trump,'" *RealClearPolitics*, August 13, 2021, www.realclearpolitics.
com/video/2021/08/13/gavin_newsom_warns_larry_elder_is_to_the_right_
of_donald_trump.html.
37. "Fighting the recall, Newsom sets a path Biden may follow," *Los Angeles Times*, September 10, 2021, www.latimes.com/politics/newsletter/2021-09-10/california-
recall-election-provides-lesson-for-democrats-fear-works-essential-politics.
38. "GOO pushes unfounded fraud claims before California recall," *U.S. News &
World Report*, September 14, 2021, www.usnews.com/news/politics/articles/
2021-09-14/gop-pushes-unfounded-fraud-claims-before-california-recall.
39. "Republicans are settling on a strategy for election losses: It was rigged!" *Van-
ity Fair*, September 13, 2021, www.vanityfair.com/news/2021/09/republicans-
are-settling-on-a-strategy-for-election-losses-it-was-rigged.
40. "'Truly Bizarre,' political experts weigh in on Larry Elder's early claims of
election fraud," *ABC10 Sacramento*, September 14, 2021, www.abc10.com/
article/news/politics/political-experts-larry-elder-early-claims-election-fraud/
103-a15c6588-6039-4d2f-9952-687f4bc76020.
41. "Falsehoods diminish trust in recall," *San Francisco Chronicle*, August 29,
2021, www.abc10.com/article/news/politics/political-experts-larry-elder-early-
claims-election-fraud/103-a15c6588-6039-4d2f-9952-687f4bc76020.

42. "New stimulus checks, rent relief, business grants: Newsom sigs more recovery bills," *Los Angeles Times*, July 12, 2021, www.latimes.com/california/story/2021-01-23/recall-newsom-effort-qanon-antivaxxer-extremist-ties.
43. "Expanded golden state stimulus, the largest state tax rebate in American history, to start reaching Californians tomorrow," *Office of the Governor*, August 26, 2021, www.gov.ca.gov/2021/08/26/expanded-golden-state-stimulus-the-largest-state-tax-rebate-in-american-history-to-start-reaching-californians-tomorrow/.
44. "California economy adds 114,000 jobs: Unemployment rate stays at 7.6%," *The Center Square*, August 23, 2021. Whether he knew it, Elder's campaign remarks were manna from Heaven for the Newsom campaign.
45. "California's consumer confidence hits new peak," *San Jose Mercury News*, July 4, 2021, www.pressreader.com/usa/the-mercury-news/20210704/282437057109030.
46. "California Roars back: Governor Newsom presents $100 billion California comeback plan, office of the governor," May 14, 2021, www.gov.ca.gov/2021/05/14/california-roars-back-governor-newsom-presents-100-billion-california-comeback-plan/.
47. Appearance on NBC4, "News conference," July 11, 2021.
48. "California doing much better with Delta variant than Florida, Texas: Here's why," *Los Angeles Times*, August 11, 2021, www.latimes.com/california/story/2021-08-11/despite-surge-california-doing-much-better-with-delta-variant-than-florida-texas-heres-why.
49. "California today: Why California has one of the lowest covid-19 rates in the nation," *The New York Times*, September 16, 2021, https://mail.google.com/mail/u/1/#inbox/FMfcgzGljvJknDHFhzHbhfMkFWkkNMhV.
50. "PPIC statewide survey: Californians and their government," September 2021, www.ppic.org/publication/ppic-statewide-survey-californians-and-their-government-september-2021/.
51. "Recall backers raise more, but Newsom's side has more cash in the bank," *CalMatters*, May 4, 2021, https://calmatters.org/politics/2021/05/newsom-recall-cash-california/.
52. "Track the millions funding the campaign to recall California's governor," *Los Angeles Times*, September 15, 2021, www.latimes.com/projects/california-recall-election-money-newsom-vs-jenner-cox/.
53. "Jerry Brown nearly matched Meg Whitman's campaign spending on TV in final weeks of race," *Los Angeles Times*, February 1, 2011, www.latimes.com/archives/la-xpm-2011-feb-01-la-me-governor-money-20110201-story.html.
54. "'Newsom sues to get party preference on the ballot," *Los Angeles Times*, June 30, 2021. www.google.com/search?q=los+angeles+times+%27A+sideshow+to+a+sideshow%27&rlz=1C5CHFA_enUS773US773&oq=los+angeles+times+%27A+sideshow+to+a+sideshow%27&aqs=chrome.69i57.18573j0j7&sourceid=chrome&ie=UTF-8.
55. "Gavin Newsom sent kids to summer camp not enforcing state mask rules," *San Francisco Chronicle*, July 28, 2021, www.sfgate.com/gavin-newsom-recall/article/Gavin-Newsom-kids-summer-camp-mask-rule-COVID-news-16344403.php.
56. See Zoltan L. Hajnal, "Why does no one vote in local elections?," *The New York Times*, October 22, 2018, www.nytimes.com/2018/10/22/opinion/why-does-no-one-vote-in-local-elections.html.
57. "Democrats try to tie Donald Trump to Newsom recall effort," *Los Angeles Times*, March 16, 2021, www.latimes.com/california/story/2021-03-16/gavin-newsom-recall-election-trump-covid-19-campaigns-republicans-democrats.

58. "Voter support for recalling Newsom remains at 36%," *Berkeley IGS Poll,* May 11, 2021, https://escholarship.org/uc/item/1m66w3d9.
59. "Gubernatorial recall election much closer among voters considered most likely to participate than among the overall electorate," *Berkeley IGS Poll,* July 27, 2021, https://escholarship.org/uc/item/27x9k5qt.
60. "Democrats worry fight against Newsom recall is too focused on TV, not enough in person," *San Francisco Chronicle,* www.sfchronicle.com/politics/joegarofoli/article/Democrats-worry-fight-against-Newsom-recall-is-16378352.php.
61. Ibid.
62. "Tracking COVID-19 in California," *Dashboard, State of California,* September 7, 2021, https://covid19.ca.gov/state-dashboard/.
63. "States ranked by COVID-19 test positivity rates," *Becker's Hospital Review,* September 3, 2021, www.beckershospitalreview.com/public-health/states-ranked-by-covid-19-test-positivity-rates-july-14.html.
64. PPIC Statewide Survey: Californians and Their Government, September 2021, https://escholarship.org/uc/item/27x9k5qt.
65. "CBS news analysis: Early ballot returns point to healthy turnout in California recall," September 9, 2021, https://mail.google.com/mail/u/1/#inbox/FMfcgzGljvJknDHFhzHbhfMkFWkkNMhV.

Chapter 8

The Struggle to Govern California

> We do not learn from experience. . . . We learn from reflecting on experience.
>
> John Dewey

Those words from Dewey could be applied to many of life's varied events, including governing California in the midst of the worst public health catastrophe in one hundred years. Clearly, the intersection of the COVID-19 pandemic, Governor Gavin Newsom's stewardship, the state's policymaking institutions, local governments, and the California electorate should be included among them.

The state's voters elected Democrat Newsom over opponent Republican John Cox by an overwhelming margin in 2018 and the new state chief executive began, as you might expect, trying to pass his ambitious agenda. The state budget was finally healthy and Newsom was fortunate to step into office with a big budget surplus. The possibilities seemed only limited by lawmakers' imaginations. Newsom's leadership style—though certainly not without its quirks and missteps in the early going—seemed well inside the bounds of normal stewardship of a complicated state. He was considered a good bet for re-election and a serious contender for higher office. True, a few outliers initiated feeble recall efforts long before the pandemic, but they generated mostly yawns. What kind of mischief could they create, anyway?

Then came the pandemic and within a few months the public became almost paralyzed with fear and anxiety from a public health tragedy that was as relentless as it was unforgiving. The human toll on California was enormous: more than 75,000 deaths from 5,000,000 cases of COVID-19 by the time of the recall election. The state's economy came to a screeching halt, causing tens of thousands of businesses to fold as close to three million Californians lost their jobs. Schools, once busy educating the state's youngest residents, took on the appearances of empty warehouses as millions of students floundered at home in a new world of uncertainty

DOI: 10.4324/9781003217954-8

for some and a sense of abandonment for others. The state's creaking public health agencies and political institutions became stretched beyond limits. At the same time, the repeated shutdowns, re-openings, and slew of COVID-19 mandates placed Newsom's once steady yet ponderous activities in and out of government under a public microscope, yielding sometimes embarrassing, hypocritical behaviors. All of this activated longstanding but often overlooked political divisions across California's vast geographic landscape. These divisions animated deep ideologically-fueled arguments about leadership and governance that eventually, when mixed with the recall—a rare but always lurking-in-the-background threat to any elected official in the state—brought the governor to the brink of a political disaster.

It was the sixth attempt that mattered. As the Newsom recall campaign gathered steam, the governor's management of the pandemic ultimately becoming the primary yardstick of his success or failure as the state's chief executive. Newsom's defenders viewed such a measurement as both unfair—after all, from a public health perspective, California coped far better than many other states during the pandemic—and unrepresentative of his stewardship. Yet for his strongest critics the pandemic emerged as a conduit through which many other older grievances and concerns could be aired, such as concerns about too much government, too much executive power, too much ignoring of the "the people's freedom." The pandemic and recall thus formed a symbiotic twosome that could toss Newsom and usher in a new political order. For Newsom opponents, the arguments may have been old, but the pandemic offered hope of getting new people to listen and sign on to the cause.

This much seems true about California's experience with the recall in the midst of a once-in-a-century catastrophe: it was about much more than Newsom, whatever his foibles. It revealed in very clear terms the state's questionable capabilities, vulnerabilities, and inconsistencies, and with that, the sheer challenges of governing the Golden State. It spoke to the political divisions that animate this state and how organized, passionate, and vocal activists and voters (even if in some cases they constitute a minority in number) can use the institutions available as a vehicle for change and shed the comfortable from power. Things that seem familiar and predictable can become very much the opposite. California is a place where things can get turned upside down.

Yet the story of the recall also exposed the fact that there are important limitations and barriers to upending the system. California's demographic change continues to produce important political effects. The state's partisan politics has become increasingly tied to national politics and national political trends. These, we'll explain, play a major part in understanding this recall election, what separates it from the last, and what it may portend for the future of California governance and politics.

Gray Davis and Gavin Newsom: Issues, Personalities, and Results

We can't end this book without a brief comparison of the Newsom recall event and the recall of California Governor Gray Davis nearly two decades earlier. Both Davis and Newsom were Democrats, and that's about where the similarities ended. Otherwise, their differences and circumstances were stark, as were the outcomes of the challenges to their power. So, what led one recall effort to succeed while the other failed?

The Davis recall attempt stemmed largely from public resentment over a series of issues, some his doing, others not.[1] Up to that time, no California governor had been recalled from office. On paper, Davis was eminently qualified for California's top elected office. Given his extensive political experience, he should have easily managed any major issue, and most certainly a recall attempt. His portfolio included stints as chief of staff in Governor Jerry Brown's first administration, followed by elections to the state assembly, state controller, lieutenant governor, and ultimately the governorship. Few candidates for the state's highest office have had such deep political experience. But overseeing the affairs of the nation's most ethnically diverse and economically robust state includes a lot more than a robust resume.

When Davis entered the governor's office on January 4, 1999, California was in relatively good shape with a state budget surplus of $8 billion, thanks to a roaring stock market. With such good fortune, Davis and the legislature invested in public education, healthcare for uninsured children, and hefty raises for state employees. Beginning in 2001, the economy slowed at first and then within a few months plummeted into a sizable recession, exacerbated by a massive burst in the state's tech sector. That meant fewer income taxes and capital gains taxes as well as a surge in unemployment. What to do?

Davis had relatively few options to set the state back into economic health. Unlike the federal government that typically engages in deficit spending during economic downturns, state chief executives are required to create constitutionally balanced budgets. That's because states don't have the credit opportunities found with the federal government. With California facing a $24 billion deficit in 2002, Davis recommended to the legislature an unenviable package of new taxes and reduced state commitments to important policy areas such as public education, health and human services, prisons, and other costly obligations.

But the legislature, much more equally divided along political party lines than during the Newsom era, often struggled with hard decisions. That didn't serve Davis's interest. At one point after feeling particularly frustrated by the legislature's lack of cooperation with his policy objectives, Davis castigated his policymaking partners sternly, saying, "It's the job of the legislature to implement my vision." That didn't sit well the members of a co-equal branch of state government. On other occasions, Davis scolded the state courts when judges overruled his executive orders, as well as other independently elected members of the executive branch. The fundamental concept of "checks and balances" just didn't fit in with Davis's approach to government in a time of crisis, and he angered other power centers as a result. Such words did not win friends for the governor.

Nevertheless, toward the end of his first term, Davis found himself with an increasingly nagging combination of problems. Ironically, most of the hitches, such as another recession-caused deficit, a plunging economy, and massive electricity crisis, were not of his doing. Clearly, those issues were important and not easily treatable. But to the voters, they were less important than something known as the "car tax," officially the annual motor vehicle license fee. Earlier, in 1998 in the waning days of the Pete Wilson governorship and a humming economy, Wilson and the legislature agreed to reduce the motor vehicle license fee by two thirds. But given the burgeoning state revenue gap approaching $24 billion in 2002, Davis and the legislature reluctantly agreed to increase the tax back to its original formula as part of the effort to close the fiscal mismatch.

That change struck a special nerve of Californians, who treasure their automobiles; it was something they could relate to in a very personal way. Grumbles turned into protests. As a result, the motor vehicle tax hike "poured gasoline on the [Davis] recall movement,"[2] noted Rob Stutzman, a Republican strategist, and that public anger fueled a sudden recall election effort as much as or more than anything else. Worse yet, the $24 billion budget deficit in 2002 grew to $32 billion by January 2003.

The stage was set for a political revolt months after Davis's re-election and within weeks opponents began plotting a recall election. Wealthy Republican Congressman Darrel Issa lit the fuse by underwriting the tedious and expensive signature-gathering process with a $2 million check, assistance the Newsom recall proponents had to do without. The signature-collecting process began in late March 2003 and completed by early July, followed by an announcement by the Secretary of State that a recall election would be held. Shortly thereafter, Lieutenant Governor Cruz Bustamante set the election for the following October.

Having burned so many political bridges, Davis had precious few allies to help him fend off the recall. Thus, when recall adversaries took out the necessary papers to begin the process just three months after his re-election, the governor was pretty much on his own. He received little help from legislative Democrats other than perfunctory support. And since California Democrats outnumbered Republicans by a relatively small margin of 45% to 35%, GOP opponents had a larger base from which to attract a "yes" vote on the Davis recall. These were not good signs for the governor.

Perhaps the most revealing precursor of Davis's thin Democratic support came from Democratic Lieutenant Governor Bustamante, who actually ran as a recall candidate with the platform "No on Recall, Yes on Bustamante." That behavior vividly exposed the division within the Democratic Party. Even organized labor, normally in lockstep with Democrats, was anything but unified on the topic; only 56% of union members voted against the recall, with 44% joining the pro-recall forces. Add to that the popularity of recall replacement candidate and winner Republican Arnold Schwarzenegger, a larger-than-life celebrity who ran as a political outsider coming in to "clean house."

Gavin Newsom operated in a different, more favorable political environment from the Davis era. True, some of Newsom's problems stemmed from questionable personal actions, but they clearly weren't seen by a majority of the public as malevolent. Public opinion polls conducted by the Public Policy Institute of California showed Newsom stayed above the critical 50% approval level throughout the entirety of the campaign.[3] He was aided by broader shifts in the electorate. Steady increases in the state's racial and ethnic diversity and average educational attainment have continued to shift the California electorate leftward in the nearly 18 years between recall elections. Today, Republicans compose just 24% of registered voters, a decline of 11% from 2003. Comparing results of the Davis recall election in 2003 with Newsom's general election in 2018 reveals only 11 (all lesser populated, more rural counties) of California's 58 counties showed a drop in Democratic support. All other parts of the state experienced increases in Democratic support. Combined, this meant Newsom had a stronger base of support from which to draw than Davis. Pockets of very vocal opponents to Newsom in the recall election didn't turn out to reflect views of the larger electorate.

Another key difference is that Newsom maintained the support of Democratic party leadership and interest groups who support the party and its candidates, including the state's major unions and the public education establishment. Organized labor provided considerable financial assistance. Substantial funding also came from the corporate sector and wealthy Democrats. Combined, these conditions provided a solid framework of valuable political collaboration and massive funding for the governor's campaign to defeat the recall. Working together instead of against one another fostered an unyielding sense of unity for the Newsom recall resistance.

Given a basic political foundation of comity rather than anger and distrust, key Democrats inside the legislature also worked to help Newsom defeat the recall. As we documented at different points in this book, there were numerous times when legislative leaders questioned Newsom's decisions and actions. But such concerns usually stemmed from bruised egos and an interest in protecting legislative prerogatives and institutional powers, rather than because of any major substantive policy disagreements. With a generally strong wall of support from the party leadership, no well-known Democrat elected to run as a replacement candidate. This was a risky play for the Democrats—they would have no major candidate to replace Newsom if he were recalled—but it proved critical to Newsom because it allowed him to keep his campaign message simple: "Say no to the recall."

What also aided Newsom is a trend political scientists have been documenting for some time now: our more nationalized and polarized politics. Even as recently as fifteen to twenty years ago, ticket splitting was more common because state voters might prefer a candidate from one party for president but a candidate of the opposite party for a state office like governor. In the context of state politics, voters placed relatively less emphasis on party and more on which candidate they thought could best tend to state concerns and bring tangible benefits to their communities. By contrast, today, as Daniel Hopkins argues in his book *The Increasingly United States: How and Why American Political Behavior Nationalized*, Americans' identities are becoming increasingly aligned with national identities rather than their state or the community in which they live. At the same time, the two major parties are becoming more polarized. They have each developed clear, distinct positions and brands around hot-button cultural issues tied to race, immigration, guns, and abortion. Importantly, this has increasingly caused voters to evaluate *state* candidates through a national lens and their (the voters') national party affiliations.[4]

What did this mean for Newsom and the recall? It meant if Newsom could nationalize the recall election he could activate voters' national political identities and thus very likely survive. He thus framed the recall around the idea that the election was a Republican power grab and a Trump takeover. "Let's call this what it is: it's a partisan, Republican recall—backed by the RNC, anti-mask, anti-vax extremists, and pro-Trump forces who want to overturn the last election and have opposed much of what we have done to fight the pandemic," Newsom said in March 2021. Even after all that had occurred over the pandemic, Newsom hit on the same anti-Trump theme that he campaigned on in 2018. It's not a coincidence that his vote share in the recall election (61.9%) uncannily mirrored his vote share in 2018 general election.

There was a clear logic behind the strategy: Democratic voters outnumber Republicans in California by a ratio of nearly 2 to 1. If enough voters viewed the election through a lens of national party identity as opposed to, say, Newsom's personal mess-ups or his many challenges with COVID-19-related governance, then the election would become less about him per se and more about the "enemy" party trying to take over the governorship. Our polarized era has given rise to what political scientists call "negative partisanship"—the idea that voters of one party see members and candidates of the opposite party as a threat and danger to the nation. By elevating the importance of national partisan identity Newsom could trigger fear in the Democratic electorate over the possibility of a Republican takeover. This became even easier when Republican candidate Larry Elder, who packaged his candidacy using familiar Trump-style rhetoric, became the leading candidate to replace him.

The California Recall: A Flawed Instrument for Democracy

Although Newsom easily survived the effort to deny him his elected position, the episode revealed some serious issues in California governance. We first turn to the recall instrument, a special election mechanism through which voters determine whether an elected public official should be removed from office before the end of his or her term. In this case, it was the means by which California's voters determined whether Governor Newsom should be separated from office.

Early in the twentieth century, reform proponents known as "Progressives" envisioned the recall as a way for the voters to keep elected officials from abusing their positions of authority. Waiting for the next election to replace an incompetent or corrupt elective official to continue could place the public in unnecessary danger, or so they argued. Thus, in 1913, California voters inserted the recall (along with the initiative and referendum) into the state constitution.

Compared with the other 18 recall states, it is incredibly easy to qualify a recall election in California. With respect to statewide officials such as the governor, petitioners must acquire valid signatures from 12% of the number of voters who participated in the previous gubernatorial election. Only two states, Montana and Virginia, require fewer signatures (10%). However, 16 states have higher recall qualification thresholds, with most calling for signatures from 25% or more of the voters.

Another concern about the California version of the recall lies with the absence of any reason for removing the elected official from his or elected position. Several states require specific reasons for beginning the recall process such as malfeasance, conviction of a felony, neglect of duty, or misuse of office. Giving a reason to propose and consider removal helps to clarify the issues for the voters who, in turn, can decide the question on its merits. In other words, it helps to make a recall election worthy of the voters' time.

Then there is imbalance between the votes the governor must win to remain in office and how few it may take to remove the chief executive. Think of it: under recall rules, the governor must acquire a simple majority plus one to continue in his or her position. At the same time, in a crowded field of replacement candidates, one could win with a plurality that could be as low as 15% or 20% of the vote or, simply put, one vote more than anyone else. This scenario didn't happen in the 2003 recall election: Arnold Schwarzenegger received 3.7 million votes compared to the 3.5 million votes for keeping Gray Davis in office. Nonetheless, as a general rule, this seems patently unfair, not to mention an undemocratic abuse of the election process. Some scholars have argued it is unconstitutional, a violation of the 14th Amendment's equal protection clause and the "one person one vote" principle.[5]

There's also the issue of the dual ballot. While the first question on the ballot decides the governor's fate, the second question is important only if the governor is recalled. Only seven states (including California) replace the governor in the same election. The rest either have separate elections at another time or use a process through which a successor is appointed. Many California voters are confused by the two-ballot election. In the Newsom recall election, more than 40% of the voters didn't even bother to select a replacement. Some of these voters were undoubtedly confused, but many were Newsom supporters who didn't want to give the question about replacement any credence by offering up their preference.

It's no wonder Californians are frustrated with the recall process. Even as far back as 2003, voters expressed dislike of the process. A survey by the Public Policy Institute of California showed 58% of voters thought the recall needed major or minor changes. Only 35% said it worked "okay the way it is." Lawmakers even introduced a state constitutional amendment to reform the recall, but the bill went nowhere.[6]

We believe there are remedies to these inter-connected problems. With respect to the percentage of petition signatures required to qualify for a recall election, a higher percentage requirement would give a sense of gravitas to the issue that it currently lacks while making it harder for relatively small minority of voters to upend a governor's term prematurely. Using the 25% required by most states would provide that seriousness and, we feel, draw more public attention to the recall effort. Another way of dealing with the signature threshold could come from requiring 15% or 20% of the total number of registered voters in the state. The point is that a larger number of signatures would underscore a more serious interest in qualifying a recall election of a statewide elected official.

Regarding the imbalance between required votes for the governor to stay in office versus to remove the governor, we believe there are a couple of potential reforms. One would be to hold two separate recall elections. The first election would focus on the incumbent and the question of whether he or she should be removed from office. The second election, if necessary, would focus on determining the governor's replacement. Another side benefit is that it would free candidates in the governor's party from looking disloyal to the governor or party if they ran since the two elections would be separate. A second reform would simply eliminate the second question altogether. Instead, should the voters elect to remove the governor, replacement should fall to the lieutenant governor who, like the governor, has been elected by the voters. The newly installed governor would nominate a new lieutenant governor who, along with the replacement governor, would serve the remainder of the term. That change would solve several problems; among them, confusion around the second ballot and the potential presence of questionable candidates who have little real interest in the position and/or little knowledge. Normally, such nuisance candidates would be dismissed in a primary, but that doesn't exist with California's replacement ballot. There's a bonus with this approach; namely, that the lieutenant governor's position would take on greater importance. Our recommendations are general and subject to modification. But the point is that constitutional change is necessary.

The Legislature's Disappearing Act From the Policymaking Process

Much of the focus during the recall campaign rightly centered on Governor Newsom's stewardship, and increasingly over his management of the COVID-19 pandemic. As the state's chief executive, Newsom and his actions predictably received far more attention than the efforts of everyone else. Still, the legislature had a place at the policymaking table, even if it were less "hands on" than the governor. So, how should we evaluate what the legislature was doing during the pandemic, especially in the first critical year?

As we documented in Chapter 5, at the beginning of the pandemic when Governor Newsom declared a state of emergency in response to the COVID-19 killer virus, the legislature gave the governor authority to spend $1.1 billion on pandemic-related items before going into an unplanned recess. Later that summer after a brief temporary period of a return to business, the legislature approved Newsom's request of another $2.9 billion to fight the pandemic.

Handing the governor blank checks to fight COVID-19 may have been necessary, but for some legislators it wasn't a sufficient use of their time or expertise. Many complained under their breath as not to offend the governor; others were openly critical. Said Assemblymember Phil Ting, chair of a budget subcommittee, "What's the point of a Legislature if we're, like the public, watching to get information? It doesn't feel very democratic to me."[7] Assemblymember Marc Berman echoed that several colleagues had tweeted their anger at the governor "on a daily basis. And I think there is unanimous agreement [among legislators] at that frustration. It's so important that we continue to be the co-equal branch of government that we are."[8] A reminder: both of these legislators were Democrats!

Considering their elected positions, Newsom's legislative colleagues had a point—to an extent. On paper, the state legislature is a co-equal branch of California government along with the executive and judicial branches. It not only sends bills to the governor, it also has the capability to overturn the governor's veto, and in the case of the governor's executive orders, reject them with an absolute two-thirds vote. Nevertheless, after the onset of COVID-19, the legislature closed down for most of the rest of the year, leaving the governor totally in charge of COVID-19 policies. As a result, the governor operated without the potential constraints and accountability that might have been required by the legislative branch.

Of course, no one could blame the state legislature for shutting down in the midst of a pandemic. But a key question is this: could there be other ways to carry out their obligations? After all, more than half of the nation's state legislative bodies managed to operate remotely as well as many local governments in California. So, why wasn't it the case in California?

Deriving the answer was no easy task. The Legislative Counsel, the legislature's legal expert, advised that "legislating remotely arguably violates the constitutional guarantee of open and public meetings."[9] But the legislature's leaders heard from others as well. Two experts at the California Constitution Center reviewed the California State Constitution and found no obstacle to remote voting and reported as much to the legislature's leaders, but no serious consideration of the idea occurred.[10] Assembly Speaker Anthony Rendon concluded that remote participation presented constitutional problems, and therefore elected to not consider remote voting. At the same time, Senate President Toni Atkins ushered through an emergency resolution that enabled senators to participate remotely as long as a Senate member convened the session in person.[11] Said Atkins, "The [state] Constitution did contemplate and direct that each house adopt rules to govern its proceedings, as we have."

That stalemate left the legislature unable to act on any possible legislation for much of the summer. It wasn't until August 2020 that both chambers got vote operations running remotely. More significantly, it left the legislature without any ability to review the governor's activities. As a result, Newsom operated without any accountability to the legislative branch. Such behavior was both selfish and irresponsible. The legislature did little to assert its policymaking role beyond public complaints. It's not as if the members were powerless. Rather, they stayed out of the policymaking fray while complaining at a distance—the California version of wanting their cake *and* eating it.

Disjointed Relationships Between the State and Local Governments

The test of government comes not when things hum along but when crises emerge. With COVID-19, California came close to failing that test. Whatever California's official "org chart" of policymaking bodies, agencies, and institutions, coordination between the state and local levels of government was anything but smooth, particularly at critical moments of dealing with the most significant health care challenge in memory.

The hemorrhaging came with state efforts to get local governments on the same response page to the pandemic. Such problems were most obvious with reactions to Governor Newsom's 60-plus executive orders ranging over a variety of areas including statewide curfews, business shutdowns, waivers for Medi-Cal participation, and a halt to renter evictions. Most local governments abided by the orders, but some openly flouted state edicts, and others offered watered down responses. Think back to boards of supervisors that refused to close businesses and sheriff's departments who, in effect, decided to create their own law, and thereby implemented their own version of what's best for their community over the collective needs of the state.

Local leaders may have viewed such behavior as the result of their interpretation of sovereignty, but their actions tested the limits of American federalism, the longstanding relationships among governments. Given that constitutionally local governments are considered "creatures of the state," local government resistance to state mandates generally has no legal standing. In other words, when the state sets policy, the local governments are expected to comply.[12] Nevertheless, from a practical standpoint, local government opposition in mostly conservative pockets throughout the state had the effects of draining badly needed energy from the overall effort to control the pandemic.

Whether a county or local agency disagreed with Newsom's emergency orders, he had the right to issue them with rare exception.[13] According to Section 8625 of the California Government Code, the governor may declare a state of emergency when "[h]e finds that local authority is inadequate to cope with the emergency." Other provisions give the governor power to expend any funds necessary to deal with the emergency and that the order extends to "each political division of the state."[14] In other words, all levels and agencies of government are compelled to abide by the governor's order should he or she declare a state of emergency.

Nevertheless, several local governments refused to obey Governor Newsom's mandates. Recall our analysis in Chapter 5 of a Superior Court judge in Sutter County who ruled that Governor Newsom exceeded his authority in ordering that ballots for the November 3, 2020 general election be sent to all registered voters via mail because of the COVID-19 pandemic.[15] By inference, the ruling placed into question the legality of all COVID-19-related executive orders issued by the governor.[16] Bear in mind that this decision came down just four days before the November 6, 2020 decision to add another 120 days to the recall petition period, and add to that infamous French Laundry episode the same night and the recall-Newsom crowd had to feel on top of the world. Together, the court decision, the signature-gathering extension, and the Newsom French

Laundry gaffe gave pro-recall groups confidence that they would succeed in turning out the governor.

Their exuberance, of course, would not last after the three-member State Court of Appeal panel ruled unanimously in May 2021 that the governor had the right to issue executive orders in times of crisis such as the pandemic. Undaunted, the pro-recall petitioners appealed to the State Supreme Court. However, the threat to the governor's emergency powers ended in August 2021, when the justices declined to hear an appeal to the Appeals Court decision.

Now that we're sure of the governor's emergency powers in managing disasters, we're left to wonder, what can be done to compel compliance short of lengthy court battles which potentially might cost thousands of lives during the process? Answering this question could be helpful in closing the incongruity between a governor's executive order and the poor response to it by local government authorities.

It seems to us that the legislature needs to step in with a solution in the form of providing meaningful penalties for local governments that resist a governor's emergency orders. Possible restraints could vary from monetary fines for the irresponsible officials to the temporary removal of those officials from office. At first glance, such penalties might appear extreme, but these would be assessed only when a governor determines a violation has been intentionally committed. The governor might even be tasked with giving the obstate government a compliance window, perhaps 30 days, before taking punitive action.

This is not to suggest that the governor should be totally unrestrained at a moment of crisis. In fact, that's why we have the courts. Should officials in a local government believe that the governor has exceeded his or her constitutional authority, they would be free to sue no differently than people sue the governor or state agencies now, although perhaps under special expedited terms. Another check on the governor could come through the legislature's vote to reverse the governor's action by the same absolute two-thirds majority required to overturn a governor's veto.

It bears repeating that this proposal is not intended to make the governor omnipotent or beyond oversight. Rather, it comes only as a means to firm up the governor's power in rare times such as COVID-19 pandemic when cooperation from all quarters is a must.

Gavin Newsom and California: A Look Ahead

With his recall rejection victory in hand, the question remains, what can be concluded about the conduct of California Governor Gavin Newsom during the state's historic public health crisis? Was Newsom's behavior responsible for bringing on the recall effort or was he an easy target when conservative supporters of the recall, who initially struggled to capture enough signatures, caught lightning in a bottle when Californians became overwhelmed from and depressed by the onslaught of COVID-19? And could anyone have done better under the circumstances?

The sixth recall effort against Newsom began similarly to the first five attempts. The assortment of people against Newsom had one theme in common—they were outsiders. Whether their issues centered on too much government regulation, taxes, immigration, school vouchers, water distribution, or myriad other longstanding complaints, the numbers of Newsom protesters were few and relegated largely to rural and more conservative areas already under duress *before* the pandemic. The efforts of *Recall Gavin 2020* generated few signatures until the Newsom French Laundry gaffe coupled with the 120-day extension. Only then was their effort rewarded with the necessary signatures. And despite Newsom's repeated claims that the campaign was a well-organized, Trump-driven Republican effort, that just wasn't the case. Official Republican leaders in the state or national party apparatus didn't become involved with the Newsom recall effort until the hard work—signature-gathering—was virtually over.

With respect to Newsom's performance, his early self-confidence was not matched by a successful pandemic campaign. After setting high expectations for a successful vaccine rollout, Newsom's administration floundered. The state's public health community was simply overwhelmed, similar to the troubles witnessed in other states. The lack of cooperation by some local governments was irresponsible and added to his woes. Occasional public disturbances by malcontents magnified a sense of public angst. And let's face it, the decision of President Donald Trump to tell the states they were on their own in the midst of a national crisis was palpable and unforgivable. But with all that, Newsom was still the face of California government, and an often red face at that thanks to a few badly timed self-generated blunders.

Still, whatever his initial difficulties and gaffes, Newsom recovered over time. He and the state's public health specialists adopted and stayed with a plan to discourage human interaction in places ranging from schools to businesses to entertainment venues. At first, Newsom lacked consistency in style, sometimes catching the public and leaders alike off guard, but downstream his approach ultimately paid off. By August 2021, California—never a leader in successfully combatting the pandemic—had the lowest per capita infection rates in the nation. Quite a turnabout.

Just as Newsom deserved blame for erratic steps and foolish behavior early on, he deserved praise for leading the state to success over time. And judging from the public opinion polls before and after the recall election, the overwhelming majority of voters ultimately agreed with the transformation of the governor's performance. We should note that he continued to usher through major parts of his agenda especially as the budget situation improved. One or two issues from this list would be impressive for any Democratic governor but Newsom got it all: stimulus checks for some of the neediest Californians, the expansion of family leave and child care, legislation that provides two free meals each day for all public school students in the state, funding for summer school and after-school programs for 2 million kids, a full year of transitional kindergarten for all four-year-olds by 2025. Though it's difficult to disentangle the effect these and other pieces of legislation had on the recall, it couldn't have hurt to produce an incredibly one-sided victory despite a flawed political process and somewhat troubled stewardship. After all, he was a Democrat delivering a Democratic agenda in a heavily Democratic state.

All of the foregoing leads to the question, what's next for Gavin Newsom and Californians? For Newsom, the path to re-election remains, assuming no political crisis of his doing. There will be few if any challengers from the Democratic Party, while defeated Republican opponents will continue to struggle in an incredibly blue state. For Californians, there will be countless other crises to take up any political slack; among them, drought, an uneven economy, an underperforming public education system, the lack of available housing, and a large homeless population.

As for the pandemic, the threat from another variant looms until such time that the scourge is stamped out not only in California and the nation but the world over. That's the nature of a global plague—no one is safe until we're all safe. And if another surge should occur, Newsom and California should be more prepared and, to the extent that is needed, recipients of the Biden administration and a much more helpful federal government.

Finally, a word on the recall. It would be wise for Californians to consider whether this instrument works well in the twenty-first century, at least in its present form. Such creations as online signature gathering, the ability to disseminate misinformation on a widespread basis, and easy access to funding sources present a California much different from that of a century ago. Yes, it's important for there to be checks on elected officials who don't live up to expectations, but that's why we have elections. And if their performances are so outrageous that the next election can't wait, then perhaps we need to apply a serious process with more initial public buy-in to begin the discussion. The state has enough routine tumult without adding any unnecessary political turmoil. Then again, similar to the unpredictable upheavals from California's earthquakes, perhaps it's asking too much to expect order in a state fraught with endless political faults.

Notes

1. Most of this section comes from the information presented in Larry N. Gerston and Terry Christensen, *Recall! California's Political Earthquake* (Armonk, NY: M.E. Sharpe Publisher, 2004).

2. "10 years later, lasting effects of the car tax clash," *KXTV* (ABC, Sacramento), June 10, 2013, www.abc10.com/article/news/politics/john-myers/10-years-later-lasting-effects-of-car-tax-clash/103-310262281.
3. "'A different California:' Recent seismic shifts could help Newsom survive a recall," *Los Angeles Times*, June 17, 2021, www.latimes.com/projects/davis-vs-newsom-california-recall-election-comparison/; it should be noted, however, that other statewide polls, including the University of California's Institute of Government Studies poll, did show Newsom drop below the 50% threshold for a period time.
4. Daniel J. Hopkins, *The Increasingly United States: How and Why American Political Behavior Nationalized* (Chicago, IL: University of Chicago Press, 2018).
5. "There is a problem with California's recall: It's unconstitutional," *New York Times*, August 11, 2021, www.nytimes.com/2021/08/11/opinion/california-recall-election-newsom.html.
6. "California, let's make the Newsom recall the last one like this," *Washington Post*, April 28, 2021, www.washingtonpost.com/opinions/2021/04/28/cailfornia-recall-election-reform-newsom/.
7. "California lawmakers deliver their harshest criticism of Newsom yet," *Politico*, May 22, 2020, www.politico.com/states/california/story/2020/05/22/california-lawmakers-deliver-their-harshest-criticism-of-newsom-yet-1285632.
8. "California lawmakers bristle at Newsom's use of executive power during coronavirus crisis," *Los Angeles Times*, June 12, 2020, www.latimes.com/california/story/2020-06-12/california-lawmakers-frustration-gavin-newsom-executive-power.
9. Quoted in "California assembly to let absent lawmakers vote during pandemic," *Imperial Valley Press*, August 4, 2020, www.pressreader.com/usa/imperial-valley-press/20200804/281651077447607.
10. David Carrillo and Stephen M. Duverney, "Why isn't California's legislature meeting remotely?," *The Recorder*, July 16, 2020, www.law.com/therecorder/2020/07/16/why-isnt-californias-legislature-meeting-remotely/?slreturn=20210829155548.
11. "Does California law allow lawmakers to vote from home? Top democrats are divided," *The Sacramento Bee*, April 30, 2020, www.sacbee.com/news/politics-government/capitol-alert/article242359886.html.
12. See Larry N. Gerston, *American Federalism: A Concise Introduction* (Armonk, NY: M.E. Sharpe Publisher, 2007), p. 106.
13. In one such exception, the U.S. Supreme Court denied Newsom the right to keep churches and other religious institutions closed during the statewide shutdown. See "Supreme court rules against Calif., doubles down on religious rights amid pandemic," *NPR*, February 6, 2021, www.npr.org/2021/02/06/964822479/supreme-court-rules-against-california-ban-on-in-person-worship-amid-the-pandemi.
14. California Emergency Act, Sections 8566 and 8568.
15. The case was *James Gallagher and Kevin Kiley vs. Gavin Newsom*, CVCS20–0912.
16. "Gov. Newsom rebuked by Sutter County court for use of executive power amid COVID-19 pandemic," *Los Angeles Times*, November 2, 2020, www.latimes.com/california/story/2020-11-02/gavin-newsom-covid-19-executive-actions-sutter-county-court-ruling.

Index

Page numbers followed by 'n' indicate a note on the corresponding page.

efforts 110–111; as candidate in
8, 118–122; compared with other
states 107–108; as Elitist 104–106;
flawed instrument for democracy
144–146; French Laundry
incident 100, 104–105, 107, 129,
148; *vs.* Gray Davis 140–144;
homelessness 103; media criticism
106–107; petition-gathering 100;
recall process 108–110; reviewing
109–110; rural discontent 102–103;
signature campaign for 99–101;
state and local governments
relationship 147–149; two-pronged
approach of California 8; victory of
Gavin Newsom 149–151
RecallGavin2020.com 99–100, 126
recessions 9
religious services 62
Remington Steele 21
Rendon, Anthony 49, 76, 79, 147
Renteria, Amanda 38
reopening, during pandemic 60–63,
122
Republicans 5, 37, 60, 61, 80, 99,
115, 130, 141
RescueCalifornia.org 117
Ribera, Tony 24
Riley, Kevin 80–81
Riverside County 82
Rolph, James, Jr. 28
runoff election 24
rural discontent 102–103
rural values 102

Sabato, Larry 115
Sacramento 30, 46, 123
Sacramento Bee 105, 107
Safer Economy framework 66
same-sex marriage 25–26, 31, 102
sanctuary city policy 26–27, 44,
101–102
Sandburg, Carl 54
San Francisco Mayor (Gavin
Newsom) 18; big ideas 27–28;
"Care Not Cash" program 23,
24–25, 28, 103; Community
Justice Center 27; elected in 2003
24; environmental programs 27;
re-elected in 2007 27; same-sex
marriage 25–26; sanctuary city 26;
sanctuary city policy 26–27

San Joaquin County 64
San Quentin prison 89, 107
Santa Clara County 54, 55
SB1 law 43
Schnur, Dan 118
Schwarzenegger, Arnold 8, 28, 38,
142, 145
SEIU *see* Service Employees
International Union (SEIU)
Service Employees International
Union (SEIU) 39, 44, 128
Shelley, Kevin 22
shelter-in-place order 55–56, 62
Shorenstein & Co. 21
single-payer health care 42, 44
Smith, Jeff 104
social distancing 68
social media 118
South, Garry 84, 105
Squaw Valley 19, 21
"state of emergency" declaration 56,
75, 146, 148
stay-at-home order 62
Steinle, Kate 26
strategy, in politics 37
Stutzman, Rob 141
SurveyUSA poll 122, 123–124
Sutter County 62

taxation: gas 43; income 10–11, 79,
140; motor vehicle 141
ticket splitting 143
Ting, Phil 76, 146
Truman, Harry 74, 90
Trump, Donald 4, 37, 40, 150; and
Gavin Newsom 57, 125; and John
Cox 41, 43; and Larry Elder
125–126; reopening during
pandemic 60–61; travel ban during
COVID-19 55
Turner, Joe 1
Twitter 59

"U" economic recovery 9
undocumented juveniles arrest 26, 44
unemployment 9, 13
universal healthcare 28

vaccine rollout 83–85
"V" economic recovery 9
ventilators 58, 75
Villanueva, Alex 124

For Product Safety Concerns and Information please contact our EU
representative GPSR@taylorandfrancis.com
Taylor & Francis Verlag GmbH, Kaufingerstraße 24, 80331 München, Germany

www.ingramcontent.com/pod-product-compliance
Ingram Content Group UK Ltd.
Pitfield, Milton Keynes, MK11 3LW, UK
UKHW021447080625
459435UK00012B/401